T0396007

International Perspectives on Science Education for the Gifted

In the spirit of encouraging international dialogue between researchers and practitioners, often working within isolated traditions, this book discusses perspectives on science education for the gifted and is informed by up-to-date research findings from a number of related fields. The book reviews philosophy, culture and programmes in science education for the gifted in diverse national contexts and includes scholarly reviews of significant perspectives and up-to-date research methods and findings. The book is written in a straightforward style for students studying international perspective modules on undergraduate, but is especially intended for masters and doctoral degrees in science education and gifted education. Gifted education has come to be regarded as a key national programme in many countries, and gifted education in science disciplines are now of major importance to economic and technological development. Despite these national initiatives and developments, there are very few discussions on gifted education in science from international perspectives. This will be a valued addition to the scholarship in this emergent field.

Keith S. Taber is Professor of Science Education at the University of Cambridge, UK.

Manabu Sumida is Professor of Science Education at the Ehime University in Japan.

Routledge Research in Achievement and Gifted Education

Books in the series include:

International Perspectives on Science Education for the Gifted
Key issues and challenges
Edited by Keith S Taber and Manabu Sumida

International Perspectives on Science Education for the Gifted

Key issues and challenges

Edited by

Keith S. Taber and Manabu Sumida

Routledge
Taylor & Francis Group

LONDON AND NEW YORK

First published 2016
by Routledge
2 Park Square, Milton Park, Abingdon, Oxon OX14 4RN

and by Routledge
711 Third Avenue, New York, NY 10017

Routledge is an imprint of the Taylor & Francis Group, an informa business

British Library Cataloguing-in-Publication Data
A catalogue record for this book is available from the British Library

Library of Congress Cataloging-in-Publication Data
Names: Taber, Keith, editor. | Sumida, Manabu, editor.
Title: International perspectives on science eduation for the gifted: key issues and challenges / edited by Keith S Taber and Manabu Sumida.Description: Milton Park, Abingdon, Oxon; New York, NY: Routledge, 2016. | Series: Routledge research in achievement and gifted education; 1Identifiers: LCCN 2015045218| ISBN 9780415737401 (hardback) | ISBN 9781315814247 (ebook) Subjects: LCSH: Science—Study and teaching. | Gifted children—Identification. | Gifted children—Education.Classification: LCC Q181.I65574 2016 | DDC 371.95/335—dc23LC record available at http://lccn.loc.gov/2015045218

ISBN: 978-0-415-73740-1 (hbk)
ISBN: 978-1-317-80390-4 (ebk)

Typeset in Galliard
by Cenveo Publisher Services

Printed and bound by CPI Group (UK) Ltd, Croydon, CR0 4YY

Contents

List of figures and tables

Figures

Tables

About the contributors

Aziz Alamri is a PhD student in the science education department at Kent State University. He received his bachelor's degree in elementary education in 2001 and his master's degree in science education in 2008. He has taught elementary science for nine years. His areas of interest include the nature of science and cultural influences on students' science understanding.

Naama Benny is a PhD student in the Department of Science Teaching at the Weizmann Institute of Science in Israel. She received her BSc and her MSc in chemistry at the Hebrew University of Jerusalem. For more than ten years she has been a teacher and the school principal of a special school for gifted students. During this period she became acquainted with research and practice in the field of gifted students' education. Her research focuses on the interactions of science teachers with gifted students in a regular classroom.

Ron Blonder is a senior researcher in the Department of Science Teaching at the Weizmann Institute of Science in Israel. She received her BSc (summa cum laude, 1993) and her PhD in chemistry at the Hebrew University of Jerusalem. She is engaged in the professional development of chemistry teachers and in research in science education focusing on chemistry and nanotechnology education. Her goal is to promote the modernization of both chemistry contents and chemistry teaching pedagogies by promoting professional development and interactions within the community of chemistry teachers. Her research focuses on chemistry teachers' knowledge and attitudes.

Sezen Camci Erdogan holds a BA in science education, MA in elementary education from Hacettepe University, and PhD in gifted education from Istanbul University. She is currently a research assistant in the Department of Gifted Education-Special Education at Hasan Ali Yucel Faculty of Education in Istanbul University. Her main research interests are curriculum development and differentiation for gifted students, science education for gifted students and teacher training for gifted students. Also she is interested in creativity, scientific creativity, gifted students' interests towards science and scientists and gender issues among gifted students.

Nancy N. Heilbronner is Associate Dean for Academic Affairs at Mercy College, New York, where she also teaches graduate courses in the Department of Educational Leadership. Dr Heilbronner is the author or co-author of a number of publications in gifted and science education, including three books: *Think Data, Think Instruments, Let's Be Scientists*, and *Ten Things Not to Say to Your Gifted Child, One Family's Perspective*, which was honored with the Parent's Choice and Texas Legacy Awards. Her research has focused on understanding the academic and career choices of students with gifts and talents in science.

Jenny Horsley is a senior lecturer and programme director at the Faculty of Education, Victoria University of Wellington. Jenny has taught in primary and middle schools before joining the university as a teacher educator. Her research interests include investigating those factors that facilitate academic success in primary and secondary school classrooms. Jenny was the inaugural Fulbright Cognition Scholar, travelling to Johns Hopkins Center for Talented Youth where she investigated the center's academic provisions for high-ability minority students.

Sandra N. Kaplan is Professor of Clinical Education at the University of Southern California. Kaplan has been Principal Investigator of four projects funded by the Jacob K. Javitis Gifted and Talented Student Education Act, Department of Education. Kaplan has been an international and national consultant for districts, state departments, and other educational agencies to provide professional development in the areas of differentiated curriculum and instruction. She has written over 40 articles and 10 books related to identifying and providing appropriate educational services to gifted students. Kaplan has been recognized for her work, receiving awards for excellence from the Council of Exceptional Children, National Association for the Gifted for Service and Achievement, and research awards from the California Association for the Gifted. She received the NAGC Legacy Award in 2013.

Gillian Kidman is Associate Professor of Science Education at Monash University in Australia. Gillian's work history includes three years as a field scientist, ten years as a secondary science and mathematics teacher, five years as a specialist science and mathematics teacher in primary schools, and most recently, fifteen years in science and mathematics teacher education. Her passion is inquiry based teaching and learning, and she was a lead writer of the Australian Curriculum: Science. Gillian is currently undertaking large scale classroom observations of inquiry-based teaching and learning in the science and humanities disciplines to determine similarities and differences in the pedagogical frameworks employed by teachers.

Lucy Kulbago is a doctoral candidate in curriculum and instruction with an emphasis on science education at Kent State University. She has a bachelor's degree in physics from John Carroll University and a master's degree in acoustics from The Pennsylvania State University. She has coached a middle school science olympiad team for nine years, and elementary school team for five years, and initiated and co-directed an elementary science olympiad competition for five years. Her areas of interest include science olympiad and physics education research.

Ching-Chih Kuo is Professor in the Department of Special Education at National Taiwan Normal University. She has been involved in gifted and talented education for over 35 years. Her areas of research and publication include classroom teaching, cognitive development of children with special needs, assessment and identification of gifted students, counseling for gifted females, preschool gifted education, and the brain and learning. Most recently the focus of her research has been on neuropsychological and imaging studies of gifted students, policy development in gifted education, and nurturing the talents of students with ASD. More inforation is available on her webpage: www.ntnu.edu.tw/spc/kuo/index.htm.

Elon Langbeheim is a postdoctoral fellow at the Mary Lou Fulton Teachers College, of Arizona State University. He studies the affordances of computer simulations in which middle school students play the role of particles in a liquid. He received his PhD from the Weizmann Institute of Science, where he conducted design-based research concerning the development of a novel curriculum on soft matter for capable high school students.

Ching-Po Lin is a professor at the Institute of Neuroscience, National Yang-Ming University. His research interests have long focused on discovering the brain connectivity that underlies human brain functions and deviations. He spent plenty of efforts in developing, validating and optimizing diffusion MRI to map structural connectivity in the living human brain. With solid imaging technologies, links between cognitive functions and structural network in elderly, dementia, schizophrenia and stroke have been studied. More recently, genetic polymorphism and functional connectivity are linked to clarify the associations between cognitive functions, genes, and brain network in healthy and disorder subjects.

Jessica A. Manzone is a research assistant on two Javits Department of Education grants to assist in the collection and analysis of data. Manzone currently teaches at USC in the Masters in the Art of Teaching program. She has been recognized for her abilities to develop and conduct presentations on the principles of differentiated curriculum to educators. Her primary professional responsibilities throughout her career have been in Title I schools working with students of diversity. Manzone has co-authored several articles related to differentiated curriculum for gifted students. Currently, she is the co-author of a publication targeting the implementation of the Common Core State Standards of mathematical practice.

William F. McComas is the inaugural holder of the Parks Family Endowed Professorship in Science Education at the University of Arkansas following a career as a biology and physical science teacher. McComas is interested in the improvement of inquiry instruction, the impact of philosophy of science on science teaching, and science for gifted learners. He is the author of scores of articles on these topics and edited *The Nature of Science in Science Education: Rationales and Strategies*. He has given more than 100 keynote speeches and workshops in more than a dozen countries. In 2012, McComas was a Fulbright Fellow at the Centre for the Advancement of Science and Mathematics Teaching and Learning in Dublin, Ireland and currently serves as the editor of *The American Biology Teacher*.

Azra Moeed is a senior lecturer and curriculum leader for science education in the Faculty of Education, Victoria University of Wellington. Azra has taught in early childhood, primary and secondary schools in New Zealand before coming to the university as a teacher-educator. Her areas of research include science education in primary and secondary schools, in particular, learning science investigation. She is currently leading a Ministry of Education funded research project in collaboration with the science team, Beyond Play: Learning through Science Investigation. Azra is also interested in researching science teacher professional development.

Bridget K. Mulvey is an assistant professor of science education at Kent State University. Her bachelor's degree in geology is from the State University of New York College at Geneseo. She then received her master's degree in geological sciences from Indiana University at Bloomington. She taught undergraduate science for over five years, and this led her to pursue teaching K–12 for five years after her master's program. Mulvey attended the University of Virginia for her PhD in science education before going to Kent State University. Her research focuses on scientific inquiry, the nature of science and technology.

Joseph S. Renzulli is Distinguished Professor of Educational Psychology at the University of Connecticut, where he also serves as the director of the National Research Center on the Gifted and Talented. His research has focused on strength-based assessment, the identification and development of creativity and giftedness in young people through personalized learning strategies, and on curricular and organizational models for differentiated learning environments. The American Psychological Association named Dr Renzulli among the 25 most influential psychologists in the world and in 2009 he received the Harold W. McGraw, Jr Award for Innovation In Education, considered by many to be the 'Nobel' for educators.

Fran Riga comes from a background of teaching science and mathematics in secondary schools in South Africa, Greece, and England. She has a BSc, PGCE, MEd and a PhD where she investigated secondary students' conceptual development in astronomy topics. She has worked on a number of research projects in the Faculty of Education, University of Cambridge in areas such as science education for the gifted, assessment, inquiry-based science education, and dialogic approaches in secondary education – contributing to academic publications associated with these projects. Areas of particular interest to her are conceptual development and associated thinking processes, education for the gifted in science, dialogic approaches to teaching and learning, adaptive learning, and research methods and methodologies.

William L. Romine is Assistant Professor of Biology Education at Wright State University (WSU) with a joint appointment in the departments of biological sciences and teacher education. Romine's research focuses on developing and utilizing measures of conceptual change within innovative instructional contexts. He is especially interested in measuring the effects of small-scale reform-based strategies that are feasible for instructors to implement under diverse time, equipment and curricular constraints. This includes use of ubiquitous technologies to help students engage with and participate in the scientific community.

Paromita Roy has a PhD in psychology from Delhi University, India and is presently Deputy Director of India's first science talent search institute, Jagadis Bose National Science Talent Search (JBNSTS). With more than 20 years of experience in working with talented science students, she has been responsible for developing programmes for them as well as teacher development through workshops and training programmes. Her areas of focus are education, psycho-social development and curriculum planning. She was the joint convener of the First International Conference on Gifted Minds, held in New Delhi and Kolkata. She is presently engaged in research on gifted education, writing on Indian gifted population and provisions, networking with talent organizations at both national and international levels.

Troy D. Sadler is Professor of Science Education at the University of Missouri (MU) with joint appointments in the College of Education and the Division of Biological Sciences. He serves as Director of the ReSTEM Institute: Reimagining & Researching STEM Education, a research and outreach center for K-12 STEM education. Sadler's research focuses on how students negotiate complex socio-scientific issues and how these issues may be used as contexts for science learning. He is interested in how issues-based learning experiences can support student learning of science and development of practices essential for full participation in modern democratic societies.

Samuel. A. Safran received his PhD in Physics from MIT, followed by a postdoc at Bell Laboratories. From 1980–1990 he was in the Complex Fluids Physics group of Exxon research and engineering and joined the faculty of the Weizmann Institute in 1990 in the Department of Materials and Interfaces. He has served as Dean of the Graduate School and as Vice President of the Weizmann Institute. His current research is in the theory of soft and biological matter. He is the author of a graduate level text on the physics of surfaces, interfaces and membranes, translated into Japanese and Chinese.

Thomas Aneurin Smith is currently a lecturer in geography at the School of Planning and Geography in Cardiff University. Prior to this, he worked at Sheffield University as a research associate for the Centre for the Study of Childhood and Youth, and as a teaching associate in the Department of Geography. He completed his PhD at Glasgow University. Tom's research interests include the interactions between people and the environment, including how environmental knowledge is reproduced; local participation in environmental management; education and pedagogies in the global South; the geographies of young people, particularly in relation to the environment; and the intersection of spiritual beliefs and witchcraft for local environmental management.

Niamh Stack lectures on developmental psychology in the School of Psychology at the University of Glasgow and is the development officer for the Scottish Network for Able Pupils (SNAP, www.gla.ac.uk/schools/education/ablepupils) which is also situated in the University of Glasgow. As part of her work in SNAP, she is involved in supporting professional knowledge exchange partnerships with Scottish Education Authorities through providing continuing professional development activities to teachers focused on gifted development. She is also actively engaged in national and international research and publication activities related to the development and education of children with high abilities.

Manabu Sumida is Professor of Science Education at the Ehime University in Japan. He holds a BA in chemistry from Kyusyu University and a PhD in science education from Hirohima Univesity. He was a visiting researcher at the University of Georgia in 1998 and visiting scholar at the University of Cambridge in 2012. He has been Director of Kids Academy Science (a special science programme for gifted young children) for six years. He is a committee member of the Japan Science Tournament and Japan Student Science Award. He was a chief editor of the first special issue of science education for the gifted in the Japan Society for Science Education journal in 2012. He is currently Regional Representative for Asia of the International Council of Association for Science Education, Executive Board of the East-Asian Association for Science Education, and Country Delegate of the Asia-Pacific Federation of the World Council for Gifted and Talented Children.

Margaret Sutherland is a senior lecturer at the University of Glasgow, Scotland, UK. She is the director of the Scottish Network for Able Pupils and Deputy Director of the Centre for Research and Development in Adult and Lifelong Learning. She has 34 years teaching experience in schools and higher education and has written extensively in the field of gifted education. Her research interests include gifted education, early years education, inclusion and education in developing countries. She has worked across the UK and with staff and students in Tanzania, Malawi, Korea, United States, Slovenia, the Netherlands, Poland, Denmark and Luxembourg.

Keith S. Taber is Professor of Science Education at the University of Cambridge, England, where he leads the Science, Technology and Mathematics Education Group. Keith has a particular interest in science provision for students of high potential within state school systems, perhaps reflecting his own experience of attending a programme of curriculum enrichment at the local teacher training college during his junior school years. Keith read chemistry before qualifying as a teacher of chemistry and physics, and then taught science in secondary schools and in further education. He joined the Faculty of Education at Cambridge in 1999, originally working primarily in science teacher preparation but more recently teaching research methods. His research mostly concerns aspects of student thinking and learning in science.

Frida D. Tungaraza has BA and MA (education) degrees from the University of Dar es Salaam, and MA and PhD (special education) degrees from The Ohio State University, USA. Her areas of interest include special needs education and inclusive education. She has conducted research in special education, and inclusive education, including those with the support of NUFU, SIDA, NORAD and PITRO. She has published numerous papers in both local and international journals. She has worked as a curriculum developer at the Tanzania Institute of Education, and taught at Bowling Green University, USA and the University of Dar es Salaam, Tanzania.

Hsiao-Lan Sharon Wang is an assistant professor at the National Taiwan Normal University, Taipei, Taiwan. Hsiao-Lan researches in the field of educational neuroscience and literacy development. Specifically, her research focuses upon reading difficulties and the application of neuroscientific techniques to the study of learning disabilities or mental disorders. She is also a clinically certified occupational therapist and a special education teacher at the secondary school level in Taiwan. Her recent work mainly uses behavioural and experimental tools to study the identification of children with learning difficulties or mental disorders in Taiwan.

Edit Yerushalmi is a professor of physics education at the department of science teaching, Weizmann institute of science. She leads the research and development of an interdisciplinary curriculum for excelling high school students – computational modeling: randomness and structure – in which students model biological and chemical systems both computationally and analytically. In addition, she is interested in cultivating reflective practice in the physics classroom. To that end she studies instructors' beliefs and designs professional development frameworks to support teachers in changing their practice. In addition, she develops e-tutors for improving students' conceptual learning in the context of physics problem solving.

Preface

Science education is not only recognized as a highly important part of the curriculum, but also is the focus of an extensive and highly active field of research. Despite this, and the considerable attention given to gifted education and high-ability studies in many parts of the world, the specific theme of education for the scientifically gifted has received relatively little scholarly attention in the literature. In particular, there is a dearth of books on this theme which are accessible to those working in education systems and which offer well-informed suggestions on how to think about and respond to the challenges that teachers and other educational professionals face in providing educational provision that fits the needs of this group of learners. One of the few exceptions, *Science Education for Gifted Learners* (also published by Routledge), explored this issue from a range of perspectives that largely derived from themes within science education practice itself. That book was written a decade ago and, sadly – and perhaps surprisingly – there has been little, if anything, in the way of new volumes with a similar focus appearing since.

Yet the question of how to meet the educational needs of the most capable learners in science classes is a pressing one – not only for those directly involved, such as students, teachers and parents, but also for the many science and science-related fields that depend upon a flow of talented young people aspiring to work in these areas, and for the economies and societies around the world that rely upon science and technology to maintain and improve lifestyles, to provide effective healthcare, to generate wealth and to protect the environment. That is, the education of the scientifically gifted is an issue of universal importance.

The present book, published as the first volume in Routledge's Research in Achievement and Gifted Education series, is intended to respond to this pressing need by offering a diverse set of perspectives on how to think about and respond to the challenge of providing suitable science education for those students we might considered gifted. The book is an international collaboration that offers ideas and examples from authors approaching the theme from different starting points, and bringing experience from a range of educational contexts.

In planning this book we have attempted to balance a desire to offer scholarly writing, of the kind that will support those seeking to do their own research in this field and students undertaking academic assignments, with a directness and readability that will appeal to practitioners such as classroom teachers, curriculum developers, outreach providers, educational administrators and policy-makers. Each chapter has its own flavour, with some being very much grounded in particular projects and experiences, and others being more aspirational and advocating potential directions for future development of the field. We are very pleased with the balance of the volume, which we hope will make a genuinely useful contribution to all those concerned with the education of the scientifically gifted.

The development of this book was facilitated by an opportunity for Manabu Sumida to spend time as an academic visitor within the Science, Technology and Mathematics Education Academic Group at the University of Cambridge. The editors are grateful to Ehime University for funding Professor Sumida's visit and to the Faculty of Education at Cambridge for inviting and hosting Professor Sumida as a visiting scholar. We would like to thank Dr Fran Riga for editorial assistance. We have appreciated the encouragement of Christina Low, our commissioning editor at Routledge, and her associates – and would like to thank the colleagues from around the world who have generously collaborated with us by writing about their work and sharing their ideas to make this volume possible.

Keith S. Taber (Cambridge, UK)
Manabu Sumida (Matsuyama City, Japan)
June 2015

1 Giftedness, intelligence, creativity, and the construction of knowledge in the science classroom

Keith S. Taber

This book presents readers with a range of perspectives on science education for the gifted. This opening chapter explores the issue of how we can best understand the concept of giftedness in relation to school science education. The chapter highlights some problems with the notion and terminology of giftedness, seeks to link the subfield of giftedness in science education with one of the key perspectives on teaching and learning science (constructivism) and presents a pragmatic notion of giftedness in science that is recommended to the science education community. From this perspective, referred to here as the educative perspective on giftedness, giftedness is a matter that should be a concern for all those with responsibilities for school science provision – whether as policy-makers, curriculum developers or classroom teachers. Giftedness, when understood in these terms, is not an elitist issue, but rather one of educational entitlement, inclusion and equity.

The problem of terminology: who are the gifted and talented?

In the title of this book we use the common term 'gifted'. However, there is no general consensus on the way that term is used across different educational contexts. Just *how gifted* a person needs to be before they are considered 'gifted' is a moot point. In some parts of the world the terms 'gifted' and 'talented' may be considered as synonymous, whereas in other educational contexts they are considered to refer to distinct groups. Sometimes students are referred to as *highly* gifted, and in some places terms such as the 'highly able' and 'high achievers' or the 'exceptionally able' are preferred to the term 'gifted'. My starting point in this chapter is a pragmatic notion of giftedness in terms of what seems most relevant to school science. This is that 'we should consider as gifted learners in science those students who, given appropriate support, are able to either: achieve exceptionally high levels of attainment in all or some aspects of the normal curriculum demands in school science… or undertake some science-related tasks at a level of demand well above that required at that curricular stage' (Taber, 2007, p. 7). These two criteria may not describe precisely the same group of students, and the second only becomes pertinent when potentially gifted learners are actually challenged to undertake tasks at a level of demand well above that required to meet normal curriculum expectations – something that is not always the case.

People can have special attributes in all sorts of particular areas of human activity. Some individuals excel in sports – for example, running exceptionally fast or having a very accurate throw of a ball. Terms such as 'gifted' and 'talented' are sometimes used in those areas, as well as in artistic fields. A person may be considered a very gifted singer or said to have a special talent in choreography, for example. In some educational contexts 'giftedness' may be a term reserved for more intellectual areas of activity: then 'the gifted' are those who excel in academic work and another term – for example, 'talented' – is used to describe those who excel in some sporting or artistic domain.

It is important to be aware that in some discourses the term 'gifted' is used to refer to people who have been identified as having particular qualities that make them gifted *per se*, whereas other commentators see giftedness in a more contextual sense as linked to a particular domain or range of activities. This book concerns giftedness *in science* – but, in practice, in many educational contexts some learners would be considered gifted in science because they have been judged as gifted *per se*, when giftedness is closely associated with notions of intelligence (and so, often, intelligence quotient, IQ) and academic ability more generally. Moreover, the label 'gifted' is often used to imply a permanent and general characteristic.

Some people do seem to perform especially well in academic studies across a wide range of fields (although this is something which maybe needs unpacking – as suggested below). However, others may have more limited areas of strength: showing exceptional performance in physics and chemistry perhaps, while doing well (but without being especially notable) in subjects such as history and literature studies. Even within science, there may be uneven performance. A student may perform exceptionally well in biology without being especially strong in physics – or even excel in organic and inorganic chemistry, while not doing quite so well in physical chemistry. And so on. People have different strengths, both across and within subject disciplines. The view taken here is that to simply label a person as gifted without reference to some sphere of human activity is too vague to be useful. This follows a tradition of work represented by scholars such as Robert Sternberg (1993, 2009), who has developed notions of giftedness that acknowledge the importance of context and of the social recognition given to certain spheres of activity where high achievement is widely considered worthy of note. This book concerns the education of those who might be considered as gifted in science – but bearing in mind that this judgement may be made in consideration of some aspects of science and need not always apply across the spectrum of scientific activities.

Where does the giftedness come from?

Another problem with terminology is that it may bring with it unwanted associations. Notions of gifts and talents may link to once common but now less well accepted – at least in some national contexts – ideas about different people being provided (for example, by God) with particular inherent abilities, perhaps with the associated expectation that they should use those gifts or talents for the good of society generally. Such ideas potentially link to notions that people are naturally different from one another such that some will always achieve less than others no matter how hard they work or what educational opportunities we provide. Nowadays, this way of thinking may be linked to genetics rather than divine providence: that is the idea that some people are just lucky enough to have 'better' genes than others.

Taken to extremes, such an idea leads to a kind of biological determinism which is unhelpful (encouraging such lines of argument as 'If we really believe it is all down to our genes, then what point is there in seeking to rise above our station?'). Strict genetic determinism is as harmful to encouraging self-improvement as belief in the divine right of kings to rule over those whose fate it was to be their subjects – that is, the medieval notion that that a king was not just in that position due to historical contingency but had been appointed to the role by God.

There is certainly a cultural element here, with people in some societies more likely to ascribe success or failure to inherent qualities and those from other countries more likely to consider application and hard work to be the more important factors. Realistically, both sets of factors are likely to be important – but, of course, we can only bring about changes in the latter. What our experience of work in education makes quite clear is that, even if there is a sense in which we are all ultimately limited by our genetics (none of us has the potential to breathe underwater without apparatus or to run at supersonic speeds, no matter what diet and training we employ), educational opportunities, and an engagement with those opportunities, can make an enormous difference to what people actually achieve in their lives. And this, of course, is not limited to our working lives, but also to the potential to access, and achieve satisfaction from, interpersonal relationships, hobbies, interests, and involvement in community and civic activity.

Any debate framed in terms of genes versus environment ('nature or nurture') tends to be unproductive. Our individual genetic make-up is certainly significant, but anything of importance to human experience is inevitably a result of genetic–environment interactions. A particular genetic feature tends to only be advantageous or disadvantageous in particular circumstances. What is clear, then, is that, whatever a person's genetics, what they will achieve will be strongly influenced by their surroundings – the opportunities they have to learn. No doubt many individuals with the genetic potential to be an Einstein or Darwin have been born at times and in places where they were not offered opportunities to become highly achieving scientists. Had Darwin been swapped at birth with the offspring of some local peasant then his educational opportunities and social standing (and lack of independent financial means) would almost certainly have kept him away from scientific work and his genetic resources would most likely have contributed to a life's work as a farm labourer rather than revolutionising thinking across a major scientific discipline. This argument is likely to resonate with the thinking of many science educators who will be familiar with constructivist ideas about learning (discussed below).

How is giftedness recognised?

There tend to be two common ways of judging that learners are gifted. One approach links giftedness with intelligence. Intelligence is itself a much debated notion (Gardner, 1993; Sternberg *et al.*, 2000) such that scholars do not agree on quite how to define or identify it. Yet there is a well-developed apparatus (indeed, perhaps industry) for measuring those aspects of intelligence that have been incorporated in IQ tests. IQ can be measured reasonably reliably and seems to be fairly stable in people over time, and does seem to offer some useful predictive value in terms of general academic achievement. However, IQ testing does have a rather colourful history – with little awareness among early testers of the risk of including culturally biased items (Gould, 1992). IQ is certainly not a completely objective measurement. As a norm-referenced instrument that sets 'average' IQ at 100, successive modifications have been required to negate the trend for increasing IQ scores over time – as educational and other social developments have made people in general 'more intelligent'.

IQ can certainly be a useful measure: for example, if looking to identify children with very high academic potential early in their school careers. The ability to solve IQ items is certainly not irrelevant to skills needed in learning science – but it is a rather blunt instrument in relation to the different ways students may perform at high levels in a school context. Given debates about the precise nature of intelligence, and what an optimum intelligence test should measure, it is important not to rely too heavily on standardised intelligence testing.

The other common way of identifying gifted learners tends to be by teacher recommendation, often supported by checklists (e.g. see Taber, 2007). Which students commonly ask probing questions and demonstrate wide interests, and regularly finish their work quickly and accurately? Which learners spontaneously make links between current teaching and other topics, other school subjects and, indeed, other aspects of their experience? Sometimes such lists refer to gifted learners having particular forms of hobbies – such as those that involve collecting and classifying objects of some kind. These types of checklist seem to have been found widely useful, but it is difficult to find research that shows they have a sound basis in anything much more than common sense.

A constructivist notion of giftedness

A perspective that has been very influential in science education when thinking about teaching and learning is constructivism. Like 'giftedness', 'constructivism' is a term that is understood in different ways by different people (Bickhard, 1998; Bodner *et al.*, 2001) – but generally science education has been influenced by a form of 'psychological' or 'pedagogic' constructivism which recognises the highly contingent nature of learning (Taber, 2009). The human brain is a system that builds up its own cognitive resources partly channelled by genetic factors, but also largely in response to specific experiences. Upbringing, social interactions with playmates, informal opportunities to engage with scientific toys and topics, as well as formal educational experiences, all feed into the developing interest in and understanding of the science presented in the curriculum. These diverse experiences provide raw materials for the developing mind to make sense of, and so influence the development of the interpretative apparatus the brain constructs to support sense-making of subsequent experiences (Taber, 2013). Human learning is interpretive, incremental and iterative (Taber, 2014) – what any particular learner thinks and can achieve, and what sense they make of particular teaching, are outcomes of a highly complex set of contingencies, as well as being the ongoing basis for further learning and development.

Implications of adopting a constructivist perspective

Adopting a constructivist notion of learning has implications for how giftedness might be understood. A constructivist perspective suggests that high levels of science achievement cannot be seen as being inevitable for any learner at birth. Neither does measured achievement at any time represent a point along some fixed trajectory of development. Those we consider gifted now might not have been so judged had their prior learning experiences been different – and it is not inevitable they should be assumed to remain gifted indefinitely once identified. Those we do not consider gifted right now may still have potential to demonstrate exceptional achievement in the future: albeit this would likely depend upon appropriate support in meeting the demands of suitable learning challenges in the meantime (see below).

The constructivist perspective, then, informs a philosophical stance for thinking about giftedness in science education. It suggests that we should not see judgements of giftedness (or, by implication, non-giftedness) as absolute. Rather a student should only be considered gifted in relation to current educational demands and by virtue of their experiential history. If educational demands change, then we may come to make different judgements of giftedness. As the learners we work with undertake further educative experiences, their resources for interpreting the world and responding to future challenges will change and, in some cases, this will lead to students deserving to be considered gifted in science when they have not been so judged previously. Such a change might seem mysterious when we are not fully aware of the contingencies at work. Certainly, there may be genetically related developmental factors at work – influencing individual differences in the precise patterns of maturation of normal brain development. Often there also will be affective and motivational factors at work that lead to a learner suddenly getting enthused and committed to a topic or to science more generally – leading, perhaps, to extensive engagement, atypically high levels of concentration and resilience in the face of intellectual challenge, and perhaps even experiencing learning as a 'flow' (Csikszentmihalyi, 1988;

Taber, 2015a). Sometimes our teaching has a significant effect: teaching that scaffolds student learning especially well can accelerate progression (Adey and Shayer, 2002) and suitably structured educative experiences can lead to changes in what a learner is ready to tackle next.

If giftedness is inherently contextual – a person is gifted in relation to some particular task demands – then there is no reason to expect that students found to be gifted in science will also be found to be gifted in, say, history or modern foreign languages. Yet, often in school systems in many countries judgement of giftedness is made in terms of whole age-related cohorts. Perhaps this is, in part, because there are key abilities or capabilities (study habits, learning strategies, etc.) which support academic learning across domains. This might relate to something like Piagetian stage developmental level (Bliss, 1995), or such matters as vocabulary, reading comprehension, etc., which no doubt correlate to everyday notions of children being considered intelligent.

However, we should also be wary of taking such global judgements of giftedness at face value. Gardner (1993), for example, has noted how academic school subjects tend to rely on a limited subset of the multiple intelligences people express. One might go further than this and ask if the kinds of tasks set for learners in school subjects are too often of a generic kind: that students may be engaged in essentially the same activities across the curriculum, but simply with the topic changed. That interpretation might suggest that school curriculum and, moreover, its transposition in the classroom (Chevallard, 1989), may commonly fail to fully reflect the different aspects of human culture it is meant to introduce young people to. The discipline of physics is different to the discipline of history or the discipline of mathematics – but (if we ignore the subject matter) this may not always be obvious from what students are asked to do in classes.

A further complication is the nature of human beings and education systems as interactive elements that respond to how they are treated. In scientific work we do not need to worry that referring to xenon as a 'noble' gas will influence its chemical reactivity – although the label 'inert' gases did for many years deter chemists from testing whether those elements could actually form compounds – or that labelling the great white shark as 'great' will give it a sense of superiority which will make it more aggressive. Yet, once we label students as being gifted (or not being gifted) we set up expectations in them, their parents, their teachers, and their classmates. Simply setting up such expectations can be an effective ways to influence educational outcomes (Rosenthal and Rubin, 1978). An interesting question that might be posed is how much of what is observed as across-the-board gifted behaviour can be explained in terms of across-the-board gifted labelling.

By the same token, labelling a student as 'gifted in science' should be considered something akin to labelling them 'tired' or 'excited' – that is, as a description of a current state reflecting present circumstances. In particular, what is seen as gifted behaviours in science classes will, in part, depend upon what is considered to be the business of the science classroom. If the science class is about the learning of a great many science facts and the algorithmic application of scientific principles, then those students with good memories, and who are comfortable when following routines and take pride in undertaking drill and practice, will demonstrate very strong performance: perhaps even strong enough to be considered to 'achieve exceptionally high levels of attainment in all or some aspects of the normal curriculum demands in school science'. However, in such a classroom regime there might other students who have would be able to 'undertake some science-related tasks at a level of demand well above that required at that curricular stage' who may go unrecognised as gifted simply because they are given few opportunities to demonstrate their potential.

Science as a creative activity

When gifted 'students' are distinguished from 'talented' students, the discrimination is often on the basis of 'academic' excellence rather than exceptional ability in a more creative activity such as dance, fine art or music. Yet creativity is needed to be highly successful in any academic field. Moreover, science is inherently a creative activity. Certainly, logical thinking is essential in scientific work, but as *a complement to* creative thinking, not an alternative. All major scientific discoveries are initially creative acts. The scientist needs to see something in a new way, to imagine a new potential pattern: only then is it possible to design research protocols to test the new idea and apply logical thinking to 'make' the discovery (Taber, 2011). School science should provide opportunities for the development of creativity (see Chapter 2 by Roy, this volume), and such opportunities may reveal gifted learners who would not be identified without such opportunities.

In terms of school science, question-posing may be one of the best contexts for allowing students to demonstrate creativity (Watts and Pedrosa de Jesus, 2007), as this is where they can use their imagination to think up possibilities (in effect, possible alternative worlds) which they can then set about testing against evidence from our actual physical world. Such testing certainly requires students to have a relevant knowledge base and to already be aware of the repertoire of laboratory techniques available, but then offers further opportunities for being creative in designing ways to test their ideas. Thus, enquiry-based science teaching (Minner *et al.*, 2010) may reveal as gifted some students who do not seem exceptional when teaching is more about learning and applying text-book accounts of canonical science.

Creativity can be expressed in different ways. Allowing students to suggest their own metaphors and analogies for scientific concepts can offer an illuminating insight into their understanding, as well as being creative and even fun (Taber, 2016). Asking students to develop their own models, or their own representations, gives them opportunities to engage in creative activities that require deep engagement with the material they are learning (Tytler *et al.*, 2013). Asking students to find the links between the present topic and previous topics – or even with other areas of the curriculum – offers a creative challenge that takes many students beyond their comfort zone. Of course, the results may be 'small c' creativity in that school students are unlikely to identify any significant links that have not already been identified by scholars – but the point of school is *personal* learning to prepare students for later life. Science, and indeed all spheres of activity, depend upon people both being able to be creative and being comfortable in being creative, and some personal creativity will prove to be 'big C' Creative and make genuinely original contributions. After all, every creative breakthrough that is publicly recognised in some domain or field started with an individual having what, to them, was a novel idea.

An educative notion of giftedness in science education

At the outset of the chapter I suggested two possible groups of students who might usefully be considered gifted. Those who 'achieve exceptionally high levels of attainment in all or some aspects of the normal curriculum demands in school science' are easily recognized. They get near-perfect marks on assignments and in tests. However, regularly getting near-perfect marks is not necessarily a good thing. If school is about learning and learning requires matching task demand to the learner's current capabilities, then we might expect effective learning to be reflected by performances clearly below our mark or grade ceilings. If the tasks set lack a high level of challenge then some of those in this group may actually be able and conscientious rather than of exceptional potential. Those who are potentially in the group that meet the second criterion, those who are 'able to undertake some science-related tasks at a level of demand well above that required at that curricular stage', will only demonstrate this potential when they are actually set tasks at a level of demand well above that formally required at that curricular stage – which again points to the need to pitch task demands to a level that will facilitate learning.

According to Vygotsky (1934/1986), the educator should not focus on what the learner can currently do well with minimal support, but rather on what the learner cannot yet do unaided, but which becomes feasible for them once suitable support is provided. From this viewpoint, effective teaching involves scaffolding learners in their 'zone of proximal development' – in providing sufficient support such that activities are both challenging and yet achievable. Learning activities are not educative if they do not allow students to eventually succeed, but nor are they educative if they lack sufficient challenge to provide a basis for moving beyond the limits of current capability (Taber, 2015b). This clearly applies to all learners (see Figure 1.1). There is a particular issue for gifted learners (able to 'achieve exceptionally high levels of attainment in all or some aspects of the normal curriculum demands in school science' or 'undertake some science-related tasks at a level of demand well above that required at that curricular stage') when the task they are asked to engage in is readily achievable without any sense of challenge. Such tasks are familiar, they are routine, they are algorithmic and they are (in Vygotsky's terms) well within the learner's zone of actual development, rather than within their zone of next development.

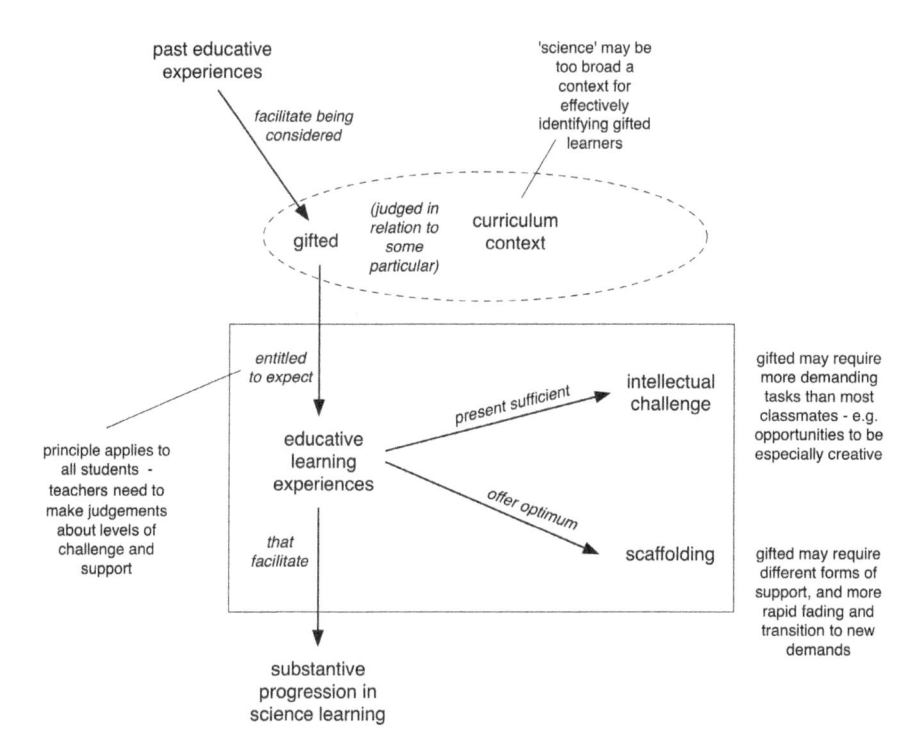

Figure 1.1 All students, including the gifted, need to be set suitably challenging learning activities

Meeting the needs of the gifted is an inclusion issue

Science learning activities, then, are truly educative only when they offer learners the right balance of challenge and support. In virtually any school class, work that is challenging for most pupils will be routine for some, just as it will be too demanding for some others unless they are offered additional support. Where students are completing set work quickly and accurately, but without being regularly taken out of their comfort zone and genuinely challenged, they will be doing all that is required of them without receiving genuinely educative learning experiences. From this educative perspective on giftedness, meeting the needs of the gifted learner is not an elitist concern, but rather is a matter of equity (Taber and Riga, forthcoming). All students are entitled to science education that is genuinely educative – which means science education they can succeed at, but not without having to stretch themselves. This requires activities that are engrossing and challenging, but which lead to genuine satisfaction as they are only completed with real effort that requires going beyond previous levels of knowledge, understanding and or skills. Arguably, we know in general terms what is needed to offer challenge to gifted learners in science classes (Taber and

Corrie, 2007), but would benefit from a good deal more research finding precisely what works well for different groups of gifted learners in various science learning contexts (Taber, 2015b).

The motivation behind a concern with the educational provision for the gifted in science relates to their entitlement to genuine educational opportunities (Taber and Riga, forthcoming). An education system should provide all learners the opportunity to develop towards their potential. Too often, in many science classes, this sense of real intellectual challenge is never experienced by some students. The present volume contains a range of perspectives on gifted education in science. A subsequent volume in this series (*Policy and Practice in Science Education for the Gifted: Approaches from diverse national contexts*) will report a range of approaches to addressing the needs of gifted learners adopted around the world. Quite a few of these contributions discuss approaches to enriching curriculum experience by offering something extra beyond the standard classroom fare. These approaches can be very effective, and when they involve moving outside school for special actives with other gifted learners this can provide a learning environment quite different from school that may be experienced as more mature, as special, as exciting (Taber and Riga, 2006). At least as important, however, are the contributions that offer ideas for how classroom teachers can manage teaching and learning within the normal curriculum to ensure gifted learners are genuinely challenged in their core school science. Whatever elective enrichment activities may be offered to the gifted, it is just as important to ensure they are included in genuinely educative learning actives during their compulsory school science lessons.

References

Adey, P., and Shayer, M. (2002). An exploration of long-term far-transfer effects following an extended intervention program in the high school science curriculum. In C. Desforges and R. Fox (Eds), *Teaching and Learning: The essential readings*. Oxford: Blackwell, pp. 173–209.

Bickhard, M.H. (1998). Constructivism and relativism: a shopper's guide. In M.R. Matthews (Ed.), *Constructivism in Science Education: A philosophical examination* pp. 99–112. Dordecht: Kluwer Academic, pp. 99–112.

Bliss, J. (1995). Piaget and after: the case of learning science. *Studies in Science Education*, 25, 139–72.

Bodner, G.M., Klobuchar, M., and Geelan, D. (2001). The many forms of constructivism. *Journal of Chemical Education*, 78 (Online Symposium: Piaget, Constructivism, and Beyond), 1107.

Chevallard, Y. (1989). On didactic transposition theory: some introductory notes. In Proceedings of the International Symposium on Selected Domains of Research and Development in Mathematics Education. Bratislava, August 1988, pp. 51–62.

Csikszentmihalyi, M. (1988). The flow experience and its significance for human psychology. In M. Csikszentmihalyi and I.S. Csikszentmihalyi (Eds), *Optimal Experience: Psychological studies of flow in consciousness*. Cambridge: Cambridge University Press, pp. 15–35.

Gardner, H. (1993). *Frames of Mind: The theory of multiple intelligences* (2nd edn). London: Fontana.

Gould, S.J. (1992). *The Mismeasure of Man*. London: Penguin.

Minner, D.D., Levy, A.J., and Century, J. (2010). Inquiry-based science instruction: what is it and does it matter? Results from a research synthesis years 1984 to 2002. *Journal of Research in Science Teaching*, 47(4), 474–96. doi: 10.1002/tea.20347

Rosenthal, R., and Rubin, D.B. (1978). Interpersonal expectancy effects: the first 345 studies. *Behavioral and Brain Sciences*, 1, 377–86. doi: 10.1017/S0140525X00075506

Sternberg, R.J. (1993). The concept of 'giftedness': a pentagonal implicit theory. *The Origins and Development of High Ability*. Chichester: John Wiley and Sons, pp. 5–21.

Sternberg, R.J. (2009). Toward a triarchic theory of human intelligence. In J.C. Kaufman and E.L. Grigorenko (Eds), *The Essential Sternberg: Essays on intelligence, psychology and education*. New York: Springer, pp. 33–70.

Sternberg, R.J., Forsythe, G.B., Hedlund, J., Horvath, J.A., Wagner, R.K., Williams, W.M., Snook, S.A., and Grigorenko, E.L. (2000). *Practical Intelligence in Everyday Life*. Cambridge: Cambridge University Press.

Taber, K.S. (2007). Science education for gifted learners? In K.S. Taber (Ed.), *Science Education for Gifted Learners*. London: Routledge, pp. 1–14.

Taber, K.S. (2009). *Progressing Science Education: Constructing the scientific research programme into the contingent nature of learning science*. Dordrecht: Springer.

Taber, K.S. (2011). The natures of scientific thinking: creativity as the handmaiden to logic in the development of public and personal knowledge. In M.S. Khine (Ed.), *Advances in the Nature of Science Research: Concepts and methodologies*. Dordrecht: Springer, pp. 51–74.

Taber, K.S. (2013). *Modelling Learners and Learning in Science Education: Developing representations of concepts, conceptual structure and conceptual change to inform teaching and research*. Dordrecht: Springer.

Taber, K.S. (2014). *Student Thinking and Learning in Science: Perspectives on the nature and development of learners' ideas*. New York: Routledge.

Taber, K.S. (2015a). Affect and meeting the needs of the gifted chemistry learner: providing intellectual challenge to engage students in enjoyable learning. In M. Kahveci and M. Orgill (Eds), *Affective Dimensions in Chemistry Education*. Berlin Heidelberg: Springer, pp. 133–58.

Taber, K.S. (2015b). Developing a research programme in science education for gifted learners. In N.L. Yates (Ed.), *New Developments in Science Education Research*. New York: Nova Science, pp. 1–29.

Taber, K.S. (2016). 'Chemical reactions are like hell because...': asking gifted science learners to be creative in a curriculum context that encourages convergent thinking. In M.K. Demetrikopoulos and J.L. Pecore (Eds), *Interplay of Creativity and Giftedness in Science*, Rotterdam: Sense, pp. 321–49.

Taber, K.S., and Corrie, V. (2007). Developing the thinking of gifted students through science. In K.S. Taber (Ed.), *Science Education for Gifted Learners*. London: Routledge, pp. 71–84.

Taber, K.S., and Riga, F. (2006). Lessons from the ASCEND project: able pupils' responses to an enrichment programme exploring the nature of science. *School Science Review*, 87(321), 97–106.

Taber, K.S., and Riga, F. (forthcoming). From each according to her capabilities; to each according to her needs: fully including the gifted in school science education. In S. Markic and S. Abels (Eds), *Inclusion in Science Education*. New York: Nova Science.

Tytler, R., Prain, V., Hubber, P., and Waldrip, B.G. (Eds). (2013). *Constructing Representations to Learn in Science*. Rotterdam: Sense.

Vygotsky, L.S. (1934/1986). *Thought and Language*. London: MIT Press.

Watts, M., and Pedrosa de Jesus, M.H. (2007). Asking questions in classroom science. In K.S. Taber (Ed.), *Science Education for Gifted Learners*. London: Routledge, pp. 112–27.

2 Creativity and science education for the gifted

Insights from psychology

Paromita Roy

Any endeavour involving discussions on the lives of human beings cannot be bereft of a commentary on the manner in which they think, feel and behave. The study of psychology is integral to understanding motivation, endeavour and achievement. Furthermore, creative expressions and achievements in the field of science and technology have gained monumental importance and relevance in modern societies and have become national yardsticks for development, economy and power. This ever-growing emphasis on the paradigms, processes, products and progress of research and practice in scientific creativity calls for better understanding of psychological aspects of scientific creativity. In this chapter, an attempt has been made to link psychological science to the manifestation and growth of creativity in science. It is hoped that this linking will lead to enriching educators, parents and society in general towards creating a better learning environment for young creative students of science, keeping in mind their psychological strengths and vulnerabilities.

Although the concept of creativity has been discussed and debated for nearly 200 years, formal research on creativity has come to the forefront in approximately the last 100 years. The extraordinary work of Terman (1928), who spoke about the 'genius', the presidential address by Guilford (1950) to the American Psychological Association titled 'Creativity', which first sowed the seeds of creativity as a scientific study and Torrance's (1962, 1974) seminal work in the field of creativity assessment provides a rich backdrop. Creativity did not become a significant topic of psychological research until after the Second World War and, when it did, it was primarily quantitative and statistical.

Psychometrics developed rapidly to quantify measures of ability, thinking and intelligence. Assessment tools for divergent thinking developed on the one hand, while, on the other hand, personality traits were correlated with creativity measures. Simultaneous developments across the areas of biographical inventories, case studies and test batteries to link ability with creativity took place. With the development of cognitive science, researchers focused on mental processes to attempt understanding creativity in terms of performance on cognitive tasks.

Psychologists and educators have expressed widely divergent views on the nature and characteristics of creative and gifted children. Creativity has been studied from various perspectives: person, product, process and place.

The perspectives of 'person' relate to personality of creative persons and their productivity across the life span; 'product' to understanding the value of the creative product in terms of its originality and use; 'process' to the stages of creative behaviour and output; and 'place' to creativity-friendly environments. The concept of little 'c' has been linked more with the person and the product whereas big 'C' has a relation with the process. Simonton (1999) emphasizes that, for an individual to be big 'C' creative, one's contribution must be judged by others as being both original/novel and functional/useful. Understanding the 'psychology behind scientific creativity' presents us with the need to recognize the domains of science, creativity and psychology separately first and then together. The theories of knowledge pertaining to these individual domains find themselves crisscrossing across a multidimensional canvas.

Amabile (1996) argued that creativity is not just about possessing domain-specific skills (like knowledge, technical skills and special talents in the domain), but also depends heavily on environmental factors such as freedom, support and positive challenges, the quality of discipline required within the domains and traits such as the ability to suspend judgement, perseverance and nonconformity, and degree of intrinsic motivation. Renzulli (1977) argued that task persistence, creativity and motivation are important psychological characteristics which should be cultivated in school programmes. Subsequently, measures of innate intellectual ability have been complemented by research on psychosocial variables relating to the manifestation of creativity. Interests, individual goals, achievement motivation, action competencies, ideational fluency, discriminating observations, superior memory, cognitive flexibility and preference for unstructured complex experiences are more important than intelligence factors (Subotnik and Steiner, 1993; Nwazuoke, 1996; Tucker, 2001).

Characteristics of creative personalities

Creative traits in students are mostly recognized when they display goal-oriented achievement. In India, for example, a majority of creative young students do not find support to either nurture the joy and excitement of their creative mindsets, nor are they provided an environment that will recognize their needs in overcoming vulnerabilities associated with asynchronous development and creativity. Society, parents and teachers treat creativity with a worrisome level of naivety, without being aware of its nuances and its demand on the person. Observations by parents and teachers in natural conditions have been predominant in studying and understanding personality of creative children. Primary characteristics like intensity, sensitivity and over-excitabilities have been attributed to them. The creative phase, many a times, is rooted and sharpened through a journey of failures or disappointments. In this phase, the creative result may take many years and the result would be unconventional. In contrast, the reproductive phase is one where success is high and results are predictable and typical. Conventional thinkers can at best be trained to be perceptive towards creative persons, processes, products and environment. The role of creative mentors is of great value and importance because only they can play a decisive role in steering creativity without which it becomes a lone battle for creative individuals in the face of passion and commitment, on the one hand, and discouragement and adversity, on the other.

As a psychologist working with talented Indian science students for more than two decades, I have observed various themes emerging with respect to psychological characteristics of such students. Two sets of personalities seem prevalent. One kind of creative science students are seen to be natural leaders, are extroverted in nature, have a 'Midas touch' and excel in academic tasks as well as extra-curricular activities. They seem well adjusted, and are often seen interacting with students of higher grades on academic issues. Due to their exuberant personalities and sharpness they often seem distracted with too many things at a time and are often at the risk of changing their preferences too often. Sometimes it becomes necessary for educators and family to 'pin them down' and counsel them towards sieving out their immediate and long-term goals. The other type of creative students shows contrasting traits. They are intense, introverted and emotionally sensitive. They display focus on definite aspects of science and prefer to gain deeper insight within that domain. In behaviour they are quiet and reserved and their 'adventure' for science is internal and guarded. They are seen to be voracious readers and prefer to be with people who share their personality and interest. For such creative students, competition is not of much interest and they are happy to be 'out of the race' and, instead, engaged in thought and rigour towards the pursuit of scientific understanding.

The qualitative difference between creative and other children and adolescents creates vulnerabilities across social and emotional domains (Bailey, 2011). As against high achievers who learn faster using the faculty of pattern recognition to their advantage, creative individuals may seem painfully slow in formal and conventional school set-ups. Because they seek nonconventional avenues/solutions, they tend to be deep thinkers rather that fast thinkers. They seem to struggle at communicating their thoughts and passion to other average peers and teachers, and become isolated. Sometimes this isolation may result in withdrawal and denial of their gifts. The Johns Hopkins University Center for Talented Youth (CTY), with its focus on research in personality and cognitive learning styles of academically talented students since 1983, found such students differing from same-age peers on cognitive style dimensions of introversion–extraversion, sensing–intuition, thinking–feeling and judging–perceiving (Mills, 1993). They expressed greater preferences for introversion, intuition and abstract thinking and tended to be higher on achievement motivation and lower on interpersonal and social concerns (Sak, 2004). The perspectives of creative individuals differ qualitatively with differences in intensities, sensitivities, idealism, perceptiveness, over-excitabilities, asynchrony, complexity, introversion, perfectionism and moral concerns (Silverman, 2005).

The notion that creativity, high ability and giftedness are extra endowments for a child and that he/she is already 'the lucky one' is strongly prevalent in most societies. Because of this notion, creative children are usually neglected on the premise that they already 'have more than the others'. Society at large expects such students to excel on their own, with minimum additional support. In dealing with gifted students, I notice a tendency of teachers and parents to believe that, just because a child is creative or talented, he/she must be capable to continue being the best – not just in the talent domain, but also in all other aspects of life. Parents often seek counselling when they realize that their child has underdeveloped competencies in certain domains like social behaviour and conflict resolution. It is not unusual to hear comments about creative young people that they are 'strange' because, on the one hand, they show advanced ability while, on the other, some skills and capabilities are seriously lacking.

In schools across India, creativity is, at best, appreciated. The role of providing talent-enriching support is often left to the home. Many a time, parents of creative and gifted children fail to identify these qualities, often labelling them 'different'. Only when the child's creative ability results in a product that is acknowledged by 'higher authorities' does it warrant attention and is it credited with importance by teachers and parents. Provisions of acceleration, enrichment, curriculum compacting, focused mentorship and advanced opportunities are few and far between and not a part of formal education. Motivated teachers, by virtue of their passion and dedication towards their craft, informally identify creative students and try to encourage and support them in their individual capacities. Sometimes a group of such teachers pool their intellectual resources to mentor such children. In many cases, when and if this happens, it is usually for those creative students who are economically disadvantaged.

Science and creativity

Initially, there was very little interest in correlating science with creativity because science was considered rational, practical and observable and creativity too vague and abstract because of its 'undefinable' status. Fields such as science and engineering have experienced a less explicit relation to creativity. But the success of science and scientists in the latter part of the twentieth century attracted researchers to contemplate hypotheses that explored domain-specific characteristics of science talent and creativity. Talent in science is unlike that in music, art, or mathematics – where specialized aptitudes can be readily recognized in the young (Csikszentmihalyi and Robinson, 1986) and prodigies in scientific research are rare (Feldman, 1991). Owing to the quantum leap society witnessed as a result of important scientific contributions in the natural sciences, like the theory of relativity, superconductivity, nuclear power, gene mapping and many such life-altering discoveries, a newfound interest in scientific creativity was born. Also, the failure to establish intelligence as the sole cause of individual creative performance led many psychologists to focus research on cognitive styles that tended to be a better predictor of creativity.

Different countries have different understandings of creativity. For example, Niu (2006) found that 'westerners' view creativity in terms of the individual attributes of a creative person, while the Chinese view it more in terms of the social influence of creative people on society. Mpofu *et al.* (2006) surveyed 28 African languages and found that only Arabic had a word that directly translated to 'creativity'. In Scandinavian countries creativity is seen as an individual attitude which helps in coping with life's challenges (Smith and Carlsson, 2006), while in Germany creativity is seen more as a process that can be applied to help solve problems (Preiser, 2006).

In common with many other countries, creativity in the Indian context is understood better through performance and products. Domain-specific performance has been the yardstick for labelling an individual as talented/creative/gifted. Research across domains to understand the general characteristics of creative behaviour *vis à vis* specific domain characteristics of giftedness has mostly been influenced by theoretical frameworks that many a times do not apply to the Indian scenario. For this reason the understanding of qualitative differences between talent, creativity and giftedness in India has remained ambiguous. The *process* of creativity and its interaction with the environment has received little attention, perhaps because the *product* of creativity has been of more interest. For example, when it comes to art and literature, it is almost always termed 'creative', but when in sports it is perceived as a talent. In academics and, especially, in science, the exceptional are almost always termed as 'geniuses'. With little understanding of why different labels are given to gifted persons, these stereotypes only get strengthened with time.

In an over-populous country like India, creativity tends to be overshadowed by the need to be economically stable and find employment. Indigenous talents in rural areas remain mostly unidentified. Exceptional talent in sports and art are comparatively more noticeable due to the skills being observable and demonstrable. But for scientific creativity to be recognized, there needs to be a formal educational set-up where talent, passion and commitment towards science can be demonstrated through structured scientific activities. Many students display out of school science proclivity through characteristics of intense curiosity, fertile imagination and a questioning attitude. However, these characteristics yield little results in a society where academic achievement is still a predominant indicator of ability.

Catering to the needs of creative science students is of low priority for India, where even basic education is a colossal challenge. Science teaching in most Indian schools is targeted, at best, towards medium-ability students and with strong emphasis to get the students to score high marks in science and mathematics so that the aggregate result looks good and projects the student as an above-average performer of scholastic ability. A majority of school teachers are trained to deliver content and concepts in science with little or no understanding about the process, pedagogy or the philosophy behind learning science. As far as creative science students are concerned, their academic needs are hardly met within the school system where, by and large, creative questions and discourses are discouraged within the classroom lest it 'disrupts a class' with 'unnecessary and outlandish' ideas. As a result, such students go through several years of formal education restricted to only expressing their abilities through examinations and evaluations that do not address their creative capabilities and needs. A few lucky students may accidentally, or with considerable effort, catch the attention of a mentor (either a teacher, or a domain expert in his or her community, or a family member) who motivates them towards creative thinking, guides them through the creative journey or provides special opportunities for creativity to blossom.

While some research reports that creative children are lively, happy, enjoy stable emotions and are admired by their peers (Coleman, 1985), other studies report that they are vulnerable to issues and situations which hamper their cognitive and affective development (Colangelo and Assouline, 2000). They may feel out-of-step with their social context and this, coupled with their heightened awareness of being different from their peers, can cause further dissonance and emotional stress. Initial results of an ongoing study by the author and her colleague (Roy and Chatterjee, 2014) on motivation, self-concept and self-portrayal of talented high-school science students from India show students facing difficulties in developing positive and realistic self-concepts, being confused in goal orientation and suffering from motivational lapses. Results also reveal that both power and affiliation needs are strong for these respondents which is a source of considerable conflict.

Science proneness (Brandwein, 1995) seems embedded in general giftedness, which develops into verbal and mathematical skills initially and, with time, translates into problem-seeking, finding and solving in specialized science fields. Predicting eminence and creative accomplishments becomes difficult when the exact nature of specific abilities is yet not well established. Lubinski and colleagues (e.g. Webb *et al.*, 2002; Lubinski *et al.*, 2006; Wai *et al.*, 2005) have found that specific mathematical and verbal abilities measured around age 13 in high-achieving students are valuable predictors of educational and occupational outcomes. The Study of Mathematically Precocious Youth (SMPY) have shown that verbal versus quantitative tilt in abilities predicts differences in domains of accomplishment, with verbal tilt increasing the probability of accomplishments in the humanities and quantitative tilt increasing the probability of accomplishments in science, technology, engineering and maths (STEM) fields (Park *et al.*, 2007; Wai *et al.*, 2005).

Early sets of observable activities in children displaying science talent are usually noticed in the form of focused high-level ability in both acquisition of knowledge and a capacity for enquiry. Some exhibit raw, unfocused giftedness in search of a purposive expression of talent and gradually exhibit a definitive focus towards science by demonstrating domain-specific interests. Creativity in different subjects may have some domain-specific traits required for expression within that domain and might, further, be likely to lead to characteristic ways in which creativity may be expressed. 'High cognitive complexity', a term proposed for creative individuals by Hollingsworth (2006), denotes the capacity to understand the world in more diverse ways than those with less cognitive complexity. Scientists with high levels of cognitive complexity tend to internalize multiple fields of science and show greater capacity to observe and understand the connectivity among phenomena in multiple fields of science. They also tend to be more tolerant of ambiguity, more comfortable not only with new but even contradictory findings which are typical of science study and practice. Klix (cited in Heller, 1993) identified psychological mechanisms like the ability to reduce complexity in problems through information processing as a characteristic feature of creative students of science.

Possessing high intelligence, domain knowledge and practical skills are considered basic requisites for a potential scientist. However, scientific creativity focuses not only on discovering or inventing concepts or products, but also on developing them to a level where 'what if' questions replace the 'why' questions. While answers to 'why' questions are sought within the domain, answers to 'what if' questions tend to transgress domains with application of abilities like intuition, imagination and unifying known knowledge with the new in a coherent manner. Sternberg and Lubart (1995) maintained that creativity includes intellectual skills to define and represent problems in new ways, analytical skills to evaluate ideas and select the best ones, practical intelligence to sell the value of the new idea to others and divergent-thinking abilities to generate many diverse ideas.

The propulsion theory of creativity, suggested by Sternberg (2006), mentions eight types of creative contributions to a domain that are divided into three major categories. The first category consists of contributions that accept current paradigms such as 1) replication and 2) redefinition (that preserve domain contributions where they are) or 3) forward incrementation and 4) advance forward incrementation (that preserve contributions and yet move the field forward in the direction it already is going). The second category of creative contributions is those that reject current paradigms such as 5) redirection and 6) reconstruction (move the field in a new direction from an existing or pre-existing starting point) or 7) reinitiation (those that move the field in a new direction from a new starting point). Finally, the third category involves 8) integration (those which combine approaches to integrate two formerly diverse ways into a single way of thinking about a phenomenon). These eight types of creative contributions are largely qualitatively distinct and quantitatively substantially different. The model is therefore suitable to measure contributions not only in qualitative terms but also in terms scientists prefer – that is, quantitatively. Use of this taxonomy to classify creative contributions seems particularly well suited to explain scientific creativity because it is compatible with the structure of science and the manner in which scientists think. These categories of creative contributions help conjure a cognitive schema for scientists and scholars in terms of defining their work as transmitting, correcting, conserving, or expanding the substance of a field to achieve a continuity of cumulative knowledge.

Research scientists are seen to possess characteristics of early independence training, are wide conceptualizers and categorizers, voracious readers and are idiosyncratic in attitude and inventive in procedure. They suffer no inhibitions in attacking a specific problem and 'are free to adopt' any course that their ingenuity is capable of suggesting to them. They value knowing what's wrong as much as what's right (Brandwein, 1995). Another characteristic frequently seen is divergent production, the ability to generate diverse yet appropriate responses to a given situation. Divergent thinking has since become a characteristic identifier for creative thinking because of the cognitive flexibility, associative and intuitive thought connected to it. The student engaged in scientific enquiry displays a 'character-rooted passion' and seeks perpetual acts of scholarship. Self-imposed by rigorous habit, their regimen exceeds the demands of schooling and even of the university. Their self-concept is sharply distinguished from the cursory identification of giftedness or talent in the young through IQ scores or other tests of ability and/or achievement.

Science talent in the young encompasses genetic, predisposing and activating factors. Genetic factors interact with environment to influence a student's ability to learn, in general, and science, in particular. Predisposing factors show up through a questioning attitude that is usually because of dissatisfaction with common explanations of reality. Activating factors comprise an environment of achievement. Attitudinal studies on motivation, self-concept, social emotional needs, self-esteem issues, achievement and school environment, societal and parental influences on creative expression in students provide valuable insights. According to Csikszentmihalyi (1996), who introduced the term 'flow' (performing an activity by being fully immersed in it), people with curiosity, persistence, low self-centredness and a high intrinsic motivation are perhaps able to achieve flow more often than an average person, and may well demonstrate gifted characteristics that are not observed in other learning situations.

One reason students are attracted to science is its inherent logical, mathematical, complex and coherent nature. However, many students (especially girls) feel drawn towards its human face. This closeness to 'person-oriented' science makes them seek out subjects or domains within science which allow them an interface between 'hard' and 'humane' science. Taber (2007) talks of science as a human and collaborative activity – eventually a part of society – which needs to be communicated. However, even today, science is often regarded as unpopular in many countries and the proportion of students interested in science education or careers is relatively low. Plausible reasons for this could be high expectations from science and scientists, lack of cultural and social support structure, lack of educational policies towards exposure to and provisions for science and a dearth of motivational training necessary/conducive to science study. In addition, students' interest in education and employment in science seems gender-specific (Sadler *et al.*, 2012). Studies about attitudes, interests and career choices in science consistently show a gender-specific pattern, with female adolescents choosing science subjects and science careers more infrequently than their male counterparts (Stoeger and Sonntag, 2009).

Psychological factors behind creativity differ with gender, and reducing gender differences in engagement with mathematics and sciences is an ongoing global challenge. Parents, peers and society play a crucial role in attitudes, stereotypes and values associated with creativity in boys and girls. One still finds society and parents steeped in misconceptions that science is better suited to boys than girls (see Chapter 9 by Camcı-Erdoğan and Riga, this volume). Many girls believe that science is a cold, difficult and impersonal subject and feel more comfortable studying literature and arts. For a long time, critical thinking skills and data interpretation were believed to be masculine abilities (Huebner, 2009).

Until recently, not enough attention has been paid to female self-related cognitions in science, leading many girls to underestimate their own talents in mathematics and the sciences and, from a motivational perspective, attribute their successes and failures in ways that further inhibit motivation (Heller and Ziegler, 1996).

In relatively traditional societies like India, the participation of women in science is way below men. The author reports that out of 744 highly talented students identified and selected in the past 55 years by India's first science talent search and nurture centre, the Jagadis Bose National Science Talent Search (JBNSTS), only 69 are women. A longitudinal study of JBNSTS scholars in terms of their achievement and eminence is presently being conducted (Roy, 2014).

Dabrowski (1902–1980) believed gifted and creative individuals possess over-excitabilities (OEs) that are inborn heightened abilities to respond to stimuli that are intellectual, psychomotor, sensual, imaginational and emotional in nature. He reported that more people with OE exist in the gifted population than in the average population. Intellectual OE in creative science students finds expression through their distinct and strong need to seek understanding and truth, to gain knowledge, and to analyse and synthesize (Dabrowski and Piechowski, 1977; Piechowski, 1979, 1991). They are, therefore, attracted to theory, meta-cognition and moral thinking, display intense curiosity, are often avid readers of diverse subjects and have sharp observational powers. Given a difficult intellectual problem, they exhibit the capability to concentrate deeper, for a prolonged period and show tenacity in solving problems. Due to this tenacious, perfectionist character, they tend to be fiercely independent in their thinking and often risk being labelled as too critical, impatient and arrogant. They may also seem rude and non-conforming. When confronted on this issue they may become agitated or lose interest and start underachieving.

Psychological insights towards nurture of creative science students

Exhibiting scientific creativity is one thing; being a successful scientist is altogether a different, though related issue. The intellectual, social, economic and cultural milestones between science giftedness and eminence in science are fraught with challenges which can be overcome by provisions of support from every possible quarter. The defining circumstances where a student, on displaying creative behaviour in science, can grow into a creative and contributing scientist seems to depend mainly on four factors: 1) the home environment in terms of socio-cultural, emotional and economic stability, 2) the school environment in terms of science teaching, provisions for creative expression and resources, 3) the student's psychological constitution, intellectual capacity and the extent of passion and task commitment for a sustained period of time, 4) opportunities for special provisions that enhance creative thought in science beyond school level and where the student is encouraged to hone divergent-thinking skills in the presence of mentors and role models.

In this section, I will focus on learning and insights from psychology that broadly encompass intellectual and emotional aspects and affect related aspects of creativity in science. High cognitive complexity, along with high intelligence, demands the psychological constitution to be in tune with the demands of being creative. Strengthening one's self-concept, self-esteem and self-analysis will add to motivational levels which, in turn, will be reflected in both the creative product and the process. Psychological science tells us that creativity is developmental and, for that very reason, it becomes crucial to ensure that the development of high cognitive complexity is in line with a matching ability. Vygotsky (1978) discussed an optimal learning environment called the 'zone of proximal development' (see Chapter 1 by Taber, this volume). According to him, when work is too easy, learners are in 'comfort zones' and eventually lose interest and, when work is too difficult, learners feel incapable and frustrated. The area between the comfort zone and the frustration zone is the one where learning takes place and is the zone of proximal development.

The initial prerequisite for creativity to survive is a stable home environment. Understanding and yet non-pampering parenting of the creative child goes a long way in the child developing into a disciplined and independent worker; a necessity for pursuing science. Because of their asynchronous development creative young people are particularly vulnerable in some developmental and maturational areas. Understanding of psychological factors which come to play in helping the child deal with this asynchrony and develop coping mechanisms needs meticulous research to inform training for parents, teachers and professional counsellors. School psychologists play an important role in creating awareness about issues that seem insurmountable by creative students in the presence of those who think that they 'ought' to be good at everything.

Ultimately, displaying creativity is an act of courage to grope in darkness and venture into areas where results may not always lead to achievement. Creative students in science need that extra help in developing a psychological make-up where they can cope with the rigorous and demanding nature of science. They must develop psychological skills that help them to focus on their passion, keep themselves relatively detached from distractions, help them to develop verbal skills to communicate what and how they think and, finally, to develop social skills needed for collaborative learning in science with other creative scientists. The capacity to push oneself in the face of the complex, exhaustive and difficult nature of the domain of science and mathematics requires honing psychological skills like task commitment, sustained energy for staying within the domain and developing the openness to interact with other domain knowledge.

Exceptional performance in the sciences is explained by cognitive psychological studies that focus on issues such as whether achievement is primarily determined by cognitive problem-solving competence or by motivation, and what leads to scientific under-achievement, and the role of social and cultural influences (Heller, 1996). Psychometric studies help to measure cognitive and non-cognitive personality traits behind scientific ability. Intelligence and creativity aspects like formal-logical thought processes, abstract thinking ability, systematic and theoretical thought processes, problem sensitivity, inventiveness and flow of ideas, flexibility and originality in creative processes and products are typical of creative people in science. Non-aptitude traits, such as intellectual curiosity, a questioning mind, intrinsic motivation, goal orientation and persistence, tolerance of ambiguity, are also seen in such people.

The biographies of a significant number of highly creative people show that they usually had supportive but rigid and non-nurturing parents. Most had an interest in their field at an early age, and most had a highly supportive and skilled mentor in their field of interest. They often chose relatively uncharted fields and devoted almost all of their time and energy into their craft, achieving a creative breakthrough in about a decade. Their lives were marked with extreme dedication and a cycle of hard work and breakthroughs as a result of their determination (Gardner, 1993; Policastro and Gardner, 1999).

Conclusion

Human resources today is precious for every nation and it is the creative 'bank' of a nation that defines the course of its development. Nations aspiring to lead, become more powerful, humane, resourceful and advanced, demand ideas that are novel, innovative and path-breaking. And, in this endeavour to forge ahead as a nation, developments in science and technology matter greatly. The only way to achieve this is to educate and nurture human resource that will be able to meet the demands of the rapidly changing and cutting-edge science and its applications. In the process of achieving this, we are confronted by the need for creative and gifted thinkers in science whose ideas and products will compete globally and create new and advanced benchmarks. Thus, the study of creativity is important not only at the individual level, but also because it has national and global ramifications. With the world becoming a complex arena of geo-political discourse, technology-oriented lifestyle, crisis management and leaps in human endeavour in every domain, creative ideas and novel ways of problem-solving are increasingly in demand. Creativity is not just an academic activity, but also one of practical, social, technological and economic relevance.

The need and challenges faced by advocates of gifted education are manifold and multidisciplinary. Primarily, the basic structure of science learning and teaching in both formal and informal educational systems needs careful restructuring. First, creative students need to be drawn to a science curriculum that motivates them to take on the challenging journey of scientific enquiry and, on the other hand, teaching and teachers need a completely new paradigm and philosophy to steer these creative students towards the pursuit of science. Second, psychologists and educators must collaborate in coming up with better and more creative ways to motivate, identify and nurture science talent, while at the same time keeping a finger on the pulse of society and the changes in perception towards such creative individuals. And, finally, a nation requires its policies to be creativity-friendly and provide an educational and social environment where expressions of creativity do not go unnoticed and uncatered for.

Linking psychological science with cognitive and behavioural aspects of science creativity will play a key role in primarily three broad areas: 1) an understanding of the interplay of psychological constructs that facilitate or thwart creative achievements in science; 2) an awareness of empirical and observational manifestations of psychological mindsets of creative scientists; and 3) the understanding of how psychological strength-building can complement science creativity nurture and vice versa. This linking needs to be done in a manner that preserves the qualitative structure of psychology as well as the logical structure of scientific arguments. In this super domain, efforts need to be made to make definitive and piercing scientific knowledge live compatibly with intuitive and plural psychological approaches and philosophies. Researchers and practitioners within this super domain must learn the art of flexibility and cooperation in thought and action and treat themselves as 'inter-related' rather than 'distinct' contributors.

References

Amabile, T.M. (1996). *Creativity in Context*. Boulder, CO: Westview Press.

Bailey, C.L. (2011). An examination of the relationships between ego development, Dabrowski's theory of positive disintegration, and the behavioral characteristics of gifted adolescents, *Gifted Child Quarterly*, 55(3), 208–22.

Brandwein, P.F. (1995). *Science Talent in the Young Expressed with Ecologies of Achievement* (report no. EC 305208). Storrs, CT: National Research Center on the Gifted and the Talented. (ERIC Documentation Reproduction Service No. ED402700).

Colangelo, N., and Assouline, S.G. (2000). Counseling gifted students. In K.A. Heller, F.J. Monks, R.J. Sternberg, and R.F. Subotnik (Eds), *International Handbook of Giftedness and Talent* (2nd edn). Amsterdam: Elsevier, pp. 595–607.

Coleman, L.J. (1985). *Schooling the Gifted*. Menlo Park, CA: Addison-Wesley.

Csikszentmihalyi, M. (1996). *Creativity: Flow and the psychology of discovery and invention*. New York: Harper Collins.

Csikszentmihalyi, M., and Robinson, R. (1986). Culture, time, and the development of talent. In R.J. Sternberg and J. Davidson (Eds), *Conceptions of Giftedness*. New York: Cambridge University Press, pp. 264–84.

Dabrowski, K., and Piechowski, M.M. (1977). *Theory of Levels of Emotional Development: From primary integration to self-actualization* (Vol. 2). Oceanside, NY: Dabor Science.

Feldman, D.H. (1991). Why children can't be creative. *Exceptionality, Education, Canada*, 1(1), 43–52.

Gardner, H. (1993). *Multiple Intelligences: The theory in practice*. New York: Basic Books

Guilford, J.P. (1950). Creativity. *American Psychologist*, 5, 444–54.

Heller, K.A. (1993). Scientific ability. In G.R. Bock and K. Ackrill (Eds), *The Origins and Development of High Ability*. Chichester: John Wiley and Sons, pp. 139–50.

Heller, K.A. (1996). The nature and development of giftedness: a longitudinal study, in A.J. Cropley and D. Dehn (Eds), *Fostering the Growth of High Ability European Perspectives*, Norwood, NJ: Ablex, p. 44.

Heller, K.A. and Ziegler, A. (1996). Gender differences in mathematics and the sciences: can attributional retraining improve the performance of gifted females? *Gifted Child Quarterly*, 40, 200–10.

Huebner, T. (2009). Encouraging girls to pursue math and science. *Educational Leadership*, 67(1), 90–1.

Hollingsworth, J.R. (2006). Organizational and psychological factors influencing creativity in basic science. Paper presented before Atlanta Conference on Science and Technology Policy, May.

Lubinski, D., Benbow, C.P., Webb, R.M., and Bleske-Rechek, A. (2006). Tracking exceptional human capital over two decades. *Psychological Science*, 17, 194–9.

Mills, C.J. (1993). Personality, learning style and cognitive style profiles of mathematically talented students. *European Journal for High Ability*, 4, 70–85.

Mpofu, E., Myambo, K., Mashengo, T., Mogaji, A., and Khaleefa, O. (2006). African perspectives on creativity. In J.C. Kaufman and R.J. Sternberg (Eds), *The International Handbook of Creativity*. New York: Cambridge University Press, pp. 456–89

Niu, W. (2006). Development of creativity research in Chinese societies. In J.C. Kaufman and R.J. Sternberg (Eds), *The International Handbook of Creativity*. New York: Cambridge University Press, pp. 386–7.

Nwazuoke, I.A. (1996). *Creativity: Understanding special education*. Ibadan, Nigeria: Creative Books.

Park, G., Lubinski, D., and Benbow, C. P. (2007). Contrasting intellectual patterns predict creativity in the arts and sciences: tracking intellectually precocious youth over 25 years. *Psychological Science*, 18, 948–52.

Piechowski, M.M. (1979). Developmental potential. In N. Collangelo and R.T. Zaffrann (Eds), *New Voices in Counseling the Gifted*. Dubuque, IA: Kendall/Hunt, pp. 25–57.

Piechowski, M.M. (1991). Giftedness for all seasons: inner peace in a time of war. Presented at the Henry B. and Jocelyn Wallace National Research Symposium on Talent Development, University of Iowa.

Policastro, E., and Gardner, H. (1999). From case studies to robust generalizations: an approach to the study of creativity. In R.J. Sternberg (Ed.), *Handbook of Creativity*. Cambridge: Cambridge University Press, pp. 213–25.

Preiser, S. (2006) Creativity research in German-speaking countries. In J.C. Kaufman and R.J. Sternberg (Eds), *The International Handbook of Creativity*. New York: Cambridge University Press, p. 175.

Renzulli, J.S. (1977). *The Enrichment Triad Model: A guide for developing defensible programs for the gifted and talented*. Mansfield Center, CT: Creative Learning Press.

Roy, P. (2014). Creativity and giftedness in adolescents. Talk presented at Think CIQ Conference, Bangalore, India.

Roy, P., and Chatterjee, A. (2014) Motivation, self concept and self portrayal of talented high school science students: their voices. Paper presented at the First International Conference on Research in Education and Curriculum Planning for Gifted Minds, New Delhi.

Sadler, P.M., Sonnert, G., Hazari, Z., and Tai, R. (2012). Stability and volatility of STEM career interest in high school: a gender study. *Science Education*, 96, 411–27.

Sak, U. (2004). A synthesis of research on psychological types of gifted adolescents. *Prufrock Journal*, 15(2), 70–9.

Silverman, L.K. (2005). *Intensitive! Intensities and Sensitivities of the Gifted: Social and emotional needs of gifted children*. Hobart: Tasmanian Association for the Gifted.

Simonton, D.K. (1999). *Origins of Genius: Darwinian perspectives on creativity*. Oxford: Oxford University Press.

Smith, G.J.W., and Carlsson, I. (2006). Creativity under the northern lights: perspectives from Scandinavia. In J.C. Kaufmann, and R.J. Sternberg (Eds), *The International Handbook of Creativity*. New York: Cambridge University Press, pp. 202–34.

Stoeger, H., and Sonntag, C. (2009). Gender differences in education: the situation of high achieving boys and girls. *News and Science*, 3, 27–35.

Sternberg, R.J. (2006). The Nature of Creativity. *Creativity Research Journal*, 18(1), 87–98.

Sternberg, R.J., and Lubart, T.I. (1995). *Defying the Crowd: Cultivating creativity in a culture of conformity*. New York: Free Press.

Subotnik, R.F., and Steiner, C.L. (1993) Adult manifestations of adolescent talent in science. *Roeper Review*, 11, 139–44.

Taber, K.S. (2007). *Enriching School Science for the Gifted Learner*. London: Gatsby Science Enhancement Programme.

Terman, L.M. (1928). *Genetic Studies of Genius: Volume I. Mental and physical traits of a thousand gifted children*. Palo Alto, CA: Stanford University Press.

Torrance, E.P. (1962). *Guiding Creative Talent*. Englewood Cliffs, NJ: Prentice Hall.

Torrance, E.P. (1974). *Torrance Tests of Creative Thinking*. Lexington, MA: Personnel Press.

Tucker, V. (2001). *Creativity for You: A training course in creativity through divergent thinking*. Bandra, Bombay: Better Yourself Books.

Vygotsky, L.S. (1978). *Mind in Society: The development of higher psychological processes*. Cambridge, MA: Harvard University Press.

Wai, J., Lubinski, D., and Benbow, C.P. (2005). Creativity and occupational accomplishments among intellectually precocious youths: an age 13 to age 33 longitudinal study. *Journal of Educational Psychology*, 97, 484–92.

Webb, R.M., Lubinski, D., and Benbow, C.P. (2002). Mathematically facile adolescents with math/science aspirations: new perspectives on their educational and vocational development. *Journal of Educational Psychology*, 94, 785–94.

3 Teaching science and gifted students

Using depth, complexity and authentic enquiry in the discipline

Sandra N. Kaplan, William F. McComas and Jessica A. Manzone

This chapter shares with others in this book an expectation that gifted students will be served well by their school science experiences, and an understanding that many gifted students have specific skills, strengths, interests, proclivities and even gifts with respect to science knowledge and its processes.

Although our goal is not a focus on the identification of gifted learners, this is a vital first step. Taber (2007), for instance, detailed some of the ways that we might identify such students through demonstrations of their metacognitive maturity (sustained interest, concentration and perseverance), high-level cognitive ability and, of course, curiosity in and about science. This last characteristic must resonate with teachers, parents and all who care about the nurturing of gifted students. Even historians have often noted the childhood interests and amateur leanings of the most important and productive naturalists and scientists, such as Conrad Gessner, John Ray, Carl Linnaeus and Charles Darwin (Appleby, 2013).

Among the most charming of the historical anecdotes that exemplify curiosity is the story of how young Charles Darwin, with a beetle in each hand, was so keen to capture a new type that he was willing to pop one of his conquests in his mouth for safekeeping. This didn't end well, for the beetle had other plans. It made its escape through the haze of a mini-explosion of acidic droplets that caused Darwin to spit out this new specimen while dropping all those he had recently captured. Of course, Darwin was interested not just in beetles but in all things science, from geology to chemistry (this last avocation gave him the nickname 'Gas', which clung to him for much of his youth). But the response of his school headmaster to these various scientific interests was sobering. Even late in life, Darwin remembered that he 'called me very unjustly a "poco curante"' (Browne, 1995, p. 33), which during that time meant someone interested only in unimportant things or trifles. How sad it would have been if the young Darwin's curiosity were extinguished by this headmaster, who was unable to recognize giftedness in science when he encountered it in such a clear and dramatic fashion. We wonder how frequently this occurs even today, when a scientifically gifted student is more interested in the natural world than in the stale lesson the teacher had in mind.

While Howard Gardner's concept of multiple intelligences has its critics, it is useful to note that his most recent list of purported strengths and preferences includes 'naturalist', which joins logical–mathematical, linguistic and bodily–kinesthetic, among others (Gardner, 1999). Even if 'naturalist' is not widely accepted as a 'true intelligence', it is clear that many students are collectors and classifiers with respect to the natural world, in much the same way that Renaissance nobles had their *Wunderkammers*, or rooms of wonder, filled from floor to ceiling with objects of delight and curiosity. What child interested in science doesn't also have his or her personally relevant collection of objects that arouse these same emotions?

Steven Chu, former US Secretary of Energy and winner of the 1997 Nobel Prize in Physics, stated that science, at its core, is about trying to make sense of the natural world. According to Chu (2013), students learn how to 'cast explanations into falsifiable themes that can be tested by experiments' (p. 3). Therefore, all learners with interests in science – even those who will not become the next Galileo, Newton, or Darwin – deserve school experiences that use science as it is intended: to organize and apply the information they have obtained to uncover patterns and make sense of the world around them. Beyond merely identifying students who are gifted in science, the challenge is how best to serve such learners in the educational setting. In this chapter, we will discuss enquiry in the discipline and the Depth and Complexity Model (Kaplan, 2005) as strategies to differentiate curriculum and instruction, as a means of responding to and developing the needs and curiosity of gifted science learners.

A conceptual framework for differentiation

Differentiating science to meet the special needs and talents of gifted learners has often been equated with the concept of 'increased academic rigour' as a way to provide such students with more advanced or sophisticated learning. In some instances, differentiating science for gifted students may mean providing them opportunities to conduct experiments and engage in similar activities that other students are not ready for. However, as understanding of the nature of giftedness and definitions of differentiation have evolved, so too have the philosophical beliefs and pedagogical models that might best provide for such learners. Presently, there are two types of differentiation for gifted students: 1) differentiation for all gifted learners as they engage in any science area and 2) differentiation for those gifted students who express and/or exhibit a proclivity towards science. Several models guide the process of differentiating curriculum for gifted learners and 'gifted potential scientists'. While each of these models is unique in its approach, all share common features. The distinction between 'gifted' and 'gifted in science' may be most important when teachers are able to diagnose such strengths and prescribe targeted learning experiences, but we will take the perspective here that all gifted learners should experience science in the most engaging and embracing ways possible.

Modification of the basic or core curriculum is often considered the foundation on which differentiation is determined (Gubbins, 1994; Gallagher, 2000). Specifically, Tomlinson and Jarvis (2009) identified adjustments to the content, processes and products as the best means to achieve differentiation. Preparation for unknown challenges in the student's future (Halpern, 1998) parallels the earlier discussion by Passow (1982) regarding the importance of ensuring that differentiation provides in-depth study and enquiry-based approaches to acquiring knowledge and understanding in new situations. The need to include instructional strategies that allow for acceleration in learning how to question and problem-solve (VanTassel-Baska, 2003) underscores the concept of differentiation as a means to provide gifted students with opportunities for the kinds of self-directed studies, such as 'science fairs', that lend themselves so well to the robust study of the sciences.

Origin and development of the Depth and Complexity Model

The origin of the concept of 'depth and complexity' can be traced to early formal schooling. Teachers have always attempted to answer questions about how best to recognize and provide for individual differences among their students; therefore, modifying the standard instructional approach with depth and complexity is a logical extension of that quest. Originally, the term 'depth' referred to the principle whereby some students were permitted to forge ahead in a field of study beyond the expectations held for others in the class. Traditionally, 'complexity' referred to curriculum designs that were 'harder' or more 'challenging' than what was typically expected that other students at the same grade level could master.

The Depth and Complexity Model originated from work supported by a Javits Grant awarded to the California Department of Education (CDE) by the US Department of Education in 1994. Educators convened by the CDE worked to address the question of what subject-area differentiation would look like for gifted students.

The answer to the question was defined by four constructs: acceleration, novelty, depth and complexity. We will discuss the first elements briefly and focus more attention on the last two aspects.

Acceleration was defined in the CDE document as expediting the means by which students acquire knowledge of the discipline. This approach emphasized the inclusion of 'big ideas' – universal concepts such as 'Systems' and 'Change' – or the theories, principles and generalizations descriptive of and/or related to those big ideas, which are essential understandings in the disciplines. Acceleration also introduced the concept of 'thinking like a disciplinarian' as the means to provide gifted students with an introduction to the formal structure and content of the disciplines. Thus, in the scientific study of plants, teachers can introduce gifted students to the universal concept of 'Systems' to direct and organize the study and further their understanding within the context of 'thinking like a botanist'. The construct of Acceleration both extends and elaborates gifted students' orientation and comprehension of the study of a topic or subject in the basic or core curriculum.

Novelty was defined as the construct that would facilitate the gifted students' opportunities to acquire and practise creative, critical, problem-solving and logical-thinking skills. Germane to the construct of Novelty was providing gifted students with the opportunity to pursue in-depth independent studies that develop their interests, aptitudes and research skills. We will discuss the use of independent study in science classes below.

As Ward (1961) stated in his early seminal work, depth and complexity involve making relationships between and among ideas, connecting those ideas to other concepts, and bridging them across the disciplines. Therefore, the Depth and Complexity Model makes use of the fact that, when approaching the study of a topic from multiple perspectives, clues or prompts will help provide greater detail and promote understanding. This occurs as students examine the subject 1) from the concrete to the abstract and from the abstract to the concrete, 2) from the familiar to the unfamiliar and from the unfamiliar to the familiar and 3) from the known to the unknown and from the unknown to the known (California Department of Education and California Association for the Gifted, 1994). According to the California Association for the Gifted (2005), as students move through the different modes of thinking, they will be in the position to form important conceptual foundations related to the subject matter.

Prompts for depth and complexity

The Depth and Complexity Model uses key words that can serve as prompts to initiate gifted students' entry into an investigation of the authentic nature of a topic or discipline. Such prompts are integrated into students' daily personal and academic lives. One way of sharing these prompts in textbooks, in classroom instruction and with students directly is through the use of terms or pictorial representations like those found on the toolbar of a computer (see Table 3.1). Students can observe and utilize such prompts daily, and they can be used to activate elements of the Depth and Complexity Model.

The prompts are derived from three sources: 1) a study of the discipline itself, 2) intellectual demands of the nature and attributes of giftedness and 3) conventional wisdom of educators and disciplinarians who understand both the nature of gifted students and the structure of the discipline. These three sources can be catalysts for defining the prompts of depth and complexity (Kaplan, 2005). Each prompt may be strongly or weakly associated with the discipline under study, but all prompts have applicable associations in all disciplines. Take, as an example, a discussion of patterns: there are patterns in the structure of poetry, in rock formations, in historical events such as revolutions and in mathematical equations. The relative use and importance of each prompt will depend on the discipline: the study of science will evoke a different suite of prompts than the study of mathematics, for instance.

Each of the prompts in Table 3.1 is represented by a graphic for several reasons. In our technological age, students are used to the graphics or symbols that depict types of applications on a computer or smartphone. Symbolic representations of language are often used as cues for young learners and English-language learners. To this end, the graphics representing the prompts provide both a universal language and universal access to language development.

Table 3.1 Facilitating understanding of depth and complexity

Note to the teacher: This chart identifies key questions, thinking skills and dimensions of depth and complexity.
Key questions can be used in the context of a lesson designed to probe understanding and to prompt students during discussions.
The *thinking skills* can be used to initiate the type of cognitive operation or thinking that will best prompt each of the dimensions of depth and complexity.
The *resources* listed are the most logical references in which to locate the type of information required by each of the dimensions of depth and complexity. Teachers can add to any of these lists as appropriate.

Icon	Prompt	Key questions	Thinking skills	Resources
	Language of the discipline	What academic language is specific to the work of an individual within the discipline? What tools does the practitioner of the discipline (sometimes called a 'disciplinarian') use?	• identify • categorize	• textbooks • biographies
	Details	What are the object's attributes? What features characterize it? What distinguishes it from other things?	• identify traits • describe • differentiate • compare and contrast • prove with evidence • observe	• pictures • diaries or journals • poetry
	Patterns	What are the recurring events? What elements, events and ideas are repeated over time? What was the order of events? How can we predict what will come next?	• determine relevant vs irrelevant • summarize • make analogies • discriminate between same and different • relate	• timelines • charts • lists
	Trends	What ongoing factors have influenced this study? What factors have contributed to this study?	• prioritize • determine cause and effect • predict • relate • formulate questions • hypothesize	• journals • newspapers • graphs • charts

(continued)

Table 3.1 Facilitating understanding of depth and complexity (Continued)

Note to the teacher: This chart identifies key questions, thinking skills and dimensions of depth and complexity.
Key questions can be used in the context of a lesson designed to probe understanding and to prompt students during discussions.
The *thinking skills* can be used to initiate the type of cognitive operation or thinking that will best prompt each of the dimensions of depth and complexity.
The *resources* listed are the most logical references in which to locate the type of information required by each of the dimensions of depth and complexity. Teachers can add to any of these lists as appropriate.

Icon	Prompt	Key questions	Thinking skills	Resources
	Unanswered questions	What is still not understood about this area, topic, study, or discipline? What is yet unknown about this area, topic, study, or discipline? In what ways is the information incomplete or lacking in explanation?	• recognize fallacies • note ambiguity • distinguish fact from fiction • formulate questions • problem-solve • test assumptions • identify missing information	• multiple and varied resources • comparative analyses of autobiographies and current nonfiction articles, etc.
	Rules	How is this structured? What are the stated and unstated causes related to the description or explanation of what we are studying?	• generalize • hypothesize • judge credibility	• editorials • essays • scientific laws • scientific theories
	Ethics	What dilemmas or controversies are involved in this area, topic, study, or discipline? What elements can be identified that reflect bias, prejudice and discrimination?	• judge with criteria • determine bias	• editorials • essays • autobiographies • journals
	Big ideas, principles, and cross-cutting themes[1]	What overarching statement best describes what is being studied? What general statement includes what is being studied?	• prove with evidence • generalize • identify main idea	• quotations • discipline-related essays

	Over time	How are ideas related between the past, present and future? How are these ideas related within or during a particular historical period? How has time affected the information? How and why do things change or remain the same?	• relate • sequence • order	• timelines • textbooks • biographies • historical documents • autobiographies
	Different points of view	What are the opposing viewpoints? How do different people and characters see this event or situation?	• argue • determine bias • classify	• biographies • myths, legends and nonfiction accounts • debates
	Impact	How does _____ influence _____? What are the effects of ____ on _____?	• affect • identify • force	• quotes • editorials • persuasive essays
	Process	What steps are used to create this? What type of procedure is involved?	• sequence • connect • link • order • arrange	• continuums • storyboards • flowcharts • timelines
	Motive	What is causing this to happen? How is the idea or work stimulated?[2]	• reason • excite • enquire • explain	• biographies • autobiographies • interviews
	Validation[3]	What information verifies this? How can this be validated?	• distinguish fact from opinion • support with evidence • authenticate • prove • document	• statistics • maps • graphs • experiments • observations

(continued)

Table 3.1 Facilitating understanding of depth and complexity (Continued)

Note to the teacher: This chart identifies key questions, thinking skills and dimensions of depth and complexity.
Key questions can be used in the context of a lesson designed to probe understanding and to prompt students during discussions.
The *thinking skills* can be used to initiate the type of cognitive operation or thinking that will best prompt each of the dimensions of depth and complexity. The *resources* listed are the most logical references in which to locate the type of information required by each of the dimensions of depth and complexity. Teachers can add to any of these lists as appropriate.

Icon	Prompt	Key questions	Thinking skills	Resources
	Context	What determines the outcome of an event? What features, conditions, or circumstances describe the situation? How does the environment shape or affect what is happening?	• define • describe • illustrate • influence	• pictures • descriptive essays • narratives • almanacs • videotapes • virtual field trips
	Translate	What are the multiple and varied meanings of the language? How is the same idea interpreted in different situations by different people?	• restate • interpret • recite • express • explain • convert • transfer	• thesaurus • dictionary • professional terms
	Original	Why is it new? What makes it new? How do time and place make it new?	• create • design • innovate • modify • redesign	• copyright laws • patents • publications showing precedence • artefacts • museum collections

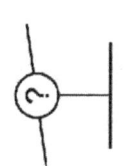

Judgement

What factors will influence what is happening?

How is the decision to be made?

- decide
- determine
- agree
- disagree
- verify
- investigate
- identify opinions to argue

- philosophical principles
- prevailing practices

Notes

[1] The *Next Generation Science Standards* (NGSS) (NGSS Lead States, 2013) in the USA feature the crosscutting concepts of (a) patterns; (b) cause and effect; (c) scale, proportion and quantity; (d) systems and system models; (e) energy and matter in systems; (f) structure and function; and (g) stability and change of systems. According to the authors of the *NGSS*, these concepts are not intended as additional content.

[2] The *NGSS* (NGSS Lead States, 2013) in the USA include engineering practices along with science practices, and there is the potential for confusion in doing so, in that the motivations of engaging in science are quite distinct from those that guide engineering.

[3] In former conceptualizations of this plan for enhancing Depth and Complexity, the term 'Proof' was used. This term is less appropriate in science than in other disciplines because, of course, one can never really prove anything of consequence in science. However, the notion of working to ensure the accuracy or voracity of an idea is highly valued in science, subsequently 'Validation' is a more appropriate way to label this concept.

Implementing the prompts

Several strategies can be used to introduce the prompts of depth and complexity to gifted students and to illustrate their utilization. Each strategy requires that the selected prompts be embedded with specific skills and content from the topic or discipline under study. The prompts require a relationship to both skills and content in order to render their meaning and activate their intent to delve into a body of knowledge. These strategies are illustrated here with examples from a science curriculum.

1. *Lesson objective:* Demonstrate, with evidence, a *pattern* to show the *process* of how rocks are formed after reading and observing information.
2. *Question strategy:* What evidence can be identified that signifies the *rules* related to the concept of 'force'?
3. *Task directions:* After viewing the video related to ecological *trends*, create a poster or persuasive essay that will influence the *judgement* of the viewer about the *ethical issues* implied or activated by knowledge of climate change.
4. *Academic language:* Common to all the prompts is their alignment with the academic language used either directly or indirectly, formally or informally, within the discipline of science. Introducing the study of the disciplines exposes students to the idea that all disciplines contain their own unique language, tools, methodology, inventions, theories and significant contributions to society (Mora-Flores and Kaplan, 2012).
   a. For example, the meaning of *patterns* is common to the disciplines of astronomy and geology. However, different *processes* in the different disciplines define *patterns* in different ways. This is an example of similarities and differences in the application of the academic language represented by the prompts.
   b. The meaning of *impact* is dependent on the *context*. For example, the *impact* of a *process* in geology differs from the *impact* of a *process* in physics. Knowledge of geology may *impact* decisions about how close to a fault line one should build. In physics the *impact* may be more esoteric, particularly if the knowledge relates to a *process* occurring in deep space or deep within the atom. This is another example of how the interpretation of academic language is dependent on the discipline.

Depth and complexity in practice: enquiry instruction and thinking like a disciplinarian

The science curriculum can be informed by using depth and complexity independently of each other, but perhaps the holistic application of these concepts together through scenarios best allows gifted students to experience science as scientists do through enquiry. Advocacy for enquiry in science teaching is almost as old as science instruction itself, and the former *National Science Education Standards* in the USA suggested that it is *the* major way to teach science because scientists so frequently engage in this practice (National Research Council, 2000). The latest or *Next Generation Science Standards* (NGSS Lead States, 2013) take a more nuanced approach to enquiry teaching by providing detail 'to better specify what is meant by enquiry in science and the range of cognitive, social, and physical practices that it requires' (p. xv). It is clear that enquiry teaching is strongly related to one of the principal investigative tools in science and to suggestions on how to enhance science teaching for the gifted by changing the degree of depth and complexity. To understand how this might be accomplished, it is useful to consider the forms of enquiry, rather than merely seeing enquiry as occurring or not occurring. At the same time, it will be useful to explore how enquiry can be part of a bigger agenda for gifted science teaching that includes helping students to 'think like disciplinarians'.

Enquiry instruction and science education

Table 3.2 shows that making some simple changes in the various roles associated with problem-solving in the laboratory results in large changes in what might be called 'cognitive load'. In very basic 'cookbook' activities in which students already know what they are supposed to find, the activity/enquiry type could be low level, perhaps a 0 or 1. When students are asked to take more responsibility for their work, the level and the depth and complexity of the activity are increased considerably, along with the potential for learning. One conclusion that is easily reached when considering the taxonomy illustrated in Table 3.2 is that it is possible to elevate both the status of the activity and its learning potential just by requiring that students take on more responsibility in terms of defining the problem, designing the problem-solving method and/or making sense of the findings. Needless to say, scientists operate almost exclusively at the highest level of this classification scheme – and gifted science learners should too.

Table 3.2 Levels of enquiry based on roles associated in problem-solving activities

Level of enquiry	*Who determines or suggests the problem?*	*Who determines the methods of investigation?*	*Who answers or solves the problem?*
0	teacher	teacher	teacher
1	teacher	teacher	student
2	teacher	student	student
3	student	student	student

Note: 'teacher' means that the classroom provides the necessary action, while 'student' means that the action comes from the learner. The implication embedded in this taxonomy is that as students are asked to take on increased responsibility, the impact on learning increases and students act more like scientists.
Source: McComas, 2005.

Authentically thinking like a disciplinarian

In the recurring conversation about the nature of educational practices, one often encounters the notion of authenticity. Unfortunately, instruction in any school discipline is fraught with many examples that do not portray the discipline accurately, leading to students' stereotypical understanding of work or study in that arena. Of course, this is true in science classes, where learning is often mediated by teachers who lecture constantly, standards that prescribe fixed learning goals, textbooks that tell and reveal without providing context and cookbook activities that are made as foolproof as possible. Some of this is likely unavoidable, but it can be minimized through the application of depth and complexity mediated through enquiry instruction. Making science instruction more authentic is quite possible by teaching students to approach concepts from an expert's point of view.

Theorists such as Bruner and Dewey reiterated the importance of curriculum that provided opportunities for students to gain abstract knowledge of the disciplines and the connections that existed between them. In other words, to assume the 'role' of the disciplinarian is to engage in the study of the discipline's language, tools and methodology. Dewey (1916) contended that the study of the nature of the discipline helps students organize information and understand that no body of knowledge exists individually and that all have larger societal implications.

Raising the level of enquiry by implementing the prompts of depth and complexity to the highest practical level allows students to think and act more like scientists while still learning the core ideas of the traditional curriculum. Fully embracing work as a disciplinarian demands that students operating at the highest and most authentic levels of the discipline must understand the 'nature of science' (NOS), the key philosophical and ideas within science that explain how knowledge is created and validated (Lederman, 1992; McComas, 1998, 2010; Osborne *et al.*, 2003). With help from a knowledgeable teacher acting as a coach, many of these key NOS principles can be learned from experience when students are working *like* scientists. However, only when students fully understand and apply key NOS principles can they work *as* scientists. Clearly, gifted students must be given as many opportunities as possible to learn and experience science and its nature by working within the discipline. Among the most authentic, realistic and powerful kinds of work that students can do in science is to participate in an independent study, often in the form of a science fair or research competition.

Science fairs, research competitions and the conduct of authentic science

Independent study or research and the presentation of projects at science fairs have been respected as important instructional practices for learning the discipline and processes of science and becoming adept as an independent learner of science. Students must be taught, through modelling and experience, to be independent researchers; there is no assumption that some set of skills is inherent in being a gifted student. Table 3.3 illustrates the relationships, either covert or overt, between the steps of independent research and the prompts of depth and complexity.

Table 3.3 The relationship of independent study to the application of depth and complexity

Syntax of independent study	Description of syntax	Connection to the prompts of Depth and Complexity
Select a topic	• Students generate a list of possible areas of focus under the umbrella of the core content standard • Students prioritize their list on a continuum of least interesting to most interesting • Students select one idea that is most interesting to become the target of their investigation	*Multiple perspectives* *Original* *Motive*
Develop a set of questions	• Students generate a set of research questions based on their selected topic • Students vary the types of questions they ask to include factual, analytic and evaluative questions • Students participate in conferences with the teacher to discuss and revise their questions	*Process* *Unanswered questions* *Translate* *Details*
Conduct research	• Students use multiple different modalities to research the answers to their questions • Students can discuss different types of evidence (quantitative and qualitative) and the relationship between evidence types and their research questions • Students can also discuss the reliability and validity of evidence as well as the importance of citations to avoid plagiarism	*Process* *Validation* *Ethics* *Judgement*
Organize information	• Students begin to organize or cull their research on the basis of the questions they asked • Students are exposed to various organizational structures and discuss the importance of aligning the desired action with the way research is organized	*Patterns* *Trends* *Context*
Present information	• Students create a presentation to share what they have learned with others • Students discuss the relationship between audience (who the information is for) and format (how the information is to be presented) • Students are exposed to various modes of presentation and discuss authentic models as related to the topic under study • Students deliver their presentation to others	*Rules* *Translate* *Context*

(continued)

Table 3.3 The relationship of independent study to the application of depth and complexity (Continued)

Syntax of independent study	Description of syntax	Connection to the prompts of Depth and Complexity
Assess information	• Students assess the results of their independent study project • Results can be assessed against the 'norm' or a teacher-created rubric, peer evaluations and student self-evaluations • Students can generate additional questions they have uncovered as a result of their research	*Judgement* *Impact* *Multiple perspectives* *Over time*

Independent study is a pedagogical practice that teachers can use to increase the academic rigour of the learning experience for gifted students. McCollister and Sayler (2010) described academic rigour as an amalgamation of the major core concepts of the disciplines and opportunities for problem-solving and reasoning. Advanced skill sets or cognitive processes such as raising questions, interpreting previously constructed hypothesizes and posing and justifying one's own argument are embedded in the steps of an independent study project. Independent study projects also offer students an opportunity to complete an original piece of work synthesized from many and varied sources.

Independent study can be implemented in three different ways to increase the academic rigour of the learning experience: 1) as the introduction to topics within the core curriculum, 2) as the reinforcement for topics currently under study and 3) as the extension or culmination of previously studied material. Independent study can be used as the catalyst for delving into the core topic under study. In this approach, teachers provide students with a general area of focus aligned with upcoming core content standards. Students' research questions can then be used to guide the unit and serve as the interest-based 'hook' that connects each learner to the content. Independent study projects that reinforce the core content could be presented concurrently with the standards-based lessons or as a truly independent activity. This strategy allows students to delve into an area of interest at the same time as they are learning about the core. What they learn independently reinforces the content presented by the standard curriculum, textbooks, or teacher.

Finally, independent study can be used to extend the core content standards. In this approach, teachers provide students with an opportunity to work on a project that serves as the culmination of what they have learned and extends the standards according to interest and aptitude. The variety of ways that independent study can be implemented in the classroom provides teachers with options for using this pedagogical practice as a strategy to differentiate learning for gifted students. Table 3.3 provides an overview of what could be called 'independent study' in almost any school subject or the 'scientific research method' in the context of science. Science teachers will recognize the phases delineated in the first column and may find the prompts from depth and complexity in the third column useful for guiding and even assessing student work.

Final thoughts

The Depth and Complexity and enquiry models are responses to the defined characteristics of giftedness as well as resources to elicit the display of the traits of giftedness in science-related learning situations. For example, the prompt of *judgement* is a response to the quandary within an enquiry study of a specific science discipline. The same prompt of *judgement* can also be applied to a student's independent study of scientific phenomena. In both situations, the prompt of *judgement* is the stimulus to articulate some of the attributes of a scientist.

There are two parallel goals regarding the teaching and implementation of the Depth and Complexity and enquiry models. The first goal is for students to internalize the meaning and nuances of the depth and complexity prompts. The second goal is to facilitate students' independent study of a topic in science. In the book *Curious Minds: How a child becomes a scientist*, Brockman (2004) describes several traits that are fundamental to becoming a scientist, including the notion that scientists are 'obsessively, passionately, almost pathologically curious' (p. 211). Brockman feels that this curiosity needs to dominate one's life. There is evidence that the Depth and Complexity and enquiry models can be the stimulus to evoke such curiosity and reinforce one of the major contributors to success in science – the ability to initiate and respond to curiosity.

References

Appleby, J. (2013). *Shores of Knowledge: New discoveries and the scientific imagination.* New York: W.W. Norton.

Brockman, J. (Ed.) (2004). *Curious Minds: How a child becomes a scientist.* New York: Pantheon.

Browne, J. (1995). *Charles Darwin Voyaging.* Princeton, NJ: Princeton University Press.

California Association for the Gifted. (2005). *Meeting the Standards: A guide to developing services for gifted students.* Whittier, CA: CAG Press.

California Department of Education and California Association for the Gifted. (1994). *Differentiating the Core Curriculum and Instruction to Provide Advanced Learning Opportunities.* Sacramento: California Department of Education.

Chu, S. (2013). Teaching science in elementary school: turning today's children into tomorrow's leaders. In *Science for the Next Generation: Preparing for the new standards.* Arlington, VA: NSTA Press.

Dewey, J. (1916). *Democracy and Education.* New York: Macmillan.

Gallagher, J.J. (2000). Unthinkable thoughts: education of gifted students. *Gifted Child Quarterly,* 44, 5–12.

Gardner, H.E. (1999). *Intelligence Reframed: Multiple intelligences for the 21st century.* New York: Basic Books.

Gubbins, E.J. (1994). When 'differentiated' becomes disconnected from curriculum. National Research Center on the Gifted and Talented. Retrieved from http://www.gifted.uconn.edu/nrcgt/newsletter/winter94/wintr941.html

Halpern, D.F. (1998). Teaching critical thinking for transfer across domains: dispositions, skills, structure training, and metacognitive monitoring. *American Psychologist*, 53, 449–55.

Kaplan, S.N. (2005). Layering differentiated curricula for the gifted and talented. In F.A. Karnes and S.M. Bean, *Methods and materials for teaching the gifted* (2nd edn),. Waco, TX: Prufrock, pp. 107–32.

Lederman, N.G. (1992). Students' and teachers' conceptions of the nature of science: a review of the research. *Journal of Research in Science Teaching*, 29, 331–59.

McCollister, K., and Sayler, M.F. (2010). Lift the ceiling: increase rigor with critical thinking skills. *Gifted Child Today*, 33(1), 41–7.

McComas, W.F. (1998). The principal elements of the nature of science: dispelling the myths of science. In W.F. McComas (Ed.), *The Nature of Science in Science Education: Rationales and strategies.* Dordrecht: Kluwer Academic, pp. 53–70.

McComas, W.F. (2005). Laboratory instruction in the service of science teaching and learning. *Science Teacher*, 72(7), 24–9.

McComas, W.F. (2010). Educating science critics, connoisseurs and creators: what gifted students should know about how science functions. *Gifted Education Communicator*, 41(3), 14–17.

Mora-Flores, E., and Kaplan, S. (2012). Thinking like a disciplinarian: developing academic language in social studies classrooms. *Social Studies Review*, 51, 10–15.

National Research Council. (2000). *Inquiry and the National Science Education Standards.* Washington, DC: National Academies Press.

NGSS Lead States. (2013). *Next Generation Science Standards: For states, by states.* Washington, DC: National Academies Press.

Osborne, J., Ratcliffe, M., Collins, S., Millar, R., and Duschl, R. (2003). What 'ideas-about-science' should be taught in school science? A Delphi study of the 'expert' community. *Journal of Research in Science Teaching*, 40, 692–720.

Passow, A.H. (1982). Differentiated curricula for gifted/talented: a point of view. In S. Kaplan, A. Harry Passow, Philip H. Phenix, Sally M. Reis, Joseph S. Renzulli, Irving S. Sato, Linda H. Smith, E. Paul Torrance and Virgin S. Ward (Eds), *Curricula for the Gifted.* Ventura, CA: National/State Leadership Training Institute on the Gifted/Talented, pp. 1–21.

Taber, K.S. (2007). Science education for gifted learners? In K.S. Taber (Ed.), *Science Education for Gifted Learners.* London: Routledge, pp. 1–14.

Tomlinson, C.A., and Jarvis, J.M. (2009). Differentiation: making curriculum work for all students through responsive planning and instruction. In J. Renzulli, E. Jean Gubbins, Kristin S. McMillen, Rebecca D. Eckert and Catherine A. Little (Eds), *Systems and models for developing programs for the gifted and talented.* Storrs, CT: Creative Learning Press.

US Department of Education. (2004). Jacob K. Javits Gifted and Talented Students Education Program: Legislation, regulations, and guidance. Retrieved from http://www2.ed.gov/programs/javits/legislation.html

VanTassel-Baska, J. (2003). Selecting instructional strategies for gifted learners. *Focus on Exceptional Children*, 36(3), 1–12.

Ward, V.S. (1961). *Educating the Gifted: An axiomatic approach.* Columbus, OH: Merrill.

4 Engagement in theoretical modelling in research apprenticeships for capable high school students

Elon Langbeheim, Samuel A. Safran and Edit Yerushalmi

Science apprenticeship programmes offer gifted and highly capable high school students the opportunity to participate in research projects in a university setting. Science apprenticeship programmes can serve the needs of these talented and curious youngsters, which are often not met in the regular school science curriculum. Such students are characterized by their motivation to apply their creativity, critical thinking and reasoning capabilities to explore in depth topics that interest and challenge them (Gardner, 2008). These needs can be accommodated via research apprenticeships that embody the complexity of authentic scientific investigations (Taber, 2007). It is thus expected that participation in cutting-edge scientific research projects foster these students' enthusiasm for learning science.

Many studies have indeed found that apprenticeship programmes nurture the capable students' motivation to learn science (Cooley and Basset, 1961, Stake and Mares, 2001). However, some studies have reported the opposite – students' disappointment with their research experiences (VanTassel-Baska and Kulieke, 1987, Burgin *et al.*, 2012). Some of the students in the latter study stated that the experience was not satisfying because the research topic was not the one they wanted; others blamed the mundane, repeated work of data collection (Burgin *et al.*, 2012). Experiencing lab research as technical work is not limited to high school research apprenticeships – it is common even among university students. An interview study with scientists who lead research groups across a variety of fields shows that there are grounds for this experience (Feldman *et al.*, 2009). The integration of graduate students in a lab progresses from an initial stage of 'novice researchers' that must be introduced to the lab's terminology, norms and practices and usually culminates in mature students who are 'proficient technicians' that are able to reliably collect, analyse and report data. Some of the graduate students, in particular, those who complete their doctorate, do evolve to a stage of 'knowledge producers' that are capable of developing their own theoretical ideas and models. Thus, gifted students, oriented to become 'knowledge producers', are prone to experience disappointment if they view their role in apprenticeship programmes as mere 'technicians'. This raises the question: how can science apprenticeship programmes provide highly capable high school students with an experience that goes beyond the technical level, thus allowing them to relate their research project to current developments in the scientific field as well as providing them with the opportunity to contribute to authentic and creative research?

The challenge in designing scientific apprenticeships that involves high school students in knowledge production (i.e. developing, using and evaluating models), is due to the hierarchical nature of scientific knowledge. Understanding scientific theory requires extensive background knowledge that high school students – even very capable ones – do not possess. For high school students, independently reading scientific papers that describe the background relevant to their project is rarely possible and, even when it is, only with substantial support to clarify related concepts and terminology. In fact, reading scientific papers is not straightforward even for undergraduate students (Van Lacum *et al.*, 2012). The following quote, from an interview with Jerry (pseudonym) who was a student in a high school apprenticeship programme, illustrates this challenge. Jerry was asked to reflect on the activities in his research experience that were most meaningful to him and replied: 'First of all, I never came across professional literature before and, since that experience, I tried to find some stuff to read myself. But I gave up (reading) because there were too many words I did not understand.'

Jerry explained that while reading professional research literature was a meaningful experience for him during the research apprenticeship, it was just too difficult without the support of his project mentor. Thus, an inherent challenge for high school science apprenticeship experiences is how to remedy the lack of mathematical and scientific background of the students; these are important prerequisites for the autonomous reading of research papers which is essential for understanding the research scope of the field.

In this chapter, we portray an educational programme entitled 'Soft and messy matter', developed to provide talented high school students with a fundamental theoretical introduction to a field that would allow them to more effectively take part in research projects in university settings. The formal course materials helped to enable students to view their project work in the context of a more general scientific effort to model the problem at hand, thus relating the students' research efforts to the overall knowledge structure of their field. We analyse the learning that took place in the programme through a case study of a pair of students. We will describe these students' achievements as well as the challenges they faced in their research. Drawing on our findings we suggest ways to better support student participation in such research apprenticeship programmes.

Introducing scientific modelling of soft matter phenomena

The 'Soft and messy matter' programme was taught and evaluated with three cohorts of capable 11th and 12th grade students who took in parallel advanced high school studies in chemistry and/or physics. The programme was carried out in Israel, where high school students in the 11th grade choose subjects which they study at an advanced level leading to a matriculation examination. Approximately 10 per cent choose to do so in physics or chemistry. The 'Soft and messy matter' programme was undertaken in addition to their regular physics and/or chemistry studies, accounted for 40 per cent matriculation credit in physics or chemistry. It took place as a biweekly, afternoon course at a university outreach centre, and targeted students from several nearby schools. The programme focused on the physical properties of Soft Matter – a growing interdisciplinary field that focuses on the structure and properties of interacting molecular systems such as fluid mixtures, colloidal dispersions, polymers and membranes (Jones, 2002).

Modelling the behaviour of soft matter is based on general principles common to many scientific disciplines, such as identifying an observable empirical pattern, analysing which variables are externally controlled or are adjusted in an independent manner by the system, and suggesting a simplified representation of the system. The theoretical set of tools used for modelling the equilibrium properties of soft matter is based on statistical thermodynamics. Students were introduced to a general modelling sequence that is shown in the flow chart of Figure 4.1. This general process was then specialized to predict the equilibrium behaviour of various soft matter systems. In all these cases, the structure and the thermodynamic behaviour of the specific system was determined via minimization of the system free energy (related to a difference of the internal energy and the entropy of the system) with respect to relevant variables.

The construction and analysis of models of soft matter phenomena calls for the expertise of practising soft matter physicists. We therefore did not expect students

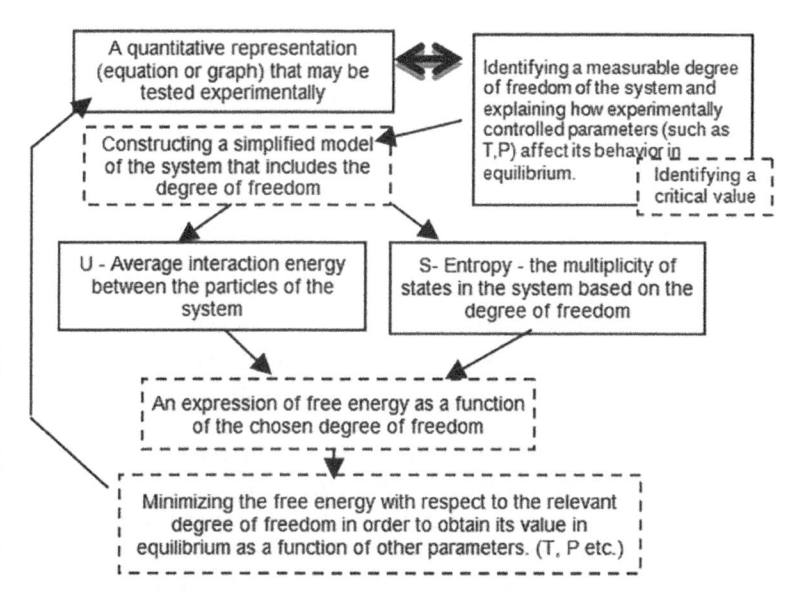

Figure 4.1 Flow chart representing a generic modelling sequence of equilibrium soft matter phenomena

to construct their models related to their projects from scratch. Instead, we engaged them in *reconstructing* a pre-existing theoretical model (Justi and Gilbert, 2002) related to the experimental phenomena or computational studies that they investigated. The term 'reconstruction' indicates that the students analysed a pre-existing model found in the scientific literature. The students were required to explicate the physical motivation for the model and how it relates to an underlying conceptual framework in terms of the general modelling process described in Figure 4.1. Reconstruction is an authentic activity performed by researchers when they review novel models proposed in research papers and scrutinize them in order to ensure their validity (Bazerman, 1988). Thus, students were expected to perceive being involved in reconstruction as a valuable objective that allowed them to catch a glimpse of scientific modelling involved in cutting-edge research.

Scaffolding the reconstruction of theoretical models in the programme

Research experiences for highly capable high school students can be thought of as settings for 'cognitive apprenticeships' (Collins *et al.*, 1989) since their central aim is to expose the student to an authentic practice of science. A central purpose of cognitive apprenticeships is to support students not only in exploring expertise in a specific context, but also to 'decontextualize knowledge so that it can be used in many different settings' (ibid., p. 459). This implies that, as a cognitive apprenticeship, the teaching in the programme should provide scaffolding – externalizing the 'cognitive and metacognitive processes that comprise the expertise' (ibid., p. 458) and directing and improving the performance of the mentee in performing these processes.

The programme was designed according to the principles of a cognitive apprenticeship for acquiring expertise in reconstructing models, by providing scaffolds that were gradually removed. The scaffolds were introduced in each of the two main parts of the programme: the classroom component and the research experience. The classroom component spanned 22 afternoon biweekly meetings starting at the beginning of the 11th grade and culminating at the end of the first quarter of the 12th grade. The research experience was conducted by pairs of students during the second and third quarters of the school year in the 12th grade. In the classroom component, the teachers presented models for several soft matter phenomena, explicating through specialized concept maps how one can particularize the approach in a manner similar to the generic modelling process that was introduced at the beginning; in both the particular and general concept maps the major intermediate steps were similar. It is important to note that while explicitly modelling soft matter phenomena was a central part of the programme, learning about the nature of a modelling process – that is, the iterative process of evaluation and revision of models – remained implicit in the instruction.

The first scaffold used in the classroom component was the aforementioned flow chart with a generic topology that represents the reasoning used by researchers to model soft matter phenomena (Langbeheim *et al.*, 2012). Flow charts along the lines of the general map shown in Figure 4.1, with details relevant to specific phenomena, were introduced by the teachers as they derived the models in the lectures. After demonstrating modelling, the students were coached to reconstruct the modelling processes in specific situations that required them to complete missing elements of the flow charts and to describe the links between the rubrics. The students were required to *reconstruct* the modelling process from the lecture slides using the map as a scaffold under the supervision of the instructor. Finally, the scaffolds were removed and students were asked to reconstruct models without using the flow charts.

The classroom component culminated in a meeting in which the students grouped themselves in pairs and chose a research topic. The projects were either experimental or computational. Computational research projects, such as the one this chapter focuses on, were performed by students who had previous programming knowledge to a level that allowed them to independently write software code. The major scaffold in the apprenticeship was a predetermined timeline that divided the project into smaller sections. During the first few meetings with the research mentor, the students discussed the background information from scientific papers or textbooks relevant to their topic and wrote an introduction to their project in which they explained the research question and the context of the study. The subsequent meetings were devoted to the experimental/computational investigation and culminated with the writing of a summary of the results. The final stage encompassed the writing of a paper that fully described the project; the paper was supposed to follow the format of the generic modelling process mentioned above. This paper was accompanied by a presentation of the project to the entire group, who provided feedback on a form with rubrics that evaluated the clarity of the argument in the presentation as well as its alignment with the modelling sequence. The feedback was used by the students to rewrite their papers and to prepare for their examinations with an external examiner. The examiner's evaluation of the project was then incorporated as 40 per cent of the students' overall matriculation grade in physics or chemistry.

Investigating student learning in the programme

Thirteen students (seven female and six male) participated in the third cohort of the programme between October 2010 and May 2012. All of the students were capable individuals; however, since this was an afternoon, elective programme, not all the students showed the same commitment to attend classes, carry out the assignments and engage in discussions. We focus on a case study of a pair of two students that stood out as highly committed. Both stood out from the rest as far as their curiosity and capabilities: Tom, who majored in both physics and computer science in his high school; and Jerry, who majored in physics and in chemistry in his high school and attended introductory maths courses at the Open University (in addition to his high school maths classes).

We examined both students' performances in the research project, as well as their retrospective thoughts about their own experiences. In our analysis of the case study, we employ the perspective of 'personal epistemologies', according to which, people evaluate and criticize their experiences through the prism of their personal beliefs and expectations of learning (Hofer and Pintrich, 2004).

The study addresses the following questions:

1. How did the students cope with their project work? What were their main achievements? What were the main difficulties they faced?
2. How did the students' retrospectively appreciate their research experience? Which aspects of their research did they criticize?

The data for our study is based on authentic classroom materials and on a semi-structured interview conducted with the case study students ten months after they finished the programme. The classroom data was obtained from videos of class discussions and written answers to worksheets. We also examined the papers that the students wrote and the email exchanges between them and their supervisors for indications of difficulties the students' expressed and the responses of their supervisors. After analysing the data, we discuss the students' perceptions of their performance in their research project and relate them to the scaffolding provided by the programme. We focus on those aspects of the projects related to the theory and practice of model-making in science.

Findings

Tom and Jerry worked on a computational project motivated by a popular talk given in the programme by a soft matter scientist who described a theoretical puzzle and a recent model developed as one solution to the mystery. The theoretical puzzle concerns the formation and stability of 'lipid rafts' – nano-sized isles of one type of lipid (saturated lipids) that phase separates from the surrounding lipids of another type (unsaturated lipids) in the cell's membrane. These 'lipid rafts' (Brown and London, 1998) play an important role in the cell function as regions in the membrane that facilitate the transfer of molecules from the cell to its surroundings. Saturated lipids comprise two 'straight' hydrocarbon chains while unsaturated comprise two 'bent' chains where the 'bending' results from double carbon–carbon bonds (see Figure 4.2). The apparent 'repulsion' between the lipids is related to the packing incompatibility of the 'straight' and 'bent' chains.

Observations of synthesized, model membranes indicated that at physiological temperatures (e.g. 37°C) the saturated and unsaturated lipids phase separate into two large domains, each of order of the system size, while the lipid rafts in the membrane of an actual biological cell appear to remain stable as nanometer-sized islands. In most phase-separating systems, such as oil and water, the two components separate into domains of the order of the system size; nanometer and even micro-sized domains are unstable. The 'puzzle of lipid rafts' refers to understanding the physical mechanism that stabilizes nanoscale rafts in the cell membrane but not in an artificial membrane. This puzzle motivated several theorists to suggest various scientific explanations.

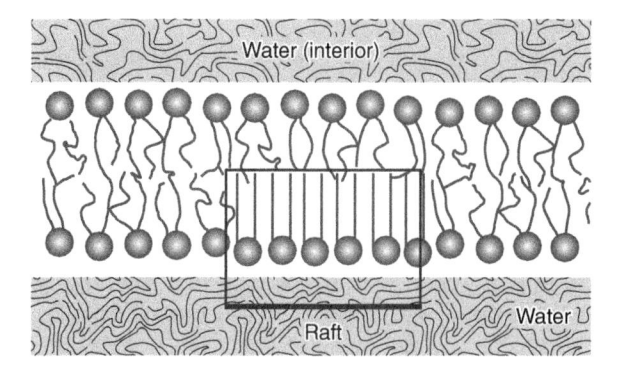

Figure 4.2 A cross-section of a lipid bilayer. The raft is the area in the rectangle with the straight chains

Note: Lipid bilayer with polar heads (spheres) that contact the aqueous phase and hydrocarbon chains that self-assemble so that they do not contact the aqueous phase and, instead, face each other.

Tom and Jerry examined one of these theoretical explanations, namely the 'hybrid lipid' model. This model suggests that the stability of the nano-sized rafts in cells might be caused by the presence of a third type of lipid – a hybrid lipid that has one saturated and one unsaturated carbon chain. The hybrid lipid allows optimal packing of each of its legs with the saturated lipids on one side and the unsaturated lipid on the other (see Figure 4.3, right-hand side). When thus oriented at the interface between the saturated and the unsaturated lipids the hybrid component can stabilize small domains in the phase-separating system. The synthetic membrane shown in Figure 4.2 does not contain hybrid lipids, comprising only stable, system-sized domains since, similar to the usual type of water-oil separation, nanometric domains were unstable.

Tom and Jerry's initial meetings with the mentor (a postdoctoral fellow whose research centred on the theory of lipid rafts) focused on modelling the mixed, lipid membrane. The postdoctoral fellow met with the students once a week over the course of a month and half. Since Tom and Jerry lived far from each other, they did much of their work separately: Tom developed the computer simulation code and Jerry reconstructed the analytical (mathematical) model. After they

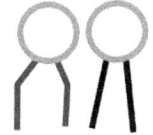 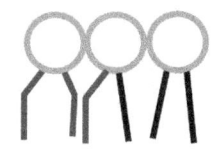

Figure 4.3 Interface between a saturated and unsaturated lipid, without (left) and with (right) a hybrid lipid in the middle

made progress on their individual tasks, they met and compared the predictions of their respective analytical and computational models.

In the first meetings, the mentor explained the central features of the Monte Carlo algorithm used to simulate the state of a system of interacting particles at constant temperature (Metropolis *et al.*, 1953). Based on the mentor's explanation, Tom, who had learned elementary programming in school, developed the code for the simulation on his own with almost no support. Tom had to choose a representation for the particles in the system and to create an output interface that predicted the equilibrium structures as a function of the system parameters (e.g. temperature, composition) that were chosen by the user. Representing the two types of lipids that phase separate was straightforward, but modelling a hybrid lipid (half saturated and half unsaturated) which has a similar size to the other two types of lipids was not trivial. Tom's idea was to represent each lipid by a square of four lattice sites. This way, each saturated lipid was represented by four blue squares, an unsaturated lipid by four red squares and the hybrid by two red squares and two blue squares, as shown in Figure 4.4.

While Tom carried out his part with little support, the project presented several challenges for Jerry, whose major role was to reconstruct the analytical model. The research paper that was the basis for the theoretical understanding of the problem (Brewster *et al.*, 2009) included many scientific ideas and terms that were not taught in class as well as some mathematical manipulations that were unclear to Jerry. Jerry initially tried to reconstruct the model by himself but got stuck at some point; the mentor consulted the teacher and they decided to scaffold Jerry's task by directing him to focus on an aspect of the derivation that was simpler. In an email, Jerry expressed his difficulty:

> **From: Jerry**
> **Subject: re: the work continues**
> **31/1/2012**
>
> 'Hi ____, I found myself sinking in confusion in an attempt to make progress. Is the 'chemical potential' the average free energy per particle?… I understood this from Wikipedia. In contrast, in lecture notes of students from the university I understood there is a term named 'Gibbs potential' which is added to the 'Helmholtz free energy' that I know.„

This email excerpt demonstrates Jerry's difficulty in clarifying a new term (chemical potential, not taught in class) that he found in the research paper.

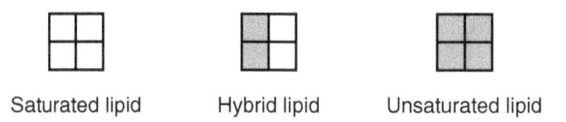

Saturated lipid   Hybrid lipid   Unsaturated lipid

Figure 4.4 Tom's idea for representing the lipids in the computer simulation

This difficulty also resonates with Jerry's comment about reading scientific papers quoted at the beginning of this chapter. Jerry's problem was clarified in the next couple of meetings with the mentor. He grappled with only a few other obstacles in reconstructing the model; those were mostly related to unfamiliar terms or mathematical tricks. With this help and redirection, in his final report Jerry was able to easily reproduce the structure of the derivation in detail and to eloquently explain its rationale.

He also compared, together with Tom, the predictions of the computational and the analytical models. The final product of Tom and Jerry's research report was an articulate, 18-page (5,300 words) paper along with a fully working computer simulation of the system. The students were examined by an experienced teacher who teaches a high school course on computational science and received a score of 100/100.

To summarize: after learning the structure of the algorithm, Tom constructed a computational model and ran it on his own with almost no support. In contrast, Jerry reconstructed the theoretical arguments presented in the research papers only after extensive, initial support from the mentors.

Students' retrospective evaluation of their research experiences

Tom and Jerry faced different challenges in their respective projects and expressed different beliefs about the nature of the activities they were engaged in. Tom and Jerry's beliefs about modelling emerged in a classroom discussion that took place even before they began their research projects. Their differing beliefs were stated even more explicitly in their responses to questions in an interview that took place after they finished their research projects. The following excerpt is taken from a class discussion concerning the general role of theoretical modelling in science.

1. Teacher: ... What, in your opinion, is the role of modelling?
2. Jerry: To *simplify* reality.
3. Teacher: But, what for?
4. Jerry: So that one can make a calculation.
5. Karen (another student): To predict what will happen in reality.
6. Jerry: The *role of modelling is to simplify a phenomenon* so that we would be able to make a calculation of it.
7. Tom: In short, *to translate reality into mathematics.*

In this excerpt, Jerry insisted that modelling is a process in which a real system is simplified, or undergoes a process of abstraction, while Tom did not mention any intermediate step of simplification in the process that relates a real, physical system to its mathematical representation. Jerry mentioned the intermediate simplification step twice, implying that he perceived it as very important step, while Tom ignored the process of simplification and concentrated on the final mathematical representation of the system which he viewed as (in principle, an exact) translation.

Tom and Jerry's beliefs were elaborated upon in the interview which took place after the completion of the research project. The interviewer asked whether they agreed with the statements they originally made during the class discussion.

275. Interviewer: Tell me if you agree with the things that you said or if you would like to say it differently now.
276. Tom: I agree.
277. Jerry: I stand behind my words.
278. Tom: What were your words?
279. Jerry: I think I said it here before.
280. Interviewer: What?
281. Jerry: That [the purpose of modelling] is to simplify reality so that one can do a calculation.

Both Tom and Jerry claimed that they maintained their previous beliefs about the role of modelling.

306. Interviewer: So you still think that modelling is like you said, to simplify reality so it that it could be calculated?
307. Jerry: So that it could be brought to a calculation. Yes.
308. Interviewer: And if you can't?
309. Jerry: If it is unsolvable [analytically]?
310. Interviewer: Yes.
311. Jerry: Look, if it is not solvable and we are working on something practical like medicines, then you can use the computer. But if we do it for theoretical physics, for the… physics and not for some application, then it is not enough.

Jerry viewed computational modelling as an approach that is appropriate only in cases where the mathematical, analytical model cannot be carried out because, in his view, only analytical models contribute to theoretical progress in physics. Jerry's approach resembles the idea of Occam's razor, which postulates that explanations for phenomena should be as parsimonious and simple as they can be. But Jerry did admit that this may not be possible in the analysis of complex systems, at least for practical purposes.

Tom, however, was mainly concerned that the simplifications of the analytical model neglected too many aspects of the system. As illustrated in the following excerpt, Tom did not really value the computer simulation that he developed because it was inherently inaccurate:

51. Interviewer: How did your simulation help answering this question? (the formation of small sized lipid rafts in equilibrium)
52. Tom: By taking a finite number of such lipids, distributing them in some random pattern, defining the interaction parameter between them and the temperature and with probabilities to

> show how the system will be in the future. *The problem is that it [the simulation] neglects all sorts of things – such as the possibility for diagonal motion.*

As seen also in the next excerpt of the interview (line 342 below), Tom expressed discomfort with those simplifications in the model that make it a less accurate representation of the actual system. We interpret Tom's approach as representing an epistemic belief that expects models to be replicas of the real system (Grosslight *et al.*, 1991; Treagust *et al.*, 2002).

The differences in Tom and Jerry's beliefs shaped their critiques of their own project. When Tom and Jerry were asked if the project was school-like or an authentic scientific investigation, they both surprisingly agreed that it was more school-like, but their explanations were not related to the fact that they were graded on the project or any other school-like feature:

338. Interviewer: OK, do you feel that what you did was similar to doing authentic science, in the enquiry project, or was it more like a 'school project'?
339. Tom: A school project.
340. Jerry: A school project.
341. Interviewer: OK, why?
342. Tom: *It was almost completely inaccurate, we neglected too many things in the computer program.*

Tom focused on his part of the project – the computer simulation – and claimed it was school-like simply because many things were neglected in it; therefore, in his opinion, its predictions were inaccurate. His criticism is based upon his belief that modelling should be an exact, mathematical representation of reality. Jerry also responded that the project was school-like, but his claim was based on his role in reconstructing the analytical model:

343. Interviewer: If you would have more time and would not be subject to time pressure so that you could continue [working on the project], would you think that it could have been a real science project?
344. Jerry: First of all, I had extensive guidance in developing the analytical model. First of all, I have the… emmm.
345. Interviewer: Do you think that every scientific investigation is a completely independent endeavour?
346. Jerry: I don't know, really, I don't know. But here I had a lot of support. It is not that I did anything by myself, *it's not that I came with some brilliant idea or something.* I don't know how I would cope alone in things without people who would help. *But it was a school-like project mainly, I think, mainly because it did not have a… real problem that I had to… a*

> *problem that I did not know how to solve, and then suddenly I knew how to solve.*

In contrast to Tom, who developed the computational model on his own, Jerry criticized his part of the project since he 'only' reconstructed a theoretical result that was previously found by others. He did not 'produce' the knowledge by himself and, therefore, did not contribute to the theory. When he was asked about his ideas to improve the project and to make it more scientifically valuable he stated:

355. Jerry: In order to do work and to be proud, I need to know not only about the specific case that I work on, but to know the theoretical background behind it more deeply.

Jerry stated that, in his opinion, in order to make an investigation more authentic, one must make a unique and discernibly original contribution; he realized that this requires previous mastery of the theoretical background. Jerry's response was rooted in his belief that an authentic scientific investigation should include a novel contribution with theoretical implications; the accuracy of the model itself was less important. With that, he was aware of the inherent problem posed by his lack of background knowledge that prevented him from being able to make such a theoretical contribution.

Discussion

Both Tom and Jerry were able to reconstruct the assumptions of the model they encountered in the research paper – a model that explained the formation and stability of lipid rafts based on interactions between saturated, unsaturated and hybrid lipids. However, solving for the time evolution of the system based on these assumptions, given the students' limited knowledge, was possible only computationally. With regard to the analytical solution, several exchanges with the mentor allowed students to merely reconstruct it.

Jerry's need for support in reconstructing the mathematical model caused him to question the quality of his part of the project. His criticism was related to his personal belief that authentic scientific enquiry requires a novel theoretical contribution – one that he could not provide at this point in his education. Framing his statements in the terms suggested in the introduction to this chapter, we conclude that he did not experience his role as a knowledge producer.

For Jerry to develop into a scientist in the future it is important that he maintains his striving for innovation and originality, since these are crucial traits for a researcher. It is possible that if Jerry had heard from scientists about how reconstructions of previously published derivations allowed them to reveal fundamental errors in those approaches, he may have better appreciated his own efforts. He might have also realized that science is not only about innovation, but also requires activities that first replicate the results of others. Moreover, in the future, his needs can be addressed in a more fundamental manner by designing programmes to routinely integrate computational modelling in research apprenticeships. Computational modelling allows students to construct and study models whose analytical solution is beyond their capabilities. To that end, we distinguish the simplification of a rich phenomenon via a more 'bare-bones' conceptual model from the use of numerical and computational tools to actually do so. Students can take part in the endeavour of producing scientific knowledge by reconstructing a conceptual model but may often have to solve the problems using computational tools.

An additional lesson can be learned from Tom's responses. His personal belief that precision is a central measure of quality led him to critique his computational solution since he realized the numerous simplifications he was forced to make in its construction. Tom's relentless questioning of less than exact approaches is valuable for a researcher. However, it also reflects an epistemology of scientific research that prevented him from appreciating his achievements. Tom's belief that modelling is equivalent to replicating reality in a mathematical form should have been challenged by his teachers and mentors. Computational models can be beneficial for comparing alternative simplifications of real systems and showing the advantages and utility of different models.

As an example, let us demonstrate how a comparison between two equivalent models can be discussed with students. Students can compare different computational models that are used to study the simple macroscopic behaviour of diffusion. The teacher and students can discuss the transitional links between alternative models (i.e. deterministic molecular dynamics models that compute all the particle trajectories using Newtonian equations of motion vs probabilistic models, such as random walks of the particles on a lattice, that greatly simplify the dynamics) in order to externalize the considerations in choosing an optimal model and approximations so that the research goals can be achieved.

Comparing two different computational models and demonstrating that model reconstruction is an essential aspect of the work of scientists are two examples of how one can explicate differing epistemologies via dialogue between a researcher-mentor and a student-apprentice. We thus encourage mentors in research apprenticeships to externalize the underlying principles of model construction and criticism in general and in their research field in particular.

References

Bazerman, C. (1988). *Shaping Written Knowledge: The genre and activity of the experimental article in science*. Madison: University of Wisconsin Press.

Brewster R., Pincus P., and Safran S. (2009). Hybrid lipids as a biological line-active component. *Biophysics Journal*, 97, 1087–94.

Brown, D.A., and London, E. (1998). Functions of lipid rafts in biological membranes. *Annual Review of Cell and Developmental Biology*, 14(1), 111–36.

Burgin, S.R., Sadler, T.D., and Koroly, M.J. (2012). High school student participation in scientific research apprenticeships: variation in and relationships among student experiences and outcomes. *Research in Science Education*, 42, 439–67.

Collins, J.S. Brown, and Newman, S.E. (1989). Cognitive apprenticeship: teaching the crafts of reading, writing and mathematics. In L.B. Resnick (Ed.), *Knowing, Learning, and instruction: Essays in honor of Robert Glaser*, Hillsdale, NJ: Erlbaum.

Cooley, W.W., and Bassett, R.D. (1961). Evaluation and follow-up study of a summer science and mathematics program for talented secondary school students. *Science Education*, 45, 209–16.

Feldman, A., Divoll, K., and Rogan-Klyve, A. (2009). Research education of new scientists: implications for science teacher education. *Journal of Research in Science Teaching*, 46(4), 442–59.

Gardner, H.E. (2008). *Extraordinary Minds: Portraits of four exceptional individuals and an examination of our own extraordinariness.* New York: Basic Books.

Grosslight, L., Unger, C., Jay, E., and Smith, C. (1991). Understanding models and their use in science: conceptions of middle and high school students and experts. *Journal of Research in Science Teaching*, 28(9), 799–822.

Hofer, B.K., and Pintrich, P.R. (Eds). (2004). *Personal Epistemology: The psychology of beliefs about knowledge and knowing.* Hove: Psychology Press.

Jones, R.A.L. (2002) *Soft Condensed Matter*, Oxford: Oxford University Press.

Justi, R.S., and Gilbert, J.K. (2002). Science teachers' knowledge about and attitudes towards the use of models and modeling in learning science. *International Journal of Science Education*, 24, 1273–92.

Langbeheim, E., Livne, S., Safran, S., and Yerushalmi, E. (2012). Introductory physics going soft. *American Journal of Physics*, 80, 51–60.

Metropolis, N., Rosenbluth, M.N., Rosenbluth, A.W., Teller, E., and Teller, A.H. (1953). Equations of state calculations by fast computing machines. Journal of Chemical Physics, 21(6), 1087–92.

Stake, J.E., and Mares, K.R. (2001). Science enrichment programs for gifted high school girls and boys: predictors of program impact on science confidence and motivation. *Journal of Research in Science Teaching*, 38, 1065–88.

Taber, K.S. (Ed.). (2007). *Science Education for Gifted Learners.* London: Routledge.

Treagust, D.F. Chittleborough, G., and Mamialo, T.L. (2002). Students' understanding of the role of scientic models in learning science. *International Journal of Science Education*, 24(4), 357–68.

Van Lacum, E., Ossevoort, M., Buikema, H., and Goedhart, M. (2012). First experiences with reading primary literature by undergraduate life science students. *International Journal of Science Education*, 34(12), 1795–821.

VanTassel-Baska, J., and Kulieke, M.J. (1987). The role of community-based scientific resources in developing scientific talent: a case study. *Gifted Child Quarterly*, 31(3), 111 15.

5 'Excuse me teacher, but you made a mistake...'
Interactions between science teachers and gifted students in a regular classroom

Naama Benny and Ron Blonder

Abstract

Intellectually gifted students think and learn differently from other students in the classroom. It is important to teach them appropriately because excellence does not emerge without appropriate help. However, the interactions between gifted students and their teachers in a regular classroom have not been extensively studied. The current study focuses on this important factor, which could either promote or hinder the development of gifted students.

In the current chapter we identify and characterize interactions between gifted students and high-school science teachers in a regular class. This study provides a rich description of the interactions and their patterns. Importantly, in this research a unique qualitative technique, Critical Incidents Technique (CIT), was used. The Critical Incidents (CIs) that were collected occurred between a science teacher and a gifted student in the class. The CIs provide insight into the teacher's world and the way they perceived their ability to teach one or more gifted students in their class. The chapter focuses on one of the identified CIs called 'Excuse me teacher, but you made a mistake...', which emerged from all the interviews and includes the following catalyst. During science lessons a gifted student comments to the teacher that he made a mistake. The comment is usually regarding the subject matter connected to the science curriculum. Different interactions are presented. The interactions reflect possible scenarios that can be developed in this situation, as they emerged from the CI analysis; they provide a rich description of the interaction. We suggest that these rich descriptions be used to make recommendations for enhancing teachers' professional development regarding fostering gifted students in a regular science class.

Introduction

Teachers and students first meet at the beginning of the school year and, from the moment that they enter the classroom, an interaction begins. The interaction consists of aspects with reference to the characteristics of students (e.g. gender and age), teachers (e.g. experience, self-efficacy and method of instruction), the activity setting, teachers and students' perceptions and beliefs about one another, the classroom environment and so on (Pianta *et al.*, 2003; Brophy and Good, 1986; Blonder *et al.*, 2014). Here we describe the interactions between science teachers and gifted students in a regular mixed-ability high-school classroom by presenting the teachers' narrative regarding the interaction.

Gifted students

What constitutes a gifted student? Numerous conceptions and countless definitions of giftedness have been put forth over the years. Nevertheless, there is no universally agreed-upon answer to this question. Giftedness, intelligence and talent are fluid concepts and may appear differently in different contexts and cultures. Even within schools we can find a wide range of personal beliefs about the word 'gifted', which has become a term with multiple meanings and many nuances. According to Passow (1981), one can learn more about the nature of giftedness by viewing responses to enrichment activities than by giving conventional tests. Conceptions of giftedness can be viewed as existing along a continuum, ranging from a very conservative view to a more flexible or multi-dimensional approach. The conservative views of giftedness focus almost exclusively on IQ test scores or other measures of cognitive ability. The multi-dimensional approaches are based on models that go beyond IQ tests. Those models involve, for example, excellence, rarity, productivity, demonstrability and the value attached to the skills/products of the individual (Sternberg and Zhang, 1995); they can also involve three interlocking clusters of characteristics, above average general ability, task commitment and creativity (Renzulli, 2012). Teachers use different criteria to identify a student as gifted. Some teachers may label a student who gets top scores as gifted; others may consider different abilities and characteristics (Ngoi and Vondracek, 2004). Gifted students are diverse within this group. There can be a variety of types and degrees of giftedness, along with socio-emotional differences, as well as a variety of cultural backgrounds and differences in learning styles and expressions of giftedness that may affect their manifestations (Wellisch and Brown, 2012; Passow, 1981).

Gifted students' characteristics are translated to their behaviours in the classroom. Unique characteristics can be transformed to unique behaviours. Sometimes those behaviours can be misinterpreted or misunderstood. Therefore, it is not surprising that the characteristics associated with giftedness can be contradictory and confusing and thus add to the problems associated with identifying them (Wellisch and Brown, 2012).

Gifted students potentially differ from their classroom peers regarding three key issues: 1) the pace at which they learn, 2) the depth of their understanding and 3) the interests that they hold (Gilson, 2009). The challenge for regular classroom teachers is to design a learning environment in which students can fully develop their abilities and interests without losing their sense of membership as part of the class (ibid.), and gifted students are no exception.

Gifted students should have access to learning opportunities that are faster paced and more complex than what is usually available in a regular classroom with mixed-ability students (VanTassel-Baska, 2003). In addition, they should continually use their high abilities in order to keep developing their academic skills (Burney, 2008). It is important to emphasize that if, during their school, years they are not provided with suitable tools for learning, they may not be able to utilize their high abilities if their self-efficacy beliefs are low (Pajares, 1996). Students' self-efficacy refers to their belief in their ability to succeed in tasks, courses, or academic activities. It influences their academic choices and the effort they expend on those activities. Students' self-efficacy beliefs are often better predictors of academic success because these beliefs mediate the effect of prior achievement, knowledge and skills on subsequent achievement (Britner and Pajares, 2006).

Differentiating and teaching the gifted learner in a regular mixed-ability classroom may still prove to be more challenging due to the factors concerning 1) the degree of differentiation required, 2) the need to provide advanced learning opportunities beyond the grade level, 3) the philosophical barriers and antipathy of teachers towards the gifted learner and their needs and 4) the lack of understanding the kind of services needed for the gifted population (VanTassel-Baska and Stambaugh, 2005).

Gifted students in the science classroom

Gifted students may have specific abilities and aptitudes rather than an evenly developed profile of strengths (Taber, 2007). In a regular science classroom we should take into consideration that there may be two different profiles of gifted students: 1) those that have a specific ability in science and 2) gifted students with other strengths who are learning school science.

Taber (ibid.) considers as gifted science learners those students who are able to 'achieve exceptionally high levels of attainment in all or some aspects of the normal curriculum demands in school science, or undertake some science-related tasks at a level of demand well above that required at that curricular stage' (p. 7). A number of characteristics of gifted learners in science have been suggested: scientific curiosity, cognitive abilities and metacognitive abilities. It has also been suggested that some gifted science learners will take on roles and exercise effective leadership in group work (ibid.). The intellectually gifted differ in their learning. They not only have exceptional thinking and learning abilities, but also use them more effectively and can more readily adopt scientific thinking (Freeman, 2003). A more practical list of characteristics has been suggested by Matthews (2012).

Gifted students in science are able to perceive relationships among different parts of a situation; they are curious about what makes things work and often are not content with simplistic explanations; they express interest in science topics at a very young age; they exhibit persistence in science-related activities; they enjoy explaining to others how things work; they have a good memory for details; they are able to generalize from seemingly unrelated details; they see the big picture; they are able to understand abstractions at a young age; and they exhibit a creative approach in projects related to science (ibid.). Note that no one student possesses the entire list of characteristics.

Excellence does not emerge without appropriate help. To reach an exceptionally high standard in any area, even the gifted students need the means to learn, which includes suitable material to work with and focused challenging instruction (Freeman, 2003). Gifted students are often naturally interested in science. Unfortunately, dull routine, recall-based assessments and lack of meaningful experiences can turn these students away from science (Taber, 2007; Matthews, 2012).

Students' personal experiences, along with their science experiences, change dramatically from fifth to twelfth grade. For instance, the topics covered in school become progressively more advanced and abstract (Watters, 2010). As students progress, especially into high school, several factors become influential: teachers' classroom practices, learning experiences in high school (ibid.), teachers' orientation towards content, epistemological beliefs, teachers' behaviours while interacting with students and the discipline-based content determine students' attitudes towards science (ibid.).

Science teachers, like all teachers, possess beliefs about teaching and learning that influence their behaviour and practice (Laplante, 1997). Understanding the nature of science and how students learn science creates a set of beliefs that guide practice and behaviour within the classroom (Bryan, 2012). Galton and Eggleston (1979) identified three communication styles in science education. 'Problem-solvers' are teachers who ask relatively many questions and emphasize problems, hypotheses and experimental procedures. 'Informers' are characterized by their rare use of questions except those requiring recall and applying facts and principles to problem-solving. 'Inquirers' can be defined as teachers who initiate interactions in class more often than other teachers; in particular, they seek information and guidance in designing experimental procedures and in implying, formulating and testing hypotheses. According to this research, the problem-solver's style was most effective for high-ability students' performance. The role of science teachers' beliefs is significantly related to how they implement the science curriculum in their classroom (Laplante, 1997). In addition to teachers' beliefs, teachers' content knowledge of science plays an important role in their science teaching (Palmer, 2006).

Teacher–student interactions

Teaching in the classroom is a complex task in a complex environment. Many factors influence the teacher, the student and what happens in class. Teacher–student interactions in the classroom occur in three different domains: emotional support, classroom organization and instructional support (Luckner and Pianta, 2011; Pianta *et al.*, 2003).

Student characteristics (e.g. academic performance, motivation and the extent of engagement) evoke various responses from teachers and impact the teacher's ability to instruct, as well as teacher–student interactions (Nurmi, 2012). Teacher–student interactions have been shown to be important for students' motivation (e.g. Davis, 2003), intellectual development and achievement.

Teachers' representations of their interactions with a specific student have been assessed with respect to three broad areas (Pianta *et al.*, 2003): 1) content or subjects; 2) how teachers view themselves in relation to the student; and 3) the affective aspect (Nurmi, 2012; Wubbels and Brekelmans, 2012).

Teachers construct general pedagogical knowledge and beliefs about classroom management, instructional strategies and subject matter. They also construct knowledge and beliefs about particular students and classrooms. Knowledge and beliefs that teachers hold become critical components in the teacher's choice to use specific methods of instruction. Constructing beliefs about students enables teachers to approach their teaching tasks professionally, interact with students and design appropriate instruction for them (Nurmi, 2012).

Students' inherent characteristics greatly influence the classroom environment and directly affect the way teachers function in class and the nature of their teacher–student interactions. For example, the students' level of academic performance plays a central role in the way teachers plan their instruction and how they implement classroom practices. However, problematic student behaviour can also greatly influence teachers' responses and teacher–student interactions (Nurmi, 2012; Pianta *et al.*, 2003). Students' misbehaviour often activates negative emotions among teachers, thereby leading to disciplinary acts (Nurmi, 2012). Teachers reported less conflict and more closeness when interacting with students that display high levels of motivation and who work with other students. When students are engaged in classroom activities and are interested in learning, teachers find teaching more enjoyable, display more teacher–student support, and report more involvement than under conditions where students are passive and uninterested (ibid.). Teachers' ratings or judgements of students are usually based on conflicts and closeness, student dependency, secure attachment to the teacher and anxious attachment to the teacher (ibid.).

However, the interactions between gifted students and their science teacher in a regular classroom have not been sufficiently studied. The current study focuses on this important factor, which could either promote or hinder the development of gifted students. For this research we attempted to identify and characterize different interactions between gifted students and high-school science teachers.

Research goals and questions

This research aims at identifying and characterizing the different interactions between gifted students and high-school chemistry teachers. More specifically, we will focus on the following question: how do science teachers describe their interactions with gifted students in their regular class when the student identifies a mistake made by the teacher?

Methodology: data collection and analysis

This research involves qualitative research methodology. The qualitative tools used consist of interviews based on CIT that was developed by Flanagan (1954). CIT involves asking respondents to identify events of experiences that were 'critical' for some purpose. These incidents are then pooled together for analysis, and generalizations are drawn from the commonalities of the incidents (Kain, 2003). CIs can be gathered in various ways, but in this approach generally the respondents are asked to tell a story about an experience they have had (Gremler, 2004). The goal of the content analysis is to obtain a classification system that provides insights regarding the frequency and patterns of those factors that affect the phenomenon of interest (ibid.).

The CI was originally defined by Flanagan (1954). It usually refers to an extreme behaviour, positive or negative. It is an incident that deviates significantly from what is considered normal or expected. The notion of 'critical' refers to the way we look at an incident and its interpretation as a significant event (Tripp, 1993). CIs, in the educational context, are not necessarily sensational events involving a lot of tensions. Rather, they may be incidents that occur every day in the classroom (ibid.) and often appear to be 'typical' rather than 'critical' at first sight, but are judged critical (ibid.; Angelides, 2001). Their classification as CIs is based on the significance and the meaning that the teachers attribute to them.

We were looking for CIs that occurred between a chemistry teacher and a gifted student in a regular mixed-ability classroom. We defined a CI as an event that confronts teachers and makes them decide on a course of action. A CI is often stimulated by students saying and doing things, and may arise through the action of the teacher; an interaction evokes responses from the teacher. These responses provide insight into the teacher's view of teaching gifted students in their regular chemistry classroom. The CIT methodology helps in viewing the interactions from the teacher's perspective, which means that it is the framework that helps the researcher identify those incidents that are significant to the teacher. A qualitative methodology of direct research, such as observations, is not fruitful from the perspective of identifying a teacher's narrative. According to CIT, a story that has been told by the teacher needs to meet some guidelines or important criteria in order to be considered as a CI: the actual behaviour is reported; the relationships of the reporter to the behaviour are clear; the relevant facts are provided; the reporter makes a clear judgement about what makes the incident critical; the reasons for this judgement are clear (Tripp, 1993; Angelides, 2001).

The interview was divided into two parts. In the first, the teachers were asked about their background (years of teaching, formal education and any additional roles in school) and about their perception of the school, the school population, their teaching ideology, school colleagues, school staff work, teaching perceptions and their relationship with students. In the second part, teachers were asked to focus on gifted students in their classroom. In order to help elicit stories about interactions with gifted students, the researcher used two kinds of cards to promote generating stories (CIs) about interactions. One type of card had definitions of gifted students, based on selected theories and models. The second type consisted of statements that other teachers said about the presence of and their interaction with gifted students in their classrooms. The teachers were asked to choose a card they felt most suits their beliefs. Then they were asked to give examples of this kind of a student from their own classroom, and to tell about the narrative of the interaction with the student. The story of the interaction refers to the following questions:

- Do you have gifted students in your classroom?
- When you said 'gifted' what did you mean?
- Can you characterize gifted students?
- How do you identify those characteristics in your classroom? Can you provide an example?
- How do you feel about the presence of gifted students in your classroom (academic, emotional, instruction, social and affective aspects)?
- Do you remember the moment that you realized that you are dealing with a gifted student? Would you please describe it?

The participants in the research consisted of 30 high-school teachers who represent a diversity of Israeli schools, teachers from urban and rural, religious and non-religious state schools, as well as Arab and Jewish schools. Twenty-five teachers were female and five were male, with teaching experience ranging from two years to over 30 years. Each interview lasted 60–80 minutes and was audio-recorded and transcribed.

Results

CIs were characterized by a triggering event that occurred during the lesson. The CI was initiated by a gifted student in a regular classroom and was followed by different responses of different teachers. The main content of the CI was used as an infrastructure for a 'bottom up' category that emerges from the data. We were able to identify 343 CIs in 27 different categories. The most common CI categories that were identified are as follows:

- A gifted student interferes with classroom management
- A question asked or comment made by the gifted student that interests the teacher
- The teacher offers help to a gifted student after the student made a mistake
- A gifted student complains about the slow teaching pace in class
- The teacher responds to the fast learning pace of a gifted student
- A gifted student is busy with something other than the lesson
- A gifted student answers a question or makes a remark, but he makes a mistake
- A gifted student present in the class elevates the teacher's motivation
- The beginning of the lesson is ruined by a gifted student
- A gifted student asks a question that the teacher has not thought about.

Two examples of CIs are described below.

The first CI primary category: a gifted student complains about the slow teaching pace in class. During a traditional chemistry lesson that includes frontal teaching and exercises, a gifted student complains that the teaching pace in the class is slow. One of the teachers described the triggering event in her own words: 'He said: "It's slow…" now I remember another student's comment. He said to me: "It is slow, it is very slow, why does it have to be that slow?".' When this happened to this teacher, she responded as follows: 'I explained… that there are different students with different abilities, that their ability to understand is at a different pace, and that I need to adjust my teaching to everyone… I do not have too much choice. Some students are not able to understand the content…' In addition to her verbal interaction with the student, she offered some options for a practice lesson:

> I try in my lessons to allow a lot of self-regulation practices so that students can express themselves, and can work by themselves… I call that differential teaching… It is clear to me, in all the groups from grade nine and up, that I can't get the same response from all the students and that every student learns at his own pace. (Teacher A.A.2)

The second example is of a commonly reported CI: the beginning of the lesson is ruined by a gifted student. At the beginning of the lesson, when a new subject is introduced, a gifted student reveals what is going to happen next and by doing so, he ruins the demonstration and the surprise is spoiled. When this happened to one of the teachers, she responded as follow:

> My gifted student ruined the surprise… and to make a long story short – he ruined the demonstration that followed… at the end of the lesson I approached him and said to him that I know that he is smart and knowledgeable but he does not have to ruin my lesson and that he has to wait until later on… I warned him in advance not to reveal the answer and to wait a bit longer and then I'll ask him. (Teacher S.S.13)

However, the most common CI that was identified was the one started with the triggering comment: 'Excuse me teacher, but you made a mistake…' More than half of the teachers participating in the research reported this CI, 19 teachers out of 30, and some of them reported this CI more than once. During chemistry lessons a gifted student tells the teacher that he or she made a mistake. The comment usually concerns the subject matter connected to the chemistry curriculum.

The following section presents a few of the teachers' responses to this interaction. In Table 5.1 we have provided the cited short dialogues representing the main wording from the teachers' interviews and representing the full interactions. A short description of the teachers' background (the years of teaching, formal education, additional roles in school, among others) and a sort summary of their teaching perceptions are also presented.

Table 5.1 Examples of teacher's responses to the interaction 'Excuse me teacher, but you made a mistake…'

Teacher	Teacher's response	Teaching educational perceptions	Teacher's background details (experience, qualifications, etc.)
Teacher R.E.9	I wrote on the board something that was related to identifying… in short he [the gifted student] said to me 'With all due respect, it can only be an oxygen atom'… Now, I was not prepared for that… I didn't realize that it can be only oxygen… I remember it vividly… I was very embarrassed; you could see it on my face right away because I blushed.	Big investment and emphasis on constructing the lesson and conducting it according to the plan. She invests in the student, any student, and refers to the chemistry group as 'my chemical family'.	21 years of experience in teaching chemistry; a BSc in chemistry and an MSc in science teaching. Role in school: chemistry coordinator at her school and technology systems assimilator.
Teacher A.A.2	One student found a mistake; he raised his hand and asked me… Because of my teaching method, in my lessons I allow the students to correct my wording… I tell them, go ahead and rephrase it.	With the 9th–10th grade students, focusing on developing students' thinking, finding relevant aspects to everyday life, developing active and self-regulating students; with the 11th–12th graders, focusing on the matriculation exams and on getting high grades. She teaches mainly using the frontal teaching style, and covers the content at a fast pace.	22 years of experience in teaching chemistry; a BSc and MSc in chemistry, a PhD in science teaching. Role in school: chemistry teacher, chemistry coordinator in school, leading innovative projects at school and responsible for technology assimilation.
Teacher R.K.10	When a student comments about my mistake – there are two options. The teacher is wrong or the student is wrong. When the student is wrong, I will explain again until she [the gifted student] will understand. When I am wrong, I say: 'Look I do not know, maybe you are right, let me check' and that's it! After the lesson I'm going to check (with the chemistry counsellor or some other expert) and later I'll give you an answer.	Focusing on creating a positive learning environment in her class. She trusts her students; however, she takes disciplinary actions when needed. She tries to get the best from every student and emphasizes the grades of the matriculation exams.	28 years of experience in teaching chemistry; a BSc and an MSc in chemistry. Role in school: chemistry teacher, an educator and vice principal of the school.

(continued)

Table 5.1 Examples of teacher's responses to the interaction 'Excuse me teacher, but you made a mistake…' (continued)

Teacher	Teacher's response	Teaching educational perceptions	Teacher's background details (experience, qualifications, etc.)
Teacher E.A.1	I can see the look on his face change: it tells me that I need to check… whether I was incorrect and what I was doing wrong… Many times I see him changing his facial expression and I say to myself 'What the heck?' I keep doing what I was doing.	Emphasizing the students' sense of what is a real chemist and developing students' thinking.	Two years of experience in teaching chemistry; a BSc in molecular biology and an MSc in science teaching. Role in school: chemistry teacher; used to be a class educator.
Teacher S.S.13	Thanks, so I'll correct it… it happens, no big deal.	Focusing on creating students' interest in chemistry, developing self-regulating students and inspiring students to excel.	14 years of experience in teaching chemistry; a BSc and an MSc in chemistry. Role in school: chemistry teacher.
Teacher Z.B.8	Good, I say – you deserve ten points, you caught me making a mistake… I'm glad that my students pay attention to what I'm writing on the board.	Focusing on students' understanding and their implementation skills. She repeats explanations over and over again, and uses a lot of exercises. She is aware of her students' personal issues and relates to them.	Over 30 years of experience in teaching chemistry; a BSc and an MSc in chemistry. Role in school: chemistry teacher and vice principal of her school.

Discussion

The CI 'Excuse me, but you made a mistake...' was followed by a spectrum of responses from different teachers to the same incident. We presented a spectrum of responses of six different teachers (Table 5.1), illustrating the following. In the first response, teacher R.E.9 feels embarrassed regarding her mistake. In the second response, teacher A.A.2 asks her students to provide an alternative explanation and to be active players in correcting her mistakes. In the third response, teacher R.K.10 needs help from an outside expert in order to be sure that she made a mistake and to extend her (and her students') knowledge. Regarding the fourth response, teacher E.A.1 responds to the student's facial expressions; first, he decides to correct the mistake and, in another interaction, he decides to ignore his students' comments. Teacher S.S.13, in the fifth response, refers to her mistakes as a 'spelling error'. In the sixth response, teacher Z.B.8 gives extra credit to students that find mistakes. For her, it is a sign that the students are paying attention to what is going on in the lesson.

A deeper analysis of the different interrelations reveals that the teacher's response depends on both the depth of their knowledge and their perception regarding the gifted students, as well as on the content matter to which the comment ('Excuse me, but you made a mistake...') referred. According to Shulman (1986), we can examine the teachers' responses with regard to different teachers' knowledge categories. We wish to emphasize two major categories of teacher knowledge – content knowledge (mainly chemistry content knowledge) and knowledge of learners (gifted students) and their characteristics – as a key to gaining more insight into the interactions, as well as the teachers' responses that were reported in the research. Mastery of the subject matter, especially content in contemporary science, enables teachers to react with self-confidence (Blonder *et al.*, 2014) to the comment. When the teachers were not sure of the answer or they lacked confidence regarding giving their answer, they tended to stop and react in a manner that did not foster developing a discourse on the comment. In some cases the teacher used the help of an external expert in order to gain knowledge and to broaden their existing body of knowledge of specific issues. Other teachers used the internet and varied sources of information in order to broaden their knowledge. Some of the teachers utilized their newly attained knowledge in class as a pedagogical opportunity to initiate a discourse in class, whereas others did not. We even found a case in which the teacher felt that she 'had been caught' in her lack of knowledge, consequently causing a physical reaction (blushing). When this happens, the teacher remembers the experience in 'vivid colour' for many years.

When the comment was made regarding the content that is covered in the curriculum, most of the experienced teachers responded immediately; they were self-assured and responded with confidence. In those cases, usually no discourse developed with the gifted students. In those cases in which discourse had been initiated, the teachers felt comfortable because they are experienced teachers that had mastered the content matter, and perhaps had even encountered the triggering comment previously, so they could anticipate the comment and already knew the best way to respond.

Science teachers in the regular classroom are expected to meet the varied needs of diverse learners and to prepare them for the national matriculation exams. Several barriers can hinder teachers in this process (VanTassel-Baska and Stambaugh, 2005). Those barriers can be reinforced when the teachers respond to the gifted student's comment 'Excuse me, but you made a mistake…' In a continuing study, we link these barriers and teachers' responses in this interaction (Benny and Blonder, under review).

Some of the gifted students have a rich content knowledge or are able to learn the content at a high pace and with a high level of understanding. This characteristic may challenge the teacher. Knowing that the student may have much more knowledge regarding the specific subject matter could be difficult for those teachers who choose to ignore the comment or refer to it outside the lesson. However, other teachers who are familiar with teaching gifted students will use this same comment as a way of reflecting on what has been said. Knowing that the gifted student has more content knowledge does not intimidate them or constitute a challenge. Instead, they listen to the comment, consider it in the wide perspective of what is being discussed in class and, in some cases, they introduce the comment with class participation, and their teaching benefits from it. As teacher P.H.6 said: 'The teacher is much more capable of dealing with those situations when she is up to date with the content knowledge.'

Gifted students need learning opportunities that challenge them. In order to achieve meaningful learning that enables students to develop their abilities, the teacher should create a supportive and enabling learning environment (VanTassel-Baska and Stambaugh, 2005). This can be challenging when the teacher is facing a situation in which a student 'finds' mistakes and publicly comments on them in class. Not all teachers can ignore this, and not all teachers can react with a smile or in such a way that the comment's 'sting' will be reduced. Positive and fostering behaviour under those conditions can be a barrier and a challenge. Giving extra points for finding a mistake or saying that 'my students pay attention to what I'm writing on the board' are ways that teachers can limit the negative nature of the comment and still maintain a proper classroom environment that allows the teacher to continue teaching. In this research, that behaviour was more common in incidents reported by experienced teachers. Few of the teachers developed indifference to the comments. A teacher's mistake is like a student's mistake; everybody makes mistakes. When a mistake is found, we correct it and nothing more. This behaviour allows the teachers to make a mistake in a secure environment. This can indicate to the students that the comment fails to become an issue. As teacher O.B.28 indicated, 'Thank you… it is good that you noticed… listen students, I'm only human and I make a mistake from time to time… it happens.' That indifference is a strategy in itself that teachers practice during the learning process at the beginning of their interaction with each class. When the learning process continues and another similar comment is made, this strategy is used again. This can go on until it is 'no big deal'.

In addition to the student's reaction, 'Excuse me, but you made a mistake...', the 32 categories of interactions between chemistry teachers and gifted students in a regular class were analysed through the theoretical perspectives presented in this chapter: teachers' knowledge and barriers for teaching the gifted student in a mixed-ability classroom (ibid.).

Conclusions and implementation

Differentiating instruction (Passow, 1982) and appropriate modification of the curriculum leads to individualizing curricula which better match individual and group learning needs, abilities and styles, usually resulting in specialized learning experiences with different learning rates, styles, interests and abilities for gifted students in a regular classroom, where the setting is challenging. That task requires knowledge, skill and time from teachers (Van Tassel-Baska and Stambaugh, 2005). This research describes the interactions between science teachers and gifted students in a regular mixed-ability classroom in high schools in Israel. The research is needed in order to be able to make recommendations for enhancing teachers' professional development, and to better understand the uniqueness of teaching gifted children in a regular classroom (ibid.). At the classroom level, teachers' behaviour while interacting with their students has been found to influence students' like or dislike for learning a subject (Matthews, 2012). Understanding the gifted students' special needs and being able to provide them with appropriate educational services in a mixed-ability classroom is a challenging professional task for most teachers (VanTassel-Baska, 2003). From our research we found that teachers should develop additional components in their professional knowledge. One major component is scientific knowledge, namely, content knowledge. The next major component is knowledge about gifted students and the how to teach them in a regular mixed-ability classroom. The third component that was found deals with teachers' interactions with gifted students and their self-confidence in their ability to teach appropriately with gifted students. Understanding the barriers teachers encounter from the teachers' point of view will enhance the effectiveness of professional development frameworks for in- and pre-service teachers (Benny and Blonder, 2016).

References

Angelides, P. (2001). Using critical incidents to understand school cultures. *Improving Schools*, 4(1), 24–33. doi: 10.1177/136548020100400105

Blonder, R., Benny, N., and Jones, M.G. (2014). Teaching self-efficacy of science teachers. In R.H. Evans, J. Luft, C. Czerniak and C. Pea (Eds), *The Role of Science Teachers' Beliefs in International Classrooms: From teacher actions to student learning*. Rotterdam: Sense, pp. 3–15.

Benny, N., and Blonder, R. (2016). Factors that promote/inhibit teaching gifted students in a regular class: Results from a professional development program for chemistry teachers. *Education Research International*, 2016, 11. Retrieved from http://dx.doi.org/10.1155/2016/2742905.

Britner, S.L., and Pajares, F. (2006). Sources of science self-efficacy beliefs of middle school students. *Journal of Research in Science Teaching*, 43(5), 485–99.

Brophy, J., and Good, T.L. (1986). Teacher behavior and student achievement. In M.C. Wittrock (Ed.), *Handbook of Research on Teaching*. New York: Macmillan, pp. 328–75.

Bryan, L.A. (2012). Research on science teacher beliefs. In K.G.B.J. Fraser, T. Campbell and J. McRobbie (Eds), *Second International Handbook of Science Education*. New York: Springer, pp. 477–95.

Burney, V.H. (2008). Applications of social cognitive theory to gifted education. *Roeper Review*, 30(2), 130–9.

Davis, H.A. (2003). Conceptualizing the role and influence of student–teacher relationships on children's social and cognitive development. *Educational Psychologist*, 38(4), 207–34.

Flanagan, J. C. (1954). The critical incident technique. *Psychological Bulletin*, 51(4), 327.

Freeman, J. (2003). Scientific thinking in gifted children. In P. Csermely and L. Lederman (Eds), *Science Education: Talent recruitment and public understanding*. Amsterdam: IOS Press, pp. 17–30.

Galton, M., and Eggleston, J. (1979). Some characteristics of effective science teaching. *European Journal of Science Education*, 1(1), 75–86.

Gilson, T. (2009). Creating school programs for gifted students at the high school level: an administrator's perspective. *Gifted Child Today*, 32(2), 36–9. doi: 10.4219/gct-2009-878

Gremler, D.D. (2004). The critical incident technique in service research. *Journal of Service Research*, 7(1), 65–89. doi: 10.1177/1094670504266138

Kain, D.L. (2003). Owning significance: the critical incident technique in research. In K. deMarrais and S.D. Lapan (Eds), *Foundations for Research: Methods of inquiry in education and the social sciences*. New York: Routledge, pp. 69–85.

Laplante, B. (1997). Teachers' beliefs and instructional strategies in science: pushing analysis further. *Science Education*, 81(3), 277–94.

Luckner, A.E., and Pianta, R.C. (2011). Teacher–student interactions in fifth grade classrooms: relations with children's peer behavior. *Journal of Applied Developmental Psychology*, 32(5), 257–66. doi: http://dx.doi.org/10.1016/j.appdev.2011.02.010

Matthews, M.S. (2012). *Science Strategies for Students with Gifts and Talents*. Waco, TX: Prufrock Press.

Ngoi, M., and Vondracek, M. (2004). Working with gifted science students in a public high school environment: one school's approach. *Prufrock Journal*, 15(4), 141–7.

Nurmi, J.-E. (2012). Students' characteristics and teacher–child relationships in instruction: a meta-analysis. *Educational Research Review*, 7(3), 177–97. doi: http://dx.doi.org/10.1016/j.edurev.2012.03.001

Pajares, F. (1996). Self-efficacy beliefs and mathematical problem-solving of gifted students. *Contemporary Educational Psychology*, 21(4), 325–44.

Palmer, D. (2006). Sources of self-efficacy in a science methods course for primary teacher education students. *Research in Science Education*, 36(4), 337–53.

Passow, A.H. (1981). The nature of giftedness and talent. *Gifted Child Quarterly*, 25(1), 5–10.

Passow, A.H. (1982). Differentiated curricula for the gifted/talented. Paper presented at the 'Curricula for the gifted: selected proceedings for the First National Conference on Curricula for the Gifted/Talented', Ventura County.

Pianta, R.C., Hamre, B., and Stuhlman, M. (2003). Relationships between teachers and children. In W.M. Reynolds and G.E. Miller (Eds), *Handbook of Psychology, Volume 7*. New Jersey: John Wiley and Sons, Inc.

Renzulli, J.S. (2012). Reexamining the role of gifted education and talent development for the 21st century: a four-part theoretical approach. *Gifted Child Quarterly*, 56(3), 150–9. doi: 10.1177/0016986212444901

Sternberg, R.J., and Zhang, L.-F. (1995). What do we mean by giftedness? A pentagonal implicit theory. *Gifted Child Quarterly*, 39(2), 88–94.

Shulman, L.S. (1986). Those who understand: knowledge growth in teaching. *Educational Researcher*, 15(2), 4–14.

Taber, K.S. (2007). Science education for gifted learners? In K.S. Taber (Ed.), *Science Education for Gifted Learners*. New York: Routledge, pp. 1–14.

Tripp, D. (1993). *Critical Incidents in Teaching: Developing professional judgement*. Hove: Psychology Press.

VanTassel-Baska, J. (2003). Selecting instructional strategies for gifted learners. *Focus on Exceptional Children*, 36(3), 1–12.

VanTassel-Baska, J., and Stambaugh, T. (2005). Challenges and possibilities for serving gifted learners in the regular classroom. *Theory Into Practice*, 44(3), 211–17.

Watters, J. J. (2010). Career decision making among gifted students: the mediation of teachers. *Gifted Child Quarterly*, 54(3), 222–38.

Wellisch, M., and Brown, J. (2012). An integrated identification and intervention model for intellectually gifted children. *Journal of Advanced Academics*, 23(2), 145–67. doi: 10.1177/1932202x12438877

Wubbels, T., and Brekelmans, M. (2012) Teacher–students relationships in the classroom. In K.G. Tobin, B.J. Fraser and C.J. McRobbie (Eds). *Second International Handbook of Science Education*, pp 1241–55, Springer.

6 Developing Blended Knowledge in science using the enrichment triad

Practical applications of an enquiry-based learning model

Nancy N. Heilbronner and
Joseph S. Renzulli

Nature and needs of gifted science learners

Max's parents knew that he was different from other boys his age. Whereas other sixth graders hurried home after school to be with friends, Max lingered to attend astronomy club meetings. At night, Max's parents would often find him searching on the internet for increasingly sophisticated concepts. He could speak knowledgably and use phrases such as the 'celestial sphere' or the 'Keppler effect'. Max loved astronomy, an interest that his parents could trace back to his sixth birthday, when they gave him a telescope. He had spent hours every night that year gazing into the lens that was focused on distant suns and planets. He had read everything about astronomy that he could get his hands on, and his parents had purchased a membership at a nearby planetarium. His greatest triumph to date was building a telescope from used parts he had ordered online. When his sixth grade science teacher announced that they would study astronomy, he rushed home to tell his parents. 'We're going to study astronomy for a whole semester in science class!' he cried excitedly. 'I can't wait to get started!'

Unfortunately, when Max's class began learning about astronomy, it was not what he had expected. The class read simple texts that covered material which Max had learned years before, and they did few investigations. When his teacher asked questions, Max blurted out answers, much to the teacher's annoyance. He grew bored and then frustrated, and his mind drifted away as he stared out the window hoping to catch a glimpse of a setting moon in the daytime sky. He could not wait to get home so he could get ready for his regular evening of star gazing.

Although Max is a fictitious student, his story is an amalgam of experiences we have encountered as we have taught and researched in the field of gifted education over the years. The dilemma Max faces is a common one experienced by many gifted science learners, and it results primarily from the mismatch between these learners' natures and needs and the regular school science curriculum. This mismatch is unfortunate, for early engagement with science is critical, and children who are talented in science know early, often as early as the age of nine or ten (Feist, 2006), that they are interested in science and would like to pursue it as a career. Maintaining this interest through appropriate, engaging science curricula would appear to increase the prospect of these students selecting a science, technology, engineering and maths (STEM) major and advancing into a STEM career.

Blended Knowledge

Seminal research (Sosniak, 1985) suggests that children with science talents have been 'mucking about' with science in one form or another since they were toddlers. Indeed, much of gifted students' early learning in STEM may be acquired essentially on their own, as opposed to in the classroom. When Max built his own telescope, he learned about the parts and assembly process required to put it together as he went along. This type of knowledge we refer to as 'just-in-time' (J-I-T) knowledge; it is the type of learning that occurs when individuals need to solve current problems. In this case, for example, Max needed to know how to procure and assemble lens components so that the telescope would function. In this day and age of rapidly evolving technology, this type of information is readily accessible through the internet and other sources, and bright young people may take advantage of a plethora of resources for learning which are more numerous and more accessible than ever before and, arguably, much more advanced than typical textbook coverage of scientific topics.

We refer to a second type of knowledge as 'to-be-presented' (T-B-P) knowledge. This type of knowledge is dictated primarily by curriculum development specialists as they attempt to agree about the type of knowledge that should be imparted in the classroom at various grade levels. The latest reform and accountability movements make efforts to standardize this type of knowledge in the USA (e.g. Common Core State Standards), and textbook publisher and testing companies make profits from producing and assessing T-B-P knowledge. To understand curricula and learning strategies, however, it is helpful to think of knowledge in the classroom as consisting of three components, depicted in Figure 6.1.

It is the combination of the following three components that we refer to as 'Blended Knowledge'. The first and perhaps simplest component of knowledge is 'Received Knowledge', or the knowledge that is traditionally delivered through textbooks, lectures, videos and more. When acquiring this component of knowledge, the learner is usually passively learning and memorizing whatever is offered to them. The second component of knowledge we refer to as 'Analysed Knowledge', or knowledge that requires the learner to engage with the material in a more active manner through a variety of cognitive processes. For example, students might apply, analyse, evaluate, categorize, interpret, integrate, extrapolate, or synthesize Received Knowledge. The third component of Blended Knowledge is 'Applied and Created Knowledge', which comes about when students use Received and Analysed Knowledge to investigate problems or to create something that is new to the individual. It should be noted here that Applied and Created Knowledge need not be new to all of mankind – the important thing to consider is that it is brought to bear on a problem that does not have a single, predetermined correct answer and it is new to the individual. For example, when

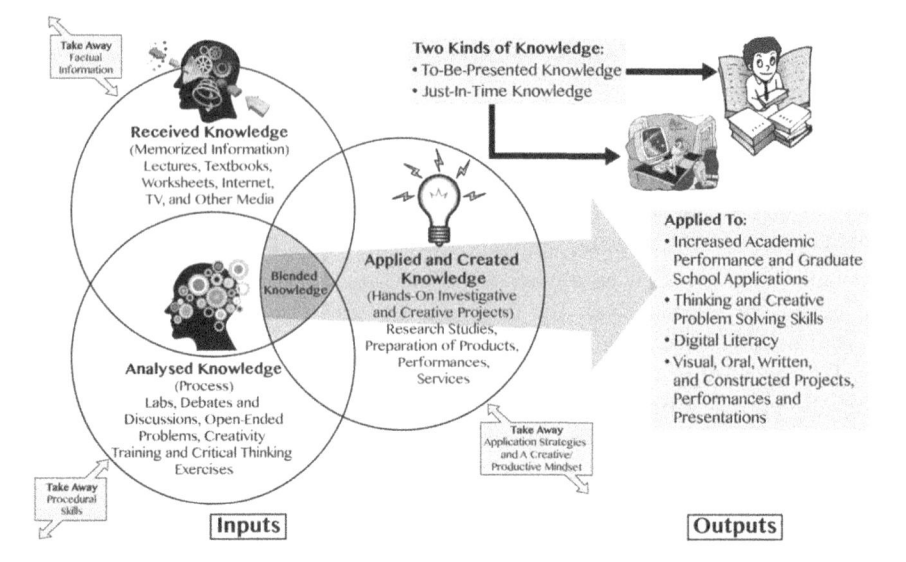

Figure 6.1 Blending levels of knowledge to promote thinking skills and creativity

a pupil writes a poem or a short story, creates an original maths problem, or designs and conducts a science investigation, he or she is creating knowledge or a product that is new to him or her. Applied and Created Knowledge represent the highest or most advanced form of learning, and it may, in a certain sense, be considered to be the end goal of higher-level learning, a goal in which students apply other components of knowledge to achieve.

In the USA, the Next Generation Science Standards (NGSS), developed by the National Research Council, the National Science Teachers Association, the American Association for the Advancement of Science and Achieve, serve as a national set of standards for the teaching of science. When closely examined, these standards relate most effectively to the concept of Blended Learning. The NGSS are categorized into Disciplinary Core Ideas (DCIs), performance expectations, cross-cutting concepts and science and engineering indicators. For example, standard 3-LS-1 is a life science standard that is appropriate for grade 3: From Molecules to Organisms, Structures and Processes. The DCI for the standard is 'Reproduction is essential to the continued existence of every kind of organism. Plants and animals have unique and diverse life cycles,' and the performance expectation reads, 'Develop models to describe that organisms have unique and diverse life cycles but all have in common birth, growth, reproduction and death' (NGSS, 2013). A cross-cutting concept is that 'Patterns of change can be used to make predictions' and the science and engineering indicator is that students need to 'develop models to describe phenomena' (NGSS, 2013). For this standard, students must be taught the Received Knowledge concerning components of reproduction, such as the fact that reproduction is necessary for life to continue, how it occurs and how it differs in species. They will then demonstrate Analysed Knowledge as they develop models of reproduction; for example, they may be asked to draw the life-cycle diagram for a flower. Applied and Created Knowledge is more sophisticated and generally occurs after the other types of knowledge have been mastered. In this case, students might be asked to invent and describe a new species of creature and account for how it will perform basic life processes that include respiration, the acquisition of energy and reproduction.

Authentic learning

The concept of Blended Learning is a natural extension of another identified type of learning that has existed in the educational community for decades – authentic learning. For learning to be considered authentic, several conditions must be met (Renzulli *et al.*, 2004). First, the learning must focus on finding and solving a real problem, and for the problem to be real, the learner must have a personal connection to the problem; this connection may be emotional or cogni-tive. Generally, students will work on authentic problems within their communi-ties; they are more likely to be emotionally vested with finding solutions to local problems. However, some students *are* motivated to solve larger problems than others – for example, what can we do about recycling in our school or commu-nity. The important idea is that there should be some feeling of personal connec-tion. The problem must also be a 'fuzzy' problem, or an open-ended one in which no single, predetermined correct answer or clear solution exists, and it must be structured in such a way that it may change actions, attitudes, or beliefs. Finally, the problem should target an authentic audience, or an audience beyond the teacher or classroom (e.g. published report, science fair, display in a public place, presentation to a science club or community group). Audiences beyond the teacher or the usual 'classroom reports' give a realness and motivation to perfect the applied or creative project. In our recycling example, students might develop a system for separating the disposal of cafeteria waste into rubbish and recyclable cafeteria material. Ideally, it is best if the students select the problem themselves. Authentic learning has been recognized as critical in fields such as science, and the Enrichment Triad Model described below naturally leads to this type of learning.

The Enrichment Triad Model

Works of theorists such as Jean Piaget (1976), Jerome Bruner (1961) and John Dewey (1910) provided the rationale for the Enrichment Triad Model (Renzulli, 1976), used in thousands of schools internationally. The model is based on a large number of creative instructional methods and curricular practices that had their origins in special programmes for high-ability students. It was developed to motivate and engage students by exposing them to various topics, areas of interest and fields of study; and to further train them to *apply* advanced content, thinking skills and investigative methodology training to self-selected areas of interest (ibid.). The Enrichment Triad is based on the ways in which people learn in a natural environment rather than the artificially structured classroom and prescribed curriculum environments that characterizes most school learning situations. The Triad Model has been adopted and adapted in thousands of schools serving diverse school populations, both nationally and internationally. Three interrelated types of enrichment experiences are embedded within the Enrichment Triad Model.

Type I enrichment: general exploratory experiences

External stimulation, internal curiosity, necessity, or combinations of these starting points cause people to develop an interest in a topic, problem, or area of study; therefore, Type I enrichment is designed to expose students to a wide variety of disciplines, topics, occupations, hobbies, persons, places and events that would not ordinarily be covered in the regular curriculum. Teachers organize Type I experiences by contacting speakers, arranging mini-courses, demonstrations, performances, videos, or by using internet-based resources such as virtual field trips. Type I experiences can motivate students to such an extent that they will act on their interests in creative and productive ways. The major purpose of Type I enrichment is to include within the overall school programme selected experiences that are purposefully developed to be motivational and to serve as invitations for more advanced-level follow-up on the parts of individuals or small groups. Type I enrichment experiences can be based on regular curricular topics or innovative outgrowths of prescribed topics, but in order to qualify as a *bona fide* Type I experience, any and all planned activities in this category must be purposefully directed towards stimulating new or present interests on the parts of individuals or small groups, and scheduled debriefings following Type I activities should reflect the invitational opportunities for student follow-up.

Type II enrichment: group training activities

Most educators agree about the need to blend into the curriculum more training in the development of higher-order thinking skills. Type II enrichment includes materials and methods designed to promote the development of thinking and feeling processes. Type II training is usually carried out both in classrooms and in enrichment programmes. It includes the development of 1) creative thinking and problem-solving, 2) critical thinking, 3) affective processes and character development skills, 4) a wide variety of specific learning how-to-learn skills, 5) skills in the appropriate use of advanced-level resource and reference materials, 6) written, oral and visual communication skills, 7) the acquisition and appropriate application of digital literacy skills and J-I-T knowledge. Type II enrichment can be blended into regular curriculum topics or offered as stand-alone experiences in regular classrooms or as part of special enrichment programmes. And they are considered an essential requirement for the *in situate* skills necessary when students are working on Type III enrichment projects described below. Type II enrichment also serves a motivational purpose similar to that discussed in connection with Type I activities. Thus, for example, students who have been taught how to measure decibels using a sound meter might be asked: 'Now that you know how to measure sound, what are some things you might like to investigate using this instrument?'

Type III enrichment: individual and small group investigations of real problems

Type III enrichment incorporates investigative activities and the development of creative products in which students assume roles as firsthand investigators, writers, artists, or other types of practising professionals. Although students pursue these kinds of involvement at a more junior level than adult professionals, the overriding purpose of Type III enrichment is to create situations in which young people are thinking, feeling and doing what practising professionals do, even if at a less sophisticated level than adult researchers, writers, or entrepreneurs. *Bona fide* Type III experiences incorporate the following four characteristics:

- personalization of interest;
- use of authentic methodology;
- no single predetermined answer;
- designed for an audience other than (or in addition to) the teacher.

Type III enrichment is the vehicle through which everything from basic skills to advanced content and process skills blend into student-developed products and services. In much the same way that all of the separate but interrelated parts of an automobile come together at an assembly plant, this form of enrichment serves as the 'assembly plant of mind'. This kind of learning represents a synthesis and an application of content, process and personal involvement. The student's role is transformed from one of lesson-learner to firsthand enquirer, and the role of the teacher changes from an instructor and disseminator of knowledge to a combination of coach, resource procurer, mentor and 'guide on the side'.

The Schoolwide Enrichment Model (SEM)

The Schoolwide Enrichment Model (SEM) is an organizational plan based on the pedagogy of the Enrichment Triad Model and includes curriculum modification procedures for high-achieving students and vehicles for examining student interests, learning styles and preferred modes of expression (Renzulli and Reis, 2010). Implementation of the SEM in diverse school districts has provided an opportunity to develop instructional procedures and programming alternatives that emphasized the need both to provide a broad range of advanced-level enrichment experiences for *all* students, and to use the many and varied ways that students respond to these experiences as stepping stones for relevant follow-up on the parts of individuals or small groups. Figure 6.2 depicts the various components of the SEM.

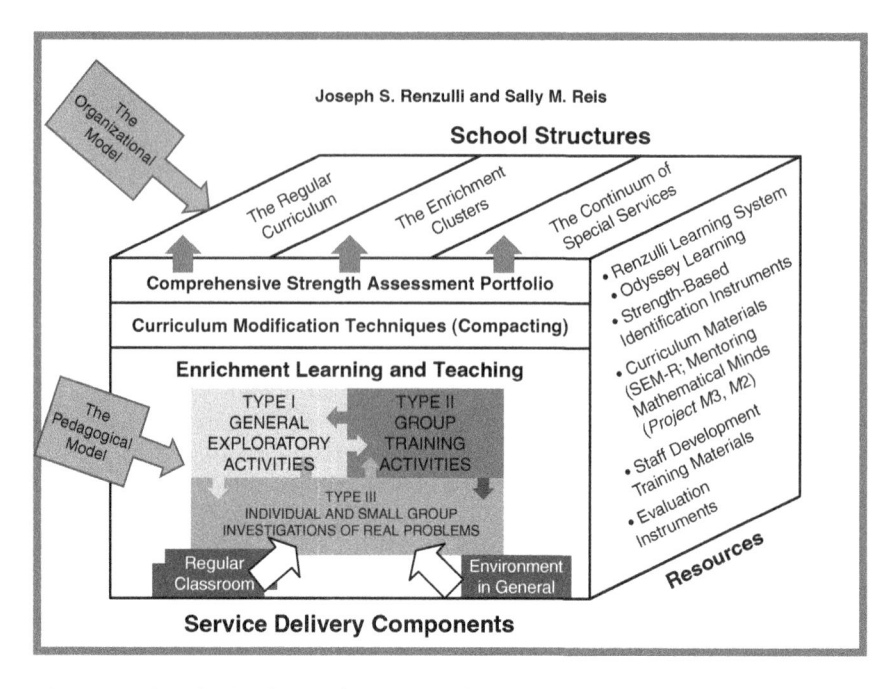

Figure 6.2 The Schoolwide Enrichment Model

Implemented at thousands of schools around the world, the SEM is designed to *infuse* high engagement enrichment activities into any and all standards-based curricular topics. A series of teaching strategies have been developed to implement the 'brand' of learning set forth in the Enrichment Triad Model. The components of the model include the following:

1. Service delivery components – these components focus on curriculum delivery:
   a. The Total Talent Portfolio is developed to help a teacher understand a child's interests, learning styles and abilities.
   b. Curriculum modification techniques allow certain activities to be condensed or eliminated because students have already mastered the content and skills required. In the place of basic activities, teachers may substitute more challenging activities.
2. Enrichment learning and teaching using the Enrichment Triad Model.
3. School structures – these components consist of the organizational structures the school uses to deliver learning to students: the regular curriculum, enrichment clusters and a continuum of special services. Regular curriculum consists of the basic skills and knowledge that we want all students to learn, but that gifted students may advance beyond. We do not recommend replacing the regular curriculum, but rather *infusing* Types I, II and opportunities for Type III enrichment into any and all regular curriculum topics. Enrichment clusters

provide students with the opportunity to interact with other students who share common interests in a topic (e.g. photography, technology, writing and more) for the purpose of defining an authentic problem and then investigating solutions to these problems. A continuum of special services might include opportunities for grade-level or subject-based acceleration, clubs and competitions sponsored by the school, extracurricular activities, mentorships and much more. For a full discussion of these and other opportunities embedded in the model, the reader is referred to Renzulli and Reis (1991, 1997, 2014).

4. Resources – these components vary from school to school, but they consist of the structures put in place to support the development and implementation of the SEM model at the school. Such components might include the SEM specialist and team leader, a professional staff development model to train teachers in SEM and more. Again, for a full discussion of the SEM model, the reader is referred to the references listed above.

Putting it all together

The integration of Blended Knowledge and the Enrichment Triad Model into authentic enquiry-based learning in the science classroom through SEM provides school administrators and teachers with an opportunity to develop hands-on curricular experiences that will engage learners in science in a meaningful way. By meaningful, we mean that students will connect with science on a cognitive and emotional level and relate learning to their experiences in the real world. What would an example of this type of learning look like in the classroom? It might help if we revisit Max, our budding astronomer; only this time, we will place him into a classroom in which the science curriculum is shaped by the Enrichment Triad Model. In addition, we will be providing examples of each of the types of Blended Knowledge.

A different scenario

This time we join Max during the first week of school. He is in Mrs D's science classroom, who is excited because she is about to begin her first year implementing the Enrichment Triad Model in science. She knows that she wants to spend the first week getting to know her students better, and so she gives them a survey called an 'Interest-a-Lyzer' (Renzulli, 1997). This instrument is designed to reveal students' interests, strengths and learning styles by asking them questions such as 'What are some of the things you would like to collect if you had the time and money?' Mrs D plans to use students' responses on the instrument to develop a Total Talent Portfolio for each student that will help her plan instruction. The students are engaged as they complete the novel questions.

Afterwards, Max approaches Mrs D's desk and chatters non-stop about his answers to some of the questions. He tells her that he would collect telescope lenses because he would like to see how they each work, or maybe he would collect many different telescope parts because he could practise putting them all together. He segues into having tried to build a telescope once and actually being able to see Mars up close through it, and how Mars appeared much redder through the telescope than it did to the naked eye, and he wondered if all planets appeared different colours and that was how artists knew how to illustrate them in science books. Mrs D notes Max's extreme interest in astronomy.

When Mrs D examines the class's Interest-a-Lyzers, she focuses again on the fact that Max appears to have a strong interest in science (and, specifically, in astronomy). She compiles a chart of the class's interests; top interests included, among others, weather, animals and… astronomy. Max is in good company! To further engage students, Mrs D decides to bring in speakers in their interest areas. She invites a meteorologist from the local television station, an astronomer from the university and a zoologist to speak. She also plans two field trips – one to the city's planetarium and another to a nature conservancy. When Max hears about the visit by the astronomer and the trip to the planetarium, he can barely contain his excitement.

The astronomy unit is scheduled to occur early in the school year, and so Max does not have to wait long. Mrs D begins the four-week unit with a pre-assessment to ascertain students' levels of knowledge about the unit's learning objectives. She administers this pre-assessment in the form of a concept map, providing students with sophisticated vocabulary and requiring that they arrange them into a coherent graphic organizer that will reveal how much the students understand about the concept. Max is able to arrange the words correctly, and even adds a few more of his own to strengthen the concept map. Mrs D decides that Max has mastered the objectives of the unit and will need additional learning challenges. She documents this mastery on a form, the Curriculum Compactor, carefully describing the unit's learning objectives, the pre-assessment she used to determine mastery of the objectives and Max's level of achievement.

Mrs D then invites the local astronomer, Dr M, to speak to the class about stars and planets, constellations and galaxies. He inspires their imaginations with colour-enhanced images of the rings of Saturn taken by the roving satellite Galileo. He presents a working telescope and allows the students to handle it and take turns looking through its eyepiece. When Max's turn to hold the telescope arrives, Max strikes up an eager conversation with Dr M, who notes Max's interest in and extensive knowledge about the telescope and invites Max to visit him at the observatory.

After Dr M's presentation, Max completes an Action Information form formally notifying his teacher of his interest in astronomy. At this point, Mrs D meets with Max to design an authentic project related to the field of astronomy. She explains to him that, because he already knows much of the content that the class will be learning in the astronomy unit, he will be using his time to work on this project. She calls it a Type III project and informs him that it should be challenging, related to his interests and require that he use many new skills (Type II skills) to accomplish it.

Max immediately knows what he wants to select for his Type III project. Recently, he had convinced his parents to take him to the observatory – the very same observatory where Dr M works. While there, he had noticed that one of the things the facility lacked was an opportunity for students to participate in hands-on activities such as telescope building. He explains to his teacher that, for his project, he'd like to construct an exhibit that the observatory might actually use – one that would allow students to construct a telescope from parts and allow them to better understand how telescopes work. After the conversation, Mrs D calls Dr M and describes Max's idea; the scientist is intrigued and immediately agrees to work with Max once a week to collaborate on the exhibit.

Max sets to work and immediately realizes this project will require a great deal of planning; he also understands that he will need to acquire some new skills during the planning phase. Specifically, he will need to develop skills in the following areas:

- Advanced research: Max will need to *research* how telescopes are constructed and how they work; he will also need to understand how similar exhibits are set up at other museums and observatories. He may visit different websites or use reference materials on telescope construction to *take notes and organize information* for what his exhibit should contain. He may also choose to *interview* curators to understand what goes into a good exhibit, learning how to collect and organize data. Or he may develop a survey that he sends out to 50 curators to help him understand what goes into a good exhibit.
- Cognitive: Max will need to *think creatively* about how his exhibit will be designed. He will also need to think critically about which aspects of the exhibit could be appropriate and which will not, evaluating the process at each stop along the way.
- How-to-learn skills: Max will need to *develop an organized plan* that constitutes an outline of his expected design. The plan will need to contain a budget for the observatory and a schedule for implementation.
- Communication skills: Finally, Max will need to *present* his plan to Mrs D and Dr M. He may select to do so using advanced presentation tools such as Animoto or Prezi.

Max develops a successful presentation and gains the enthusiastic support of his teacher and the scientist, who make some suggestions about the presentation, which Max incorporates. Next, Max must present his ideas to the observatory's director and gain approval. He has calculated a reasonable budget for the exhibit and so the director sees merit in the project and allows Dr M to continue to work with Max.

Now the real work must begin. Max spends the next several months researching, planning, creating and organizing his exhibit. His classmates help the effort by contributing their talents and materials as well. At the end of the project, the observatory holds an open house to introduce Max's new exhibit, and he watches as students from surrounding schools tour the observatory and take turns putting telescopes together. Max turns to Dr M to tell him that he has an idea for how to turn the exhibit into an App, and Dr M smiles.

Max's story does not end there. Because of his passion, he is able to further develop his telescope, refining it to pick up pulses of light from farther and farther away. One day, as his head is bent over his work, he discovers a new way of refining the telescope's lens in a way he had never come across in a textbook. Excitedly, he calls Dr M, who encourages him to pursue his thoughts about a better telescope. Eventually, Max plans to enter his invention in the International Science and Engineering Fair – a lifelong passion is born.

Summary

This second scenario is an application of authentic, enquiry-based learning. Max worked on the solution to a problem that was complex, messy and intended for an audience outside the classroom. He developed a set of J-I-T skills when he was required to research, organize information, evaluate and think critically and creatively as he constructed the exhibit. These J-I-T skills and knowledge frequently occur naturally as we go about solving real-world problems, as opposed to the T-P-B skills and knowledge that Max would acquire had he participated in the regular curriculum. Because Max had to move away from the passive world of Received Knowledge, he became a more active and engaged learner. Not that Max did not benefit from previous T-P-B skills Received Knowledge – he did, and he even applied them as he developed the exhibit. In this area, however, he had moved beyond the benefits that the regular curriculum could provide. By applying previous learning, he was able to master the Blended Knowledge components of Analysed Knowledge and Creative or Applied Knowledge. He engaged with the material (Received Knowledge) in an active manner and through a variety of cognitive processes (Analysed Knowledge), and applied that knowledge to create something new (Created or Applied Knowledge). Again, the product was not new to all mankind, but it was new to Max.

Conclusion

Whether we like it or not, the mainly prescribed, standards-driven regular curriculum is a reality and we are not arguing against the importance of Received Knowledge or for a radical replacement of what has and will continue to be the mainstay of formal education in the future. We are suggesting, however, that a theory-based enrichment model (the Enrichment Triad) and an organizational plan (the Schoolwide Enrichment Model) can be infused into traditional approaches to schooling. Every school and classroom contains bright young people like Max. For these students to achieve their potential, some easy-to-implement modifications will help us to avoid them becoming bored, provide the levels of challenge and personalization, and create the motivation to seriously consider pursuing STEM careers. An added payoff is that all students will benefit from the three major goals of an enrichment-based model – enjoyment, which leads to engagement, which, in turn, leads to enthusiasm for learning.

References

Bruner, J.S. (1961). The act of discovery. *Harvard Educational Review*, 31(1), 21–32.

Dewey, J. (1910). *How We Think*. Lexington, MA: DC Heath. doi:10.1037/10903-000

Feist, G. (2006). The development of scientific talent in Westinghouse finalists and members of the National Academy of Sciences. *Journal of Adult Development*, 13(1), 23–35.

NGSS (Next Generation Science Standards) (2013). Next Generation Science Standards: For states, by states. Retrieved from http://www.nextgenscience.org/next-generation-science-standards

Piaget, J. (1976). *The Grasp of Consciousness: Action and concept in the young child*. Trans by S. Wedgwood. Oxford: Harvard University Press.

Renzulli, J.S. (1976). The Enrichment Triad Model: a guide for developing defensible programs for the gifted and talented. *Gifted Child Quarterly*, 20(3), 303–26.

Renzulli, J.S. (1997). *The Interest-a-Lyzer: A family of instruments*. Waco, TX: Prufrock Press.

Renzulli, J.S., and Reis, S.M. (1991). The schoolwide enrichment model: a comprehensive plan for the development of creative productivity. In N. Colangelo and G.A. Davis (Eds), *Handbook of Gifted Education*. Boston: Allyn and Bacon, pp. 111–41.

Renzulli, J.S., and Reis, S.M. (1997). *The Schoolwide Enrichment Model: A how-to guide for educational excellence* (2nd edn). Mansfield Center, CT: Creative Learning Press.

Renzulli, J.S., and Reis, S. (2010). The Schoolwide Enrichment Model: a focus on student strengths and interests. *Gifted Education International*, 26(2–3), 140–57.

Renzulli, J.S., and Reis, S.M. (2014). *The Schoolwide Enrichment Model: A how-to guide for educational excellence* (3rd edn). Waco, TX: Prugrock Press.

Renzulli, J.S., Gentry, M., and Reis, S.M. (2004). *A Time and Place for Authentic Learning*. Retrieved from http://gifted.uconn.edu/wp-content/uploads/sites/961/2015/02/Authentic_High-End_Learning.pdf

Sosniak, L.A. (1985). Becoming an outstanding research neurologist. In B.S. Bloom (Ed.), *Developing Talent in Young People*. New York: Ballantine Books, pp. 348–408.

7 Engaging learners in the analysis of scientific literature

A practical strategy for enhancing gifted students' interest in science

William L. Romine and Troy D. Sadler

Conceptual change is a multidimensional framework of concern for all students, including those labelled as gifted. While many studies have addressed epistemological and ontological dimensions of conceptual change, affective aspects receive comparatively little attention in educational research (Treagust and Duit, 2008). When it comes to gifted students, interest in learning and pursuing careers in science should be a construct of significant concern; gifted students are among those with the greatest potential to become successful scientists. Unfortunately, efforts to get gifted students interested in science are not integrated into typical classroom environments.

In light of the goal to help all students become scientifically literate (AAAS, 1989, 1993), instructors are pressured to teach to the majority (Gallagher *et al.*, 1997). These approaches may address important needs in terms of maximizing the reach of science education initiatives, but they do not necessarily inspire passion for science and excitement for pursuing science careers among the most talented students. The proportion of degree-seeking students choosing to pursue science, technology, engineering and mathematics (STEM) studies has shown little growth (Maltese and Tai, 2011), indicating that efforts to direct gifted and talented students towards STEM studies and careers have had limited success.

For example, in a recent project, our research team studied a technology-enhanced biotechnology curriculum for high school biology students. The intervention was successful in terms of supporting student learning of core principles in the biological sciences, and results suggested that the learning experience was significantly more impactful for lower-level students relative to their more academically successful peers (Sadler *et al.*, 2013). Despite the learning gains, the intervention had no discernible impact on student interest in science and careers in science (Romine *et al.*, 2014; Sadler *et al.*, 2015). Classroom observation data and teacher feedback suggested that some of the same dimensions of the intervention that supported learning among the lower-level students frustrated many of the more talented students (Eastwood and Sadler, 2013; Sadler *et al.*, 2014).

Another factor limiting gifted students' access to innovative instruction is that funding for efforts to improve STEM education is directed largely at high-risk students within underprivileged communities. While the intention to reach all students and focus on underserved youth is noble, it comes with the drawback that gifted students and their special learning needs are often ignored – a majority of gifted students of all ages are condemned to boring, repetitive classrooms (Gallagher *et al.*, 1997).

A student is often identified as 'gifted' through measures of characteristics we associate with 'giftedness', such as extensive knowledge recall and logical ability (Watters and Diezmann, 2003). However, Watters and Diezmann (ibid.) argue that these are of little value in the twenty-first century if they are not used to generate the capacity for original thought, creativity and reasoning through meaningful learning activities. Extracurricular activities and clubs are often used as a way to supplement classroom activities to encourage gifted students to develop these capacities. For example, programmes such as Odyssey of the Mind, Science Olympiad and First Robotics Competition present opportunities for extending K-12 students' learning experiences and involving them in higher-level learning and problem-solving. Organizations such as Future Health Professionals (HOSA) have been developed to enrich middle and high school students' experiences with health and biology education, and increase interest in health professions. Both in-class and extracurricular opportunities are also built into some government funded programmes such as the National Science Foundation (NSF)-funded Mission Biotech (Sadler *et al.*, 2013) and the Howard Hughes Medical Institute (HHMI)-sponsored Maps in Medicine (O'Malley, 2011). In addition, STEM schools have emerged from the idea that all subject areas, including reading, writing and history, can be taught in the context of topics in science, technology, engineering and mathematics, and can help better prepare students for STEM professions (Scott, 2012).

Much of the effort behind offering gifted and talented students enquiry-based learning experiences at the college level has focused on engaging these students in authentic scientific research. Foundations such as the HHMI (through its undergraduate education grants) and the NSF (through its Research Experiences for Undergraduates (REU) programmes) have created new infrastructure on college campuses throughout the USA for connecting undergraduate students with research experiences in the laboratory groups of active science and engineering scholars (Desai *et al.*, 2008; Sadler and McKinney, 2010). Subotnik *et al.* (1993) found that access to research opportunities is among the most powerful factors in motivating talented students to pursue scientific studies and careers. These programmes have vastly expanded the access of talented students to authentic science experiences, but the programmes tend to be competitive and reach relatively few students. The same can be said for large-scale funded curricular interventions, which require significant sums of money for both material resources and qualified faculty and staff (Gess-Newsome *et al.*, 2003).

While educational efforts like those described above have reached many gifted students, there are many more without awareness of or access to opportunities with the potential to excite and generate new levels of interest in STEM studies and careers. Extracurricular opportunities such as authentic research experiences are an important part of an overall strategy for engaging gifted students in meaningful STEM experiences; however, extracurricular programmes will always fall short of reaching a majority of gifted learners. We propose that opportunities for engaging STEM learning and enquiry must also occur within science classrooms to ensure that all gifted learners can build their STEM literacy and interest. We see engaging experiences conducted within STEM classrooms as an important complement to extracurricular programming.

Purpose of the study

Integrating research into the science classroom can sound like an intimidating endeavour. However, enquiry can take many forms, from guided to completely open, and the varying approaches to enquiry can be effective in facilitating conceptual change (Sadeh and Zion, 2009). Furthermore, scientific enquiry experiences can be effective for supporting science learning and development of students' science self-efficacy (Yoon, 2009). In the context of an introductory non-majors undergraduate environmental science course, we contrast open and guided enquiry approaches to analysing scientific literature in facilitating interest in learning, careers and attitudes around environmental science. We chose to evaluate the integration of scientific literature into a classroom because we believe this is something that can be done to facilitate both guided and open enquiry in most classrooms regardless of laboratory or equipment constraints.

Sample and design

We utilized a longitudinal quasi-experimental design to track the comparative effects of guided and open enquiry approaches to reading scientific literature on undergraduate students' interest in science and technology over half of a semester. A sample of 91 students from a non-majors environmental science core class was taken. Students' interest was measured at three time points (pre, middle and post) through the final eight weeks of the semester using the Rasch-validated Student Interest in Technology and Science (SITS) instrument adapted for the environmental science context (Romine and Sadler, 2014).

Thirty students from a single classroom participated in a guided enquiry approach. This group was assigned to read a single journal article, 'Can a collapse of global civilization be avoided?' (Ehrlich and Ehrlich, 2013), over the final eight weeks of the semester. The instructor gave five quizzes of five to seven questions over the respective sections of the article approximately every two weeks. These quizzes focused on recalling aspects of the article, and served the primary purpose of holding students accountable for reading the assigned sections before coming to class. Students were also expected to come to class with their own discussion questions which served as a basis for the in-class discussions.

Sixty-one students participated in an open enquiry approach. These students were asked to identify an aspect of environmental science that interested them and find, read and review an academic article that addressed that interest. Original research, literature reviews, or meta-analyses were available options for students. At the beginning of the assignment, the instructor showed students how to locate academic articles using library databases like EBSCO and publically available databases like Google Scholar, and explained how to distinguish between academic and non-academic literature. A five-page literature review was completed by students and given in at the end of the semester. The five pages included a half-page summary of the introduction, a one-page summary of the methods, a one-page summary of the results, a 1 to 1.5-page summary of the discussion and a 1 to 1.5-page personal critique of the article.

Statistical model

Student responses on the SITS instrument provided measures for four affective variables: 1) interest in learning science, 2) interest in using technology to learn science, 3) interest in environmental science careers and 4) attitudes towards environmental science. Students' locations along each of the four scales were measured in logits derived from the Rasch model. The logit scale is normalized to 0 with a variance of 1, and serves as a convenient common metric by which gains across all subscales can be compared. Multi-level linear mixed models using an unstructured random effects covariance structure (Hedeker and Gibbons, 2006) were implemented using the SAS statistical package to evaluate differential change with respect to each scale between the two interventions. Time (coded: pre = 0, middle = 1, post = 2) and the treatment-by-time interaction were defined as continuous within-subjects variables, and treatment (coded: guided enquiry = 0, open enquiry = 1) was defined as a categorical between-subjects variable. The intercept and time were also treated as random effects, meaning that they were allowed to vary freely between students. Significance of time, treatment and the treatment-by-time interaction were evaluated using the Type 3 F-test. Regression coefficients were used to determine the direction of the relationship for significant parameters.

Results

Student interest at the beginning of the intervention

In the above model, the intercept is indicative of the average location on the Rasch logit scale for students using the guided enquiry approach at the start of the project. Since the Rasch logit scale is centred at 0, this can be interpreted as students starting significantly above or below the centre of the scale. Interest in using technology to learn science ($F_{1,113.3} = 8.05$, $p = 0.005$), careers in environmental science ($F_{1,121.6} = 21.25$, $p \ll 0.001$) and attitudes towards environmental science ($F_{1,102.6} = 44.55$, $p \ll 0.001$) had significant intercepts. These showed positive average beginning locations for interest in using technology to learn science (b = 1.39 $SE_b = 0.49$) (Figure 7.1) and attitudes towards environmental science (b = 4.03, $SE_b = 0.60$) (Figure 7.2), and a negative average location for interest in environmental science careers (b = -2.32, $SE_b = 0.50$) (Figure 7.3).

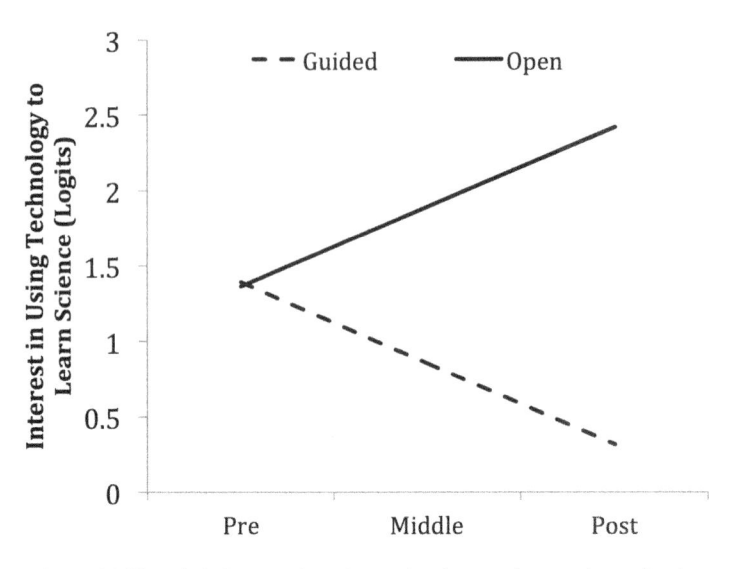

Figure 7.1 Trends in interest in using technology to learn science for the open and guided
enquiry groups

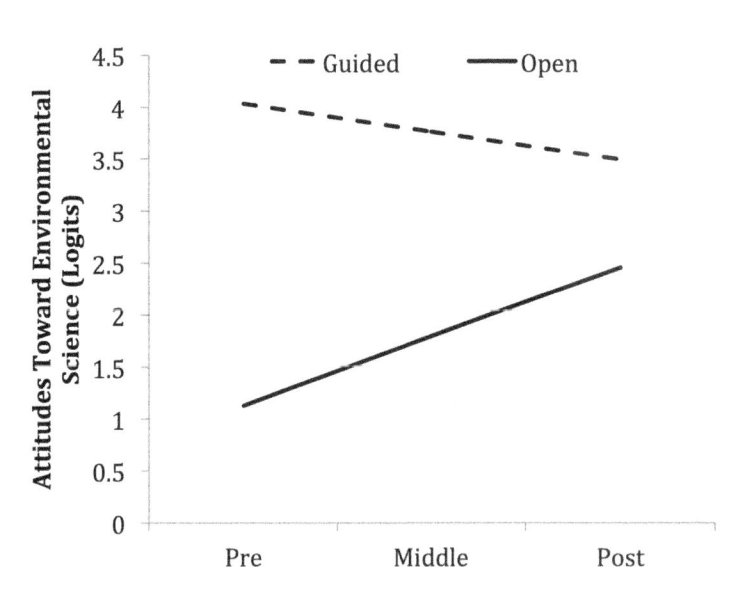

Figure 7.2 Trends in attitudes towards environmental science for the open and guided
enquiry groups

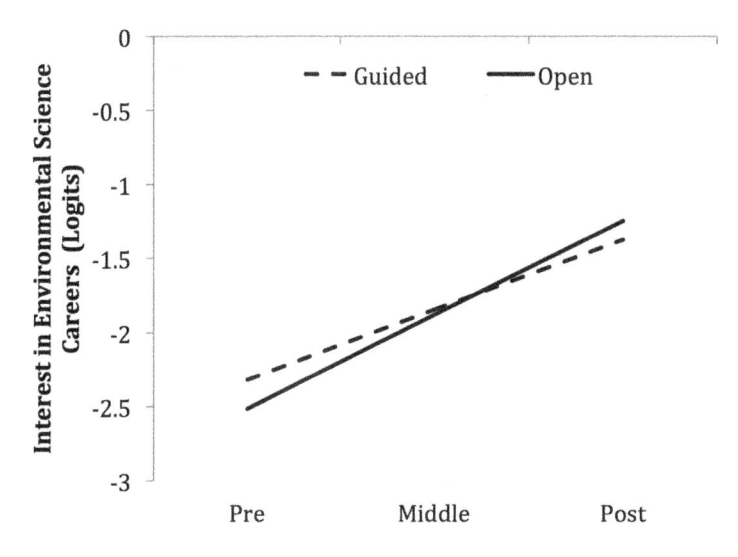

Figure 7.3 Trends in interest in environmental science careers for the open and guided enquiry groups

The treatment effect in the above model tests the extent to which the open enquiry group was significantly different from the guided enquiry group at the beginning of the intervention. The only significant treatment parameter was found for attitudes towards environmental science ($F_{1,100.6} = 15.62$, p << 0.001). Attitudes towards environmental science (Figure 7.2) was an average of 2.91 logits lower at the beginning of the intervention in the open enquiry group than the guided enquiry group (b = –2.91, $SE_b = 0.74$).

Differential effects of the interventions

The effect of time for interest in using technology to learn science ($F_{1,109.6} = 3.25$, p = 0.074) and careers in environmental science ($F_{1,86.9} = 3.24$, p = 0.075) was significant at the $\alpha = 0.10$ level. The coefficient was negative for interest in using technology to learn science (b = -0.54, $SE_b = 0.30$), meaning that interest decreased significantly in the guided enquiry group (Figure 7.1). A positive regression coefficient for interest in environmental science careers (b = 0.47, $SE_b = 0.27$) indicates significant positive growth in the guided enquiry group across the intervention. A non-significant treatment-by-time interaction ($F_{1,83.6} = 0.26$, p = 0.61) for interest in environmental science careers indicates that gains in the open enquiry group were statistically similar to those found in the guided enquiry group (Figure 7.3).

Significant differential effects between the two approaches were found for interest in using technology for learning science ($F_{1,104.9} = 8.71$, p = 0.004) and attitudes towards environmental science ($F_{1,173.7} = 4.34$, p = 0.039). A positive interaction parameter for interest in using technology for learning science ($b = 1.07$, $SE_b = 0.36$) indicates that gains in this construct were significantly higher in the open enquiry group than in the guided enquiry group. Figure 7.1 shows that while interest dropped in the guided enquiry group, students in the open enquiry group gained interest across the eight weeks. Gains in attitudes towards environmental science were also significantly larger for the open enquiry group ($b = 0.94$, $SE_b = 0.45$) than the guided enquiry group. While attitudes in the open enquiry group increased across the eight weeks, a slight decrease was found in the guided enquiry group (Figure 7.2). Although this result is intriguing, it is most likely due to a ceiling effect since attitudes in the guided enquiry group were significantly higher than those in the open enquiry group at the beginning of the intervention.

Discussion

Results from this study demonstrate that both guided and open enquiry approaches can affect change in interest in science for all students. It is interesting that while students in this study began with relatively low interest in careers in environmental science, the data suggest that both guided and open enquiry approaches facilitated growth in interest in science careers across half of a semester. While this change was not significant at the traditional 0.05 alpha level, we must remember that personal interest in STEM careers is built through a lifetime of experience (Alexander and Jetton, 1996), making demonstrable change within the course of a few weeks notoriously difficult.

Interest in using technology for learning science underwent the largest differential change between guided and open enquiry approaches. Given the structure of the interventions, we would not suggest that this difference in gains is due to the respective guided and open approaches themselves, but rather how these were implemented. Specifically, using the internet as a learning tool, where students were required to identify a specific area of interest related to environmental science and find an academic article on the internet matching that interest, was central to the open enquiry approach. Students in the guided enquiry group were assigned a single article to read by the instructor, and these students were not given explicit instruction on or experience with using the internet for research. This left Powerpoint as the sole learning technology that the guided enquiry group experienced in the classroom. To a science instructor interested in helping students become well-informed, interactive citizens in an increasingly STEM-focused community, this result is heartening. It shows that something as simple as integration of explicit instruction on how to use the internet for research into an otherwise traditional classroom setting can help to improve students' conceptions about the utility of technology as a learning tool. On the flip side, our data show that if an instructor uses technology only for traditional lectures and essays, then students will become increasingly resistant to utilizing technology for scientific enquiry. With computers and smart phones becoming ubiquitous across all school environments, reading and analysis of scientific literature can be integrated into any science class. Whether an instructor tells students what to explore or requests that students define their own learning journey, academic search engines like EBSCO and Google Scholar make the well of knowledge virtually limitless.

The data presented here were collected on non-science major undergraduate students taking their core science requirement. At first glance, this does not seem to serve as a representative sample for gifted students. This leads us to ask, what would a representative sample look like? Does giftedness imply the ability to reason mathematically? Does it imply exceptional verbal ability? How about creative achievement? Would a student who possesses some, but not all, of these traits be considered gifted or deficient? To what extent can we even trust our measures of those traits which we associate with giftedness?

Given lack of agreement on what the label of 'gifted' actually means (Sternberg and Davidson, 2005), purposeful sampling of 'gifted' students would have been a dubious endeavour. Further, such a sample would not be reflective of a real classroom, which is a mixture of students with varying backgrounds, abilities and interests. To reach gifted students within traditional classroom contexts, we must develop activities targeted at students considered to be gifted which do not alienate the remainder of the students. We show that guided and open enquiries related to reading and analysis of academic literature works to support affective change across a diverse student body within an otherwise traditional classroom environment. We posit that if these types of assignments work to increase interest in such a diverse group as undergraduate science non-majors, then they would also likely work for undergraduate science major and high school students. Future studies will be needed to either support or refute these positions.

Reading and analysis of scientific literature is one of many scientific practice-based activities that can be integrated into traditional classroom contexts at a variety of academic levels to reach gifted students and improve their interest in science. While small classroom assignments do not get the publicity of high-dollar research experiences and curricular overhauls, we must remember that there is no substitute for quality classroom instruction. Let us engineer our classrooms so that extracurricular activities complement, instead of supplement, classroom instruction. No matter how we define 'gifted', efforts to move away from the boring, repetitive classroom towards instruction centred on challenging, practice-based enquiry assignments like those described here will likely serve as the most powerful factor in getting our most talented youth interested in STEM studies and careers.

References

AAAS (American Association for the Advancement of Science) (1989). *Science for All Americans: Project 2061*. New York: Oxford University Press.

AAAS (1993). *Benchmarks for Science Literacy*. New York: Oxford University Press.

Alexander, P.A., and Jetton, T.L. (1996). The role of importance and interest in the processing of text. *Educational Psychology Review*, 8(1), 89–121.

Desai, K.V., Gatson, S.N., Stiles, T.W., Stewart, R.H., Laine, G.A., and Quick, C.M. (2008). Integrating research and education at research-extensive universities with research-intensive communities. *Advances in Physiology Education*, 32(2), 136–41.

Eastwood, J. L., and Sadler, T. D. (2013). Teachers' implementation of a game-based biotechnology curriculum. *Computers and Education*, 66, 11–24. doi: 10.1016/j.compedu.2013.02.003

Ehrlich, P.R., and Ehrlich, A.H. (2013). Can a collapse of global civilization be avoided? *Proceedings of the Royal Society B: Biological Sciences*, 280(1754), 20122845.

Gallagher, J., Harradine, C.C., and Coleman, M.R. (1997). Challenge or boredom? Gifted students' views on their schooling. *Roeper Review*, 19(3), 132–6.

Gess-Newsome, J., Southerland, S.A., Johnston, A., and Woodbury, S. (2003). Educational reform, personal practical theories, and dissatisfaction: the anatomy of change in college science teaching. *American Educational Research Journal*, 40(3), 731–67.

Hedeker, D., and Gibbons, R.D. (2006). *Longitudinal Data Analysis*. New Jersey: John Wiley and Sons.

Maltese, A.V., and Tai, R.H. (2011). Pipeline persistence: examining the association of educational experiences with earned degrees in STEM among US students. *Science Education*, 95(5), 877–907.

O'Malley, J. (2011). The Maps in Medicine program: an evaluation of the development and implementation of life sciences curriculum. Doctoral dissertation, Saint Louis University, Saint Louis, MO.

Romine, W.L., and Sadler, T.D. (2014). Measuring changes in interest in science and technology at the college level in response to two instructional interventions. *Research in Science Education*, 1–19.

Romine, W., Sadler, T.D., Presley, M., and Klosterman, M.L. (2014). Student Interest in Technology and Science (SITS) survey: development, validation, and use of a new instrument. *International Journal of Science and Mathematics Education*, 12(2), 261–83.

Sadeh, I., and Zion, M. (2009). The development of dynamic inquiry performances within an open inquiry setting: a comparison to guided inquiry setting. *Journal of Research in Science Teaching*, 46(10), 1137–60.

Sadler, T.D., and McKinney, L.L. (2010). Scientific research for undergraduate students: a review of the literature. *Journal of College Science Teaching*, 39(5), 68–74.

Sadler, T.D., Romine, W.L., Stuart, P.E., and Merle-Johnson, D. (2013). Game-based curricula in biology classes: differential effects among varying academic levels. *Journal of Research in Science Teaching*, 50(4), 479–99.

Sadler, T.D., Eastwood, J.L., Romine, W. and Annetta, L. (2014). Mission biotech: using technology to support learner engagement in STEM. In R.E. Yager and H. Brunkhorst, *Exemplary STEM Programs: Designs for Success*. Arlington, VA: NSTA Press.

Sadler, T.D., Romine, W.L., Menon, D., Ferdig, R.E., and Annetta, L. (2015). Learning biology through innovative curricula: a comparison of game- and nongame-based approaches. *Science Education*, 99(4), 696–720.

Scott, C. (2012). An investigation of science, technology, engineering and mathematics (STEM) focused high schools in the US. *Journal of STEM Education: Innovations and Research*, 13(5), 30–9.

Sternberg, R.J., and Davidson, J.E. (Eds) (2005). *Conceptions of Giftedness*. New York: Cambridge University Press.

Subotnik, R.F., Duschl, R.A., and Selmon, E.H. (1993). Retention and attrition of science talent: a longitudinal study of Westinghouse Science Talent Search winners. *International Journal of Science Education*, 15(1), 61–72.

Treagust, D.F., and Duit, R. (2008). Conceptual change: a discussion of theoretical, methodological and practical challenges for science education. *Cultural Studies of Science Education*, 3(2), 297–328.

Watters, J.J., and Diezmann, C.M. (2003). The gifted student in science: fulfilling potential. *Australian Science Teachers Journal*, 49(3), 46–53.

Yoon, C.-H. (2009). Self-regulated learning and instructional factors in the scientific inquiry of scientifically gifted Korean middle school students. *Gifted Child Quarterly*, 29, 1–14.

8 The nature of science and the teaching of gifted learners

Keith S. Taber

There has been an international movement within science education promoting more emphasis within school science on teaching about the nature of science (NOS). There are good reasons to include teaching about the NOS in the school curriculum for all learners, and these are briefly rehearsed below. However, the main argument of the present chapter concerns the potential for teaching focused on NOS for meeting the educational needs of the most able learners: those sometimes labelled as 'gifted'. It is argued that, by its nature, teaching about NOS offers opportunities to engage and challenge those learners who are judged to be gifted in science.

How should we plan the science curriculum?

Readers of this book are very likely to recognize that science deserves, or the sciences deserve, a place in the compulsory school curriculum that children are expected to study as part of their formal education and preparation for adult life. There are various arguments that can be made to support this view.

- Societies need a supply of scientists, engineers and technologists, and others working in science-dependent areas, and work in such areas can be rewarding (and usually pays decent, if unexceptional, salaries). Young people should be encouraged to consider such work, and be prepared to qualify for it. (I will call this the *economic rationale.*)
- School should introduce young people to all the major aspects of their culture – music, painting, literature, etc. Science is an important part of human culture that all young people should learn about. (I will call this the *cultural rationale.*)
- Science has very important applications and implications – for economies, for medicine, for the environment, etc. Young people will enter an adult world where they will have a role to play as consumers, voters and (potentially at least) civic activists, expected to take positions on important questions about the resourcing and regulation of, and the use of the products of, science. (I will call this the *civic rationale.*)

- School is largely about moral and intellectual development and schooling should offer opportunities for young people to engage in and develop their thinking skills. (I will call this the *developmental rationale.*)

These are all important arguments. Consideration of the purpose (or purposes) of science education should inform decisions about the nature of the science curriculum (what is to be taught and hopefully learnt) and decisions about what should be included in school science will be influenced by the relative weighting given to the different purposes that are recognised.

The first rationale listed above, the *economic rationale*, is an important one, but does not intrinsically imply any particular curriculum content. By custom and practice, however, there are often expectations about what should be included in school science, and these may link to what universities or other institutions that determine post-compulsory programmes (degrees, diplomas, apprenticeships, etc.) feel they would like to see as prior learning. That is, there is often a 'top-down' pressure on the school curriculum from 'above'. Where prior learning is assumed by teachers then it can be essential for students to actually have developed this as prerequisite knowledge to support effective further learning (Taber, 2015). However teachers in higher-level institutions often expect they will need to do some re-teaching of expected prior learning, and in any case there is no 'in principle' reason why some material currently taught in school could not be moved to post-compulsory courses (if, for example, it is recognised as being of limited interest and relevance to most students and/or being material than many students struggle with).

The liberal studies argument (i.e. the *cultural rationale*) that everyone should be exposed to science because it is part of their culture (Snow, 1959/1998) is an important argument – but it is not obvious that many of the topics commonly taught in school science are required to meet this purpose. Arguably every educated person should appreciate the principle of conservation of energy, be aware of the particulate theory of matter and appreciate the general principles of natural selection. It is not so obvious that many of the other things we tend to teach in school science lessons – say Coulomb's law, oxidation numbers, or flame test colours – come into the category of being essential for engaging in culture. That is not to say there might not be arguments for teaching such topics, but someone can be considered reasonably cultured without knowing (as one example) which metal has salts that colour a flame lilac.

The applications/implications argument (the *civic rationale*) is an important one. We might want people to know enough about how nuclear power stations work to appreciate arguments about their advantages and potential risks, and to appreciate why antibiotics will not help when they have a viral infection. There is a difficulty here in knowing precisely what knowledge base is going to be pertinent for the key social issues decades ahead (although energy and the environment are likely to remain key areas of concern). Arguably here, though, a specific knowledge base in science topics is no more important (and perhaps less so) than a good understanding of 'how science works' (Toplis, 2011) and so how evidence is used to develop, and sometimes challenge and modify, scientific knowledge (Millar and Osborne, 1998).

The final purpose considered above (the *developmental rationale*) concerns how education can support development as much as specific learning. In this regard one aspect of NOS has traditionally been considered potentially important as part of the development of students' thinking skills. Science poses hypotheses that are tested by setting up careful experimental tests to provide data that can potentially confirm or disconfirm the hypothesis (but see comments below about experimental testing). This is a logical process and science is often held up alongside mathematics as being the curriculum areas that can support the development of logical thinking skills.

It is well known that school-age students often have considerable difficulty in 1) designing fair tests for scientific hypotheses and 2) making appropriate logical deductions about hypotheses from data sets generated from suitable experimental tests. This, however, reinforces the value of these kinds of activities in supporting the development of 'scientific thinking skills' that can later be applied to make logical decision in real-life contexts. Some students, however, latch on to the logic of fair testing much earlier than their peers and have few difficulties in seeing how particular hypotheses might be tested or in making valid deductions from the results of testing. This might be good grounds to consider these students as gifted in science, and accordingly to recognise that activities based around straightforward fair testing which are challenging many of their classmates have insufficient demand to be genuinely educative for these gifted learners (see Chapter 1 by Taber, this volume).

What is the nature of science?

The NOS concerns the processes by which science sets about developing scientific knowledge, and therefore also concerns the nature of the knowledge generated. That science poses hypotheses and uses experimental methods to test them is certainly part of NOS. This aspect of NOS is often well represented in the curriculum – if sometimes in such a fragmented and bowdlerized form that the activities lose any sense of reflecting authentic scientific practice (Taber, 2008). However, there has been much scholarship in the history, philosophy and sociology of science (Gilbert and Mulkay, 1984; T.S. Kuhn, 1996; Lakatos, 1970; Latour and Woolgar, 1986; Popper, 1934/1959) which suggests that:

- many areas of science are seldom able to employ genuine experimental work (i.e. intervening in nature) and have to rely on observing 'natural experiments';
- scientific work seldom consists of simple, clear-cut experiments that prove critical to the acceptance or rejection of scientific hypotheses (things are usually a lot messier than this);
- scientific research tends to occur within ongoing research programmes, so that each study adds incrementally to a slowly developing (and often complex) evidence base;

- research programmes necessarily rely upon some grounding assumptions that are not tested but have to be assumed within the programme (so all observations are theory-laden to some degree);
- no experimental test is ever sufficient to prove a hypothesis correct, as there will always be other possible explanations that fit the data (even when no one has thought them up yet, and they may seem much less plausible);
- no experimental test absolutely refutes a hypothesis outright, but only the combination of the hypothesis with various other assumptions – about the theory of the experimental and analytical apparatus used; about the apparatus functioning, or chemicals being pure or power supplies not being interrupted; about technicians following protocols in setting up the experiment; about observers correctly noting outcomes, etc. (so it is always possible to explain away a negative result.);
- the acceptance of scientific ideas in the wider community may be a slow process, which depends in part upon rhetorical and other extra-experimental factors, and individual scientists may have (theoretical, metaphysical, empirical) commitments or personal biases which influence their evaluation of the evidence. Scientists are also imperfect human beings.

Given the complexity of genuine scientific work, it is clearly often appropriate for teachers to somewhat simplify accounts of how scientific ideas have developed in order to match the needs of the students they are teaching (Taber, 2008). When we are teaching gifted learners, however, much less simplifying and cleaning up of the full scientific story may be appropriate than when teaching most students.

All students need to learn about NOS

If our purposes for teaching science suggest we should empathise current scientific ideas and help students understand them, these various complexities could be considered as unwelcome 'noise' that could make the 'signal' more difficult for students to appreciate. Teaching as a rhetoric of conclusions (Schwab, 1962) focuses on what scientists currently think is probably the case so students can learn lots of science (that is, lots of science content) without too many NOS (that is, process-related) complications. However, it has increasingly been argued that a key purpose of science education is to meet a *civic rationale*, so that people leaving the school system can engage (individually and collectively) in decision-making processes about such matters as whether to put effort into recycling their rubbish; whether to support more wind and solar 'farms'; whether public resources should be spent cutting carbon dioxide emissions; and so forth. This requires making sense of scientific arguments, and being suitably sceptical about all claims while trusting in the value of science to offer strong evidence-based arguments to inform decision-making. This is not trivial when the public rely on the media for their scientific information. There are many examples that could be considered, but here I discuss two: one of global importance, and the other of deep personal relevance to many people.

There is very little doubt among scientists who work in the area that the climate is changing, and that anthropocentric inputs into the atmosphere are a contributing factor. Yet clearly there is uncertainty about how much the climate will change, and how fast; and how much of the change is due to human activity, and so about how much difference we could make by changing human behaviour. A few scientists will therefore argue (against a general consensus) that there is no need to invest vast resources, and to compromise industrial productivity and international development, to reduce greenhouse emissions. A complex understanding of NOS is needed to make sense of this without dismissing human influence on climate change as 'just a theory' – an idea that some scientists have but which has not been 'proved'.

A key issue then for science education is the status of scientific knowledge. Students commonly think science teaches facts, and they often see scientific ideas to come in two flavours (Lederman and Lederman, 2014; Taber *et al.*, 2015). The first flavour is often labelled as 'theories', but students often take it to mean little more than guesses, hypotheses, hunches, etc. that scientists have come up with. In everyday life people will commonly say 'It is just a theory', meaning just a suggestion or idea. But in science theories are not 'just' someone's ideas but rather are 'consistent, comprehensive, coherent and extensively evidenced explanations of aspects of the natural world' (Qualifications and Curriculum Authority, 2007). Students generally think that theories are still 'just theories' because they have not been fully tested yet. Once it has been 'proved' (which, as suggested above, is not a term justified by a contemporary understanding of NOS), what *was* a theory becomes something else – often considered a law of nature which has factual status. But, in science, laws are not proved theories: laws report widely reproduced patterns/relationships observed in natural phenomena rather than being explanatory schemes. Students need to appreciate the nature, origins, and status of scientific knowledge if they are make sense of, and engage with, issues such as climate change. Scientists' knowledge about climate change *is* theoretical, uncertain and provisional – but necessarily so, because all scientific knowledge is inherently of that nature.

An area of personal relevance to a large proportion of the world's learners is the relationship between science and religion. A subgroup of scientists who are themselves atheists have run a very public campaign in some countries to try to persuade the public that science is inherently an atheistic endeavour and that, because some religious leaders may dismiss well-grounded scientific ideas, religion is therefore the enemy of science and reason.

A quite nuanced understanding of NOS is needed to appreciate that these arguments are based on metaphysical assumptions that inform these particular scientists' personal notions of what science *should* be (Taber, 2013), but that other active, professional research scientists operate with a different (metaphysical) understanding of science. Some other scientists will share with their atheist colleagues the scientific practice of excluding supernatural causes from scientific explanations, yet still believe in a creator God as an ultimate cause that lies behind (and so complements) scientific accounts of the world.

Understanding this area of interaction between science and the wider society also requires learners to distinguish between the stances of those religious groups which accept science in principle and expect to interpret scripture to be consistent with empirical experience of the world, and so-called 'fundamentalist' faith positions which consider scripture as literal and technical accounts of the natural world which must be privileged over scientific accounts when the two do not seem consistent. Just as there are some scientists trying to persuade us that science implies a complete denial of the supernatural, there are some well-funded religious groups trying to persuade us of the truth – of religious accounts – and the incorrectness of scientific theories by careful selection and interpretation of 'evidence' to fit their preferred view of the world (such as museums that present an alternative account of natural history to fit young earth creationism).

The question of how science relates to religion(s) is clearly a complex and subtle matter. Research suggests that secondary school students generally have a less nuanced notion of how science relates to religion (Taber *et al.*, 2011) and of why different people might take different positions on such questions (Billingsley *et al.*, 2013). Indeed, formal philosophy of science is often considered too abstract and theoretical to include in school science – after all, many secondary-age learners struggle enough with applying the principles of fair testing to clear-cut simplified data sets.

Yet these two examples show why understanding the nature of scientific knowledge (its status as generally reliable but always somewhat provisional; how it is constructed through research programmes and dialogue within the scientific community) and the metaphysics of science (how understandings of science are informed by values and beliefs brought from outside science itself) may be very important for people to make sense of socio-scientific issues such as climate change, and when considering their own attitude to and engagement with science (for example, in relation to a personal faith background).

Teaching about NOS as a strategy to meet the needs of the gifted learner

As suggested above, science – alongside mathematics – has traditionally been considered to encourage logical thinking. This ignores the creative aspects of science which are equally important (see chapters 1 and 2 of this volume). However, even in terms of the logical requirements of science, the examples above demonstrate how rational decision-making involving science in the adult world involves much more nuanced and complex thought processes than the simple algorithmic deductive thinking that often suffices when considering typical experimental work in school science.

There is a good deal of research into the kind of thinking needed for dealing with the complex and messy data of real-life issues and problems: what is sometimes called post-formal thinking (Arlin, 1975; Kramer, 1983) – that is, going beyond what Piaget (1970/1972) labelled formal operational thinking, and moving towards what is sometimes labelled as wisdom (Sternberg, 2009).

Different studies have shown a common pattern to such development (D. Kuhn, 1999), and that it typically continues well beyond schooling so that even university students at elite schools are often still developing in this area (Perry, 1970). Young children may not clearly distinguish between knowledge of the world and the world itself, and when they first acquire the distinction they tend to see ideas as simply correct or wrong – akin to accepting or rejecting a hypothesis on the basis of a clear-cut critical experimental test.

When faced with the reality of the world not fitting such a simple dichotomy there tends to be a shift to a more relativistic position – that all views are simply opinions, and that if we cannot tell which are right or wrong then there is no basis for making principled judgements between them. From such a stance, everyone is entitled to their opinion, and adopting a position is simply a matter of personal taste. In one of the examples considered above this would translate to interpreting different scientists arguing over climate change as implying that science cannot tell us the truth on the issue (which is correct in an *absolute* sense), and therefore cannot guide us (which does not follow), as every opinion on the matter is equally valid/invalid and deserving/undeserving of our consideration (clearly unhelpful given what is at stake). Similarly, if learners feel that atheism is a scientific prerequisite (as a few vocal scientists argue), but one that can be ignored according to taste, then they might assume that other (genuine) scientific values such as being open-minded and sceptical can be ignored when inconvenient.

Moving beyond this to adopt a personal value system which is consistent and principled while remaining open to critical review (a bit like scientific knowledge itself) is a target which some learners may never approach during their school career (Krathwohl *et al.*, 1968). Intriguingly, a study of college students in the USA by Palmer and Marra (2004) concluded that the shift from the absolutist stage to the relativist stage occurred later in the context of studying natural sciences than in the humanities and social sciences. Perhaps that is because school science tends to limit itself to considering the one current canonical model, theory or interpretation that relates to a particular scientific question, whereas other areas of the school curriculum present students with uncertainty and alternative perspectives on a more regular basis.

Now if we prioritise the *developmental rationale* for science in the school curriculum, which sees a key role of science teaching being to support the intellectual development of young people, then we may draw two general conclusions from this analysis. The first is that science teaching which embraces NOS with its complexity and nuances, and admits consideration of how scientific ideas have been developed; and why they are (provisionally) accepted, and what limitations they may have; and which explores socio-scientific issues where scientific knowledge has to be examined in the light of personal value positions (therefore, for example, understanding the affordances and limitations of genetic testing is necessary, but not sufficient, to decide whether expectant parents *should* have their unborn baby tested for serious genetic conditions) has potential to give students opportunities to engage with and develop more advanced thinking. The second conclusion, however, is that, for most school-age students, such themes will be very challenging and that they are only likely to successfully engage in them with considerable scaffolding of tasks by teachers.

The corollary of this conclusion, however, is that these contexts that may easily prove especially challenging for most learners, and so may lead to failure and frustration without careful support from the teacher, may well be just the kind of activities that offer sufficient complexity and nuance to provide genuine challenge for the gifted learner (cf. Chapter 1). In summary then:

- teaching about NOS can respond to the *civic rationale* for teaching science for all students
- teaching about NOS can also respond to the *developmental rationale* for teaching science
- without careful structuring and sequencing, NOS activities may be pitched at too high a level for many school-age learners
- the high level of challenge inherent in considering NOS in the classroom may provide contexts to engage gifted students and provide them with genuinely educative learning activities.

Approaching the teaching of NOS in school science

This perspective suggests we should look to include more material relating to NOS in school science for all students, but that this may, in particular, be an area where we can genuinely challenge and develop the thinking of gifted students. There are many suggestions available for how to incorporate more NOS-based teaching in school science, such as the use of more authentic enquiry-based activities (Lawson, 2010) or adopting nuanced case studies from the history of science that reflect the complexity of how scientific knowledge is actually developed (Allchin, 2013). It may also be possible to develop materials that effectively model for learners aspects of more complex scientific thinking – perhaps along the lines that the Philosophy for Children programme has achieved for more general philosophy – in that case through sequences of carefully designed children's novels (Trickey and Topping 2004). The key issues for effective teaching of most learners will be the usual concerns about pacing the introduction of ideas, offering relevant context, carefully scaffolding learning tasks, regular reinforcement, etc.

For gifted learners themes from philosophy of science may be intrinsically interesting as they are the students who will commonly already be asking 'How do we know?', 'Can we ever be sure?', 'Does a theory or model always apply?', 'How can we identify the implicit assumptions behind a scientist's conclusions?' and so forth. Therefore gifted students may be primed to engage in such abstract questions when many of their classmates may need to be provided with strong and more concrete motivations for venturing into such areas.

Moreover, engaging in such abstract issues need not mean shifting from familiar ways of class teaching. There certainly is scope with the gifted to set them more independent projects, such as preparing for presentations, class debates, peer-tutoring and the like (Taber and Riga, forthcoming). However, teaching about the NOS can look like teaching any other kind of science topic in terms of class activity. For example, the author organised an after-school enrichment programme for learners considered by their schools as gifted in science known as ASCEND (Able Scientists Collectively Exploring New Demands). A key focus of the programme was NOS themes – the demarcation question in science; the scientific method; the nature of explanations in science; the nature of scientific laws; interdisciplinary work in science; socio-scientific issues; the nature of scientific models; analogy in science (Taber, 2007). Some aspects of the ASCEND programme were designed to be different from normal school experience. So, for example, the 14–15 year-old 'delegates' were treated as far as possible as adult visitors to the University, with a conference-type registration with refreshments. Activities were generally extended group work, with minimal intervention from teaching staff – and, in particular, the activities were designed to engage thinking about science which was expected to be unfamiliar from studying the standard curriculum fare.

Yet the actual format of the activities reflected the kinds of tasks that are normal in schools. For example, consider the first two ASCEND activities: 'What is science?' and 'Is there a method to science?' The 'What is science?' activity is a card-sort activity that asks a small group of students to agree on whether a range of activities count as science, or not: a theme which has much vexed philosophers of science. This sounds straightforward, but need not be for two reasons. First, most school-age students never consider the demarcation issue formally, so have no explicit criteria for what might be considered a science. The activity therefore helps make their implicit thinking explicit. A single student undertaking a card sort could simply decide that town planning, gardening, or water diving are, or are not, scientific activities – but in a group they have to offer and support their reasoning. Of course, an added complication is that, with a little bit of imagination (something gifted learners tend to engage readily), it is possible to find reasons why any activity *could* be considered scientific. This is an activity that any group of students could engage with, but which, despite having a very simple structure, offers potential to engage high-level thinking and argumentation. Indeed, the activity was adopted to use with science teachers in another project as an example of a dialogic activity. The science teachers found the activity as engaging as the school students.

The second example, asking 'Is there a method to science?', was an attempt to teach some philosophy of science perspectives on the nature of scientific method, but again through the kind of structured group activity commonly used in secondary schools. The students were asked to complete a table which asked them to match three perspectives on scientific method (labelled as 'induction', 'falsification' and 'paradigm shifts') with the names of an associated philosopher, a motto describing their approach and another motto describing how scientific progress is understood in that perspective. Students were not expected to have prior knowledge, but were provided with a brief description of each of the three perspectives to read. This then was what is sometimes referred to as DART (a direct activity related to text). Each group was also given a flow chart reflecting the approach as an alternative form of representation and asked to also match these to the perspectives.

Due to the high level of structuring of this part of the activity, it could be accessible to a broad ability range, and not just the most gifted learners, even though the topic is very abstract. However, a follow-up task asked the student groups to next consider ten historical vignettes concerning particular scientific episodes, and to evaluate the three perspectives as descriptions of how science proceeds, using the vignettes as evidence. This task was genuinely highly challenging, as, generally, the vignettes did not offer clear support for any one of the perspectives, but often included elements that could be interpreted as best fitting parts of different perspectives. To complete this activity, students have to engage with abstract models, and evaluate them based on a very messy data set. Yet the nature of the activity – group discussion to complete a task structured through texts provided by the teacher – would not look out of place in most school science lessons.

Conclusion

It is difficult to consider we are teaching science if what we actually teach is little more than a catalogue of canonical ideas detached from the processes by which they have come to be considered as scientific knowledge. Authentic science teaching has to engage with the processes of science as well as the outputs. There are strong justifications for incorporating more NOS teaching in the curriculum. Future scientists need an appreciation of NOS, and the most able students may be actually engaged in science through NOS activities better meeting their intellectual needs, and so perhaps become more likely to pursue science studies and careers (the *economic rationale*). While the theories of science permeate the social world in which students will live (the *cultural rationale*), the true culture of science concerns values and processes more than subject matter. So we want students to develop the scientific attitude, at least as much as know some science. In terms of taking their place as engaged members of democratic societies (the *civic rationale*), we need young people to be able to understand and critique scientific evidence and argumentation and that means appreciating process as well as content.

This chapter has, however, particularly argued for the *developmental rationale*, that NOS offers nuanced complexity of the kind that provides contexts for developing higher-level thinking. This is important for *all* learners, although NOS-based activities may need to be carefully introduced and scaffolded to be accessible to *most* learners. Many gifted learners in science classes find classroom tasks often lack sufficient challenge for them to be genuinely educative for them and these students are often ready to engage in authentic NOS learning activities without requiring excessive simplification and densely structured scaffolding. For developing these gifted students, having the NOS themes embedded in complex and messy context and the lack of clear definitive answers are important features of the task. Just as they so often are in science itself.

References

Allchin, D. (2013). *Teaching the Nature of Science: Perspectives and resources.* Saint Paul, MN: SHiPS Educational Press.

Arlin, P. K. (1975). Cognitive development in adulthood: a fifth stage? *Developmental Psychology*, 11(5), 602–6.

Billingsley, B., Taber, K.S., Riga, F., and Newdick, H. (2013). Secondary school students' epistemic insight into the relationships between science and religion: a preliminary enquiry. *Research in Science Education*, 43, 1715–32. doi: 10.1007/s11165-012-9317-y

Gilbert, G.N., and Mulkay, M. (1984). *Opening Pandora's Box: A sociological analysis of scientists' discourse.* Cambridge: Cambridge University Press.

Kramer, D.A. (1983). Post-formal operations? A need for further conceptualization. *Human Development*, 26, 91–105.

Krathwohl, D.R., Bloom, B.S., and Masia, B.B. (1968). The affective domain. In L.H. Clark (Ed.), *Strategies and Tactics in Secondary School Teaching: A book of readings.* New York: Macmillan, pp. 41–9.

Kuhn, D. (1999). A developmental model of critical thinking. *Educational Researcher*, 28(2), 16–46.

Kuhn, T.S. (1996). *The Structure of Scientific Revolutions* (3rd edn). Chicago: University of Chicago Press.

Lakatos, I. (1970). Falsification and the methodology of scientific research programmes. In I. Lakatos and A. Musgrove (Eds), *Criticism and the Growth of Knowledge.* Cambridge: Cambridge University Press, pp. 91–196.

Latour, B., and Woolgar, S. (1986). *Laboratory Life: The construction of scientific facts* (2nd edn). Princeton, NJ: Princeton University Press.

Lawson, A.E. (2010). *Teaching Inquiry Science in Middle and Secondary Schools.* Thousand Oaks, CA: Sage.

Lederman, N.G., and Lederman, J.S. (2014). Research on teaching and learning of nature of science. In N.G. Lederman and S.K. Abell (Eds), *Handbook of Research on Science Education* (Vol. 2). New York: Routledge, pp. 600–20.

Millar, R., and Osborne, J. (1998). *Beyond 2000: Science education for the future.* London: King's College.

Palmer, B., and Marra, R.M. (2004). College student epistemological perspectives across knowledge domains: a proposed grounded theory. *Higher Education*, 47(3), 311–35.

Perry, W.G. (1970). *Forms of Intellectual and Ethical Development in the College Years: A scheme.* New York: Holt, Rinehart and Winston.

Piaget, J. (1970/1972). *The Principles of Genetic Epistemology.* Trans. by W. Mays. London: Routledge and Kegan Paul.

Popper, K.R. (1934/1959). *The Logic of Scientific Discovery.* London: Hutchinson.

Qualifications and Curriculum Authority (2007). *Science: Programme of study for key stage 3 and attainment targets.* London: Qualifications and Curriculum Authority.

Schwab, J.J. (1962). The teaching of science as enquiry (The Inglis Lecture, 1961). In J.J. Schwab and P.F. Brandwein (Eds), *The Teaching of Science.* Cambridge, MA: Harvard University Press.

Snow, C.P. (1959/1998). The Rede Lecture, 1959: The two cultures. *The Two Cultures.* Cambridge: Cambridge University Press, pp. 1–51.

Sternberg, R.J. (2009). A balance theory of wisdom. In J.C. Kaufman and E.L. Grigorenko (Eds), *The Essential Sternberg: Essays on intelligence, psychology and education.* New York: Springer, pp. 353–75.

Taber, K.S. (2007). *Enriching School Science for the Gifted Learner*. London: Gatsby Science Enhancement Programme.

Taber, K.S. (2008). Towards a curricular model of the nature of science. *Science and Education*, 17(2–3), 179–218. doi: 10.1007/s11191-006-9056-4

Taber, K.S. (2013). Conceptual frameworks, metaphysical commitments and worldviews: the challenge of reflecting the relationships between science and religion in science education. In N. Mansour and R. Wegerif (Eds), *Science Education for Diversity: Theory and practice*. Dordrecht: Springer, pp. 151–77.

Taber, K.S. (2015). Prior Knowledge. In R. Gunstone (Ed.), *Encyclopedia of Science Education*. Berlin-Heidelberg: Springer-Verlag, pp. 785–6.

Taber, K.S., Billingsley, B., Riga, F., and Newdick, H. (2011). Secondary students' responses to perceptions of the relationship between science and religion: stances identified from an interview study. *Science Education*, 95(6), 1000–25. doi: 10.1002/sce.20459

Taber, K.S., Billingsley, B., Riga, F., and Newdick, H. (2015). English secondary students' thinking about the status of scientific theories: consistent, comprehensive, coherent and extensively evidenced explanations of aspects of the natural world – or just 'an idea someone has'. *The Curriculum Journal*, pp. 370–403.

Taber, K. S., and Riga, F. (forthcoming). From each according to her capabilities; to each according to her needs: fully inclusing the gifted in school science education. In S. Markic and S. Abels (Eds), *Inclusion in Science Education*. New York: Nova Science.

Toplis, R. (Ed.). (2011). *How Science Works: Exploring effective pedagogy and practice*. Oxford: Routledge.

Trickey, S., and Topping, K.J. (2004). 'Philosophy for children': a systematic review. *Research Papers in Education*, 19(3), 365–80. doi: 10.1080/0267152042000248016

9 Gifted females in science

Sezen Camci-Erdogan and Fran Riga

> My daughter, an honors student who was later admitted to the biology honors program at the University of Connecticut, was experiencing difficulty in an Honors Physics class of 10 students. Only two females were in the class and when I contacted her teacher (a male) he threw up his hands and told me that females were never good at physics! I wonder if part of the problem might have been his attitude and lack of understanding?
>
> O'Keefe (as cited in Reis, 1987)

It has long been acknowledged that gifted females are under-represented in careers that encompass the physical sciences and technology. A deeper understanding of the reasons for, and the impact of, this under-representation is crucial for implementing effective instruction, mentoring, career planning and enabling social adaptation. In this chapter we shall examine some ground-breaking/landmark *models* that try to explain why girls tended not to choose careers in the physical sciences, computers and engineering. We shall then look at some of the *factors* highlighted within the research literature that are thought to contribute to the gender differences observed among gifted students. Finally, by taking stock of the above-mentioned models and factors/reasons, we assess the *progress* that has been made over the last 25 years or so, and make recommendations for future practice based on the research evidence provided/discussed.

Before proceeding, it is fitting to explain what we mean by a 'gifted learner' within the context of school science. Taber (2007) defines those students that are gifted learners as either being able to 'achieve *exceptionally* high levels of attainment in all or some aspects of the normal curriculum demands in school science' or those able to 'undertake some science-related tasks at a level of demand well above that required at that curricular stage' (p. 7, emphasis original). Taber differentiates between *able learners* and *the gifted* suggesting that the former are 'capable of meeting current curriculum demands to a high level in science', whereas the latter exhibit this capability to *exceptional* level. Where *able learners* are 'self-evident in most classrooms', Taber also posits that *gifted learners* may not be – 'The gifted learners are capable of the exceptional, but may only be exceptional when given the right opportunities and encouragement' (pp. 7–8).

Gifted students seem naturally drawn to science possibly because science taps into their natural curiosity and imagination (Smutny and Von Fremd, 2004).

The discrepancy in the numbers of males and females pursuing careers in the sciences, especially the physical sciences, has long been recognized (Lubinski and Benbow, 1992). Taking engineering as an example, the landmark studies of Maccoby and Jackin (1974) predicted that approximately twice as many engineers would be expected to be male as female if spatial reasoning ability is considered a valid predictor of engineering qualification. Interestingly, writing in 1996 in Germany, Heller and Ziegler noted that, in fact, 'there are *30 times* as many male engineers' as female (Heller and Ziegler, 1996, p. 201, emphasis original). Although research carried out in some developed countries seems to suggest that females are closing the gap with males in many areas of achievement and interest – for example, there are just as many bright females in challenging biology, chemistry and physics classes as bright males (Campbell and Clewell, 1999), this trend is by no means a worldwide phenomenon (Else-Quest *et al.*, 2013; Kerr and Kurpius, 2004; Stake and Nickens, 2005).

On this note, studies have also shown that, although gifted females might be successful in scientific endeavours (especially at school), the majority do not choose to pursue careers in science (Silverman, 1993; Summers, 2005) and, hence, the number of gifted women practising careers in the fields of science, mathematics and engineering remains at lower levels than their male counterparts. Many women may be equally or more talented than men in science, yet they do not choose to study science as majors in their undergraduate years and do not go on to pursue careers in these fields (Blickenstaff, 2005) to the same degree as men. Quoting Kerr *et al.*,

> Gifted girls can show great achievements in high school; yet, those achievements do not necessarily translate to the workforce in their adult years. Career choices are still gendered; as such, it seems as if the pay gap in the workforce will not disappear soon.
>
> (2012, p. 650)

Kerr and Kurpius (2004), too, contend that equal numbers of gifted females and gifted males might *plan* careers in physics, medicine, law and other fields once dominated by males, but *realizing/undertaking* a career in these fields is not the same thing as *planning*. They support their claim using statistics from the National Science Foundation (National Science Board, 2000), which indicate that in 2000, in the USA, there were still twice as many male graduates in the physical sciences and engineering as female graduates. Heilbronner's (2013) suggestion that the picture regarding the representation of females in science, technology, engineering and mathematics (STEM) fields is 'more nuanced' seems to make sense – 'for women are represented well in some STEM fields (such as biology) and not in others (such as computer science)' (p. 39).

Research into whether gender-specific variations among gifted people are related to ability, motivation, or gender stereotyping with regard to social expectations has indicated that 'gifted girls are more at risk than boys in suffering from the negative impact of gender discrimination' (Camci, 2011). A study comparing sixth grade girls' and boys' achievement, self-concept, interest and motivation in mathematics (in a sample of equal numbers of gifted and average-ability students), showed that gender differences in self-concept, interest and motivation were more prevalent in the gifted group than the average-ability group, with both gifted and average-ability girls showing lower levels of self-concept, interest and motivation than their male counterparts (Preckel *et al.*, 2008).

The research literature puts forward a range of models that might help to explain the under-representation of gifted women in science, mathematics and engineering. Several studies suggest that this under-representation of gifted females in science may be associated with their performing better in verbal domains (such as literature, language, writing, etc.) than gifted males. Other studies, which show that (gifted) males perform better in scientific fields than gifted females, appear to corroborate these findings (Benbow *et al.*, 2000; Lubinski and Benbow, 1992; Olszewski-Kubilius and Lee, 2011).

In order to improve talent in science and solve this problem of under-representation of females, educators, mentors and parents must understand the critical factors that affect women's participation in science fields (Heilbronner, 2009). Under-representation in science should not be perceived as inevitable for gifted females – it should be challenged with a view to change!

Models explaining gender differences among gifted students

Model 1: the differences in achievement/performance and cognitive ability model

In the USA, the 2013 Scholastic Aptitude Test (SAT) maths test results showed high school boys continuing to out-perform girls in mathematics – a trend that has persisted for over 40 years. Moreover, boys outnumbered girls by a ratio of 2.28:1 in the highest-scoring student group – that is, those scoring 790–800 (Perry, 2013). If such statistics are anything to go by, the traditional model that suggests that gender differences are based on ability differences (because male students seem to consistently out-perform female students in secondary school assessment tests in STEM subjects) still lingers to the present day, despite being contested in numerous studies over the last 20 years or so.

Among gifted students, findings have generally proved to be inconsistent, making it difficult to convincingly identify a prevailing trend in performance between boys and girls. Where some research shows boys doing better than girls (Colangelo *et al.*, 1996), other studies show girls getting higher grades than boys (Freeman, 2004; Lubinski and Benbow, 1992). There are yet more studies that reveal that girls and boys achieve comparable/similar grades (Schober *et al.*, 2004; Roznowski *et al.*, 2000). Such findings appear to underscore Heilbronner's contention of a 'more nuanced' picture (2013), and hence deserve closer scrutiny.

Recent reports published in the USA suggest that changes may be underway in that country, especially with regard to gender differences in subject *preferences* at colleges. Many more girls are now taking mathematics and science courses in US colleges than ever before, with girls seemingly out-performing boys in the majority of high school subjects, especially in verbal test scores (Goldin *et al.*, 2006). Even the mean and standard deviation in performance on mathematics test scores now seem to be only slightly higher for males than for females (Niederle and Vesterlund, 2010, p. 129). Nevertheless, the picture is more complex than might first appear. Xie and Shauman (2003) report that, over the last two decades, the ratio of boys to girls who have scored in the top 5 per cent in their high school mathematics courses, has remained steady at 1:2 – a finding corroborated by Ellison and Swanson (2009). Internationally, too, a similar trend seems to be evident with regard to performance in mathematics.

> In the 2003 cycle of the Programme for International Student Assessment (PISA), which investigates mathematical literacy in 15-year-old students, gender differences in mathematics in favour of males were found in almost all of the participating countries.
>
> (Preckel *et al.*, 2008, p. 148)

Although Benbow and Stanley's (1980) assertion that gender differences in mathematics reasoning ability pointing to an innate male superiority may not hold water in today's world, statistics such as the 2013 SAT maths scores are still difficult to make sense of. Since the mid-1980s, the gender differences observed in *achievement* trends have been thought to be mediated by suggestions that:

> women have lower expectations for success, are less confident in their achievement-related abilities, are more likely to attribute their failures to lack of ability, are less likely to attribute their success to ability, and are more likely to exhibit a learned helpless response to failure.
>
> (Eccles, 1987, pp. 166–7; see also Betz and Hackett, 1981; Dweck, 1986, Parsons *et al.*, 1976)

Recent research, showing that males and females respond differently to competition, seems to be providing some evidence that it may not be a case of girls lacking ability (e.g. in mathematics), but rather that males and females respond differently to 'competitive test-taking environments' (Niederle and Vesterlund, 2010, p. 130). In an experiment conducted at the Harvard Business School, Niederle and Vesterlund found that when women were guaranteed equal representation among the winners of a competition the fraction of female entrants increased from 29 per cent to 64 per cent. This finding concurs with Huguet and Regner's (2007) conclusions when investigating girls' participation in tasks measuring mathematical ability. They found that girls competing in all-girl groups performed better than their counterparts competing in mixed-gender groups. Niederle and Vesterlund suggest that 'the gender gap in math test scores may exaggerate the math advantage of males over females', and then go on to observe, 'there is reason to suspect that females are failing to realize their full potential or to have that potential recognized by society' (pp. 130–1).

Model 2: Eccles's expectancy-value model

Eccles's work on students' *motivation* in taking on a task, seeing it through and the degree of success in performing it/the task has had a huge impact on understanding the gender differences highlighted in the preceding section. Eccles's expectancy-value model, which highlights the issue of *choice*, has been described as the most comprehensive model for addressing questions such as why girls show a preference for the social and biological sciences rather than the physical and engineering sciences (Eccles, 1987, 2011, p. 154). The model was specifically developed to examine gender differences in educational and occupational choices (Eccles, 1987, 1994; Wigfield and Eccles, 2000). According to this model, achievement-related choices are directly influenced by 1) an individual's expectations of success in the task and 2) the value an individual subjectively assigns to a task. Exponents of this theory 'argue that individuals' choices, persistence, and performance can be explained by their beliefs about how well they will do on the activity and the extent to which they value the activity' (Wigfield and Eccles, 2000, p. 68).

Eccles's theoretical model has also been applied to gifted learners (Eccles and Harold, 1992). Comparing the findings from two longitudinal studies conducted approximately 50 years apart (begun in the 1920s and 1970s respectively), Eccles and Harold noted that the pattern of gender differences in educational pursuits were strikingly similar. While girls did as well as boys in verbal tests, boys performed better than girls in mathematics – 'giftedness in math is more common and more extreme among boys' (p. 5). Although much research has been carried out in the intervening years, the problem still remains with us today – to quote Eccles, 'I find it particularly interesting that we are still studying the underrepresentation of women in STEM fields' (Eccles, 2011, p. 514).

Factors contributing to gender differences among gifted students

Attitudes

Over the years many researchers have deliberated about the reasons why gifted boys generally seem to out-perform gifted girls in STEM subjects. Students' attitudes to mathematics and science subjects have been investigated/examined as it was suspected that students' different attitudes might be giving rise not only to such distinct preferences, but possibly also to the differing levels of achievement between the genders. From the early 1980s, there were indications that students' attitudes towards science were becoming fixed at as young an age as nine years old (Harvey and Edwards, 1980; Ormerod and Wood, 1983, Taber, 1991).

Studies by Taber with students just entering secondary school suggested that 'boys and girls have different interests within science' by the time they reach the age of 11 or 12, with boys tending to opt for topics of a mechanical nature and girls preferring topics related to health science (Taber, 1991, p. 250, 1992). Furthermore, the attitude of girls towards science is documented as becoming increasingly negative with increasing age – and with the gap widening (Baram-Tsabari *et al.*, 2006; Caleon and Subramaniam, 2008; Ford *et al.*, 2006).

If students' attitudes to science become fixed before they arrive in secondary school, and these attitudes affect students' preferences and their achievements in science, then the question that comes to mind is: *where do these attitudes stem from?* Much of the research has focused on the *society* (or social environment) students are raised in and the *gender roles* which this society might impose on them – 'some type of socialization factors are at work discouraging girls from science before the age of 11 or 12' (Hill *et al.*, 1990, p. 301). Although Hill *et al.*'s work focused on black females in the USA, Campbell and Connelly (1987), reporting on white (Caucasian) and Asian-American females and males taking advanced courses in mathematics and science, also arrived at similar conclusions. Some of the comments from males in this latter study were as follows:

> Math and science are a lot of work, and girls just don't want to put in the work. Girls aren't logical. Girls do more with their friends. Girls just care about their hair – how they look. Girls just can't grasp numbers. Girls don't seem to have the patience. Girls shy away from abstract thinking. Girls just follow the leader. Girls like humanities, not science.
>
> (Ibid., p. 217)

Adams (1996), discussing Hill *et al.*'s and Campbell and Connelly's work rightly concludes: 'Hearing remarks such as these on a daily basis from antagonistic male peers would certainly not serve to make gifted girls feel comfortable in class or encourage them to continue their math and science studies!' (p. 452).

Parent and teacher influences

The influence and expectations of *parents* seem to impact on a girl's choice of studying science (Dickens, 1990; Manis *et al.*, 1989; Callahan *et al.*, 1996). Among gifted adolescent girls, strong correlations were found between the girls' self-concept and their parents' expectations regarding succeeding or failing (Dickens, 1990). Moreover, parents were found to discourage their daughters from majoring in science subjects until they demonstrated a genuine inclination for science – only then were parents seen to encourage them (Callahan *et al.*, 1996).

Parents and teachers were also found/seen to encourage certain behaviours in boys – behaviours such as inquisitiveness, assertiveness, enquiry and activity – but to discourage these same behaviours in girls (Luftig and Nichols, 1991; Olszewski-Kubilius and Kulieke, 1989; Silverman, 1993). Silverman (1993) goes further and ascribes the under-representation of gifted females in science to social expectations and social pressure. This is a finding supported by Sart (2014), who found that, in a sample of 490 18–24-year-olds, 96 per cent stated that their social environment had influenced their choice of career path.

Summers (2005), in contrast, is hesitant in assigning too much credence to the premise/hypothesis that 'little girls are all socialized towards nursing and little boys are socialized towards building bridges'. He suggests that it was easier to attribute the lack of females in science careers to socialization issues when there were none in these fields, but it is substantially more difficult to blame socialization issues when females increasingly *do* enter these professions, only to 'drop out' later. It seems that more research is required to identify the reasons why some gifted females working in science and related fields are leaving their chosen professions prematurely. It may be that cultural differences among different nations might be at play here or, as Heilbronner (2013) suggests, reasons for leaving in the early stages of their careers might be related to self-efficacy issues (discussed below).

Self-concept, interest, motivation/self-image/self-esteem

With social expectations and its pressure of being a good woman, mother, wife etc., it is no wonder that gifted girls are often confused about what career they want to pursue. Moreover, high-stakes testing situations may present further barriers for young women who lack confidence in their abilities (Rebhorn and Miles, 1999). Often, gifted females become disappointed at the first difficulty or problem in science courses, and they decide they cannot achieve success in scientific coursework due to this perceived lack of ability (Klein and Zehms, 1996). Research indicates that not only does the self-esteem of gifted females decline in early adolescence (AAUW, 1991; Klein and Zehms, 1996), but these girls also tend to be less confident in their own views, less assertive and are less tolerant to criticism (Brown and Gilligan, 1992). Some 25 years ago, Kramer's longitudinal study of ten gifted adolescent girls warned that 'Self-perceptions that lead girls to devalue their abilities may limit their future aspirations, and, as a result, decrease the contributions of a significant group in our society' (1991, p. 359). More recently, a study comparing gifted and average-ability students in Germany found that 'For all the measures of self-concept, interest, and motivation, gender differences were larger for gifted than for average-ability students' (Preckel *et al.*, 2008, p. 153), with gifted girls having lower levels of self-concept, interest and motivation in mathematics than the gifted boys in the sample. What is more, it seems that girls believe they need to work harder to attain high grades in mathematics than boys do (Lupart *et al.*, 2004).

A study looking at the potential obstacles undergraduate women might face studying science and engineering courses in the USA pinpointed the two most important obstacles facing women as being 'women's self-confidence' (an individual obstacle) and 'classroom climate' (an institutional obstacle) (Fox *et al.*, 2011). Gifted females would need opportunities to interact with peers of similar interests and abilities to overcome feelings of isolation and low self-esteem (Watters and Diezmann, 2003).

Although there are indications that the gap in achievement in STEM subjects between boys and girls seems to be closing (especially at high school level), as Summers (2005) has observed, females tend to leave their chosen STEM field prematurely when compared to males. In 2004, Kerr and Kurpius conducted an intervention study in Arizona, specially developed to improve career prospects of girls from minorities and from low-income backgrounds – girls who were potentially gifted in mathematics and science (the Talented At-Risk Girls: Encouragement and Training for Sophomores, or TARGETS, project). Focusing on 'enhancing career identity and exploration, building science self-efficacy and self-esteem and reducing risky behaviours' (p. 85), they reported very favourable findings in their sample of over 500 girls over a seven-year period. Respondents' 'self-esteem, school self-efficacy, and future self-efficacy increased from pre-test to 3- to 4-month follow-up' (ibid.); girls tended to research more information about careers and were more likely to stick to their choice of a non-traditional career.

At this point, we also consider the effect that families might have on the self-concept and success of their children. Citing from Phillips (1987), Reis and Hebert (2008) assert that females' science/mathematics self-concept is related to the expectations of the family. Reis (1995) suggests that a family's comments will often negatively affect females for many years, even if they have left home. Moreover, according to Ryan (1999), gifted females may well be obliged to make a choice between high academic achievement and sexual attractiveness. Hence, while families may encourage their sons on the subjects of science, mathematics and leadership, females' interests in these subjects are considered as unusual and they usually are not supported.

Another influence during one's secondary school years is that of one's peer group. Buescher *et al.* (1987) suggest that females are more likely to hide their abilities during these years. Females in secondary school with high capacity for academic study are disinclined to 'leave' their friends in order to be more successful in academic subjects. According to Greene (2003), talented females hide their abilities and play the 'accepted' role of a woman because they worry that males would not like them or they would not appear feminine. Pressure from a girl's peers requires her to groom herself for a relationship and establish a commitment as quickly as possible. The 'culture of romance' focuses her attention on her attractiveness rather than her intelligence. She realizes that high grades or commitment to a science major might do little for her reputation among her peer group; in fact, her friends may not even know what her major is (Holland and Eisenhart, 1990, as cited in Kerr and Kurpius, 2004). The research literature suggests that, with increasing age, girls are less interested in science than boys are (Catsambis, 1995; Shymansky and Kyle 1988; Simpson and Oliver, 1990; Weinburgh, 1995).

Gender stereotypes/roles

Empirical evidence suggests that gender-stereotyped career interests are established among young girls by second grade (Silverman, 1986) and that attitudes and stereotypes are responsible for young females' disinterest in science (Farenga and Joyce, 1998). A body of empirical research emerging in the late 1990s identified a so-called 'stereotype threat' effect (Brown and Josephs, 1999; Steele, 1997; Walsh *et al.*, 1999). This 'describes how knowledge of a negative stereotype about one's own social group can lead to behavioral outcomes that reinforce the stereotype' (Hyde and Kling, 2001, p. 374). Evidence from data based on Graduate Record Examinations (GRE) and SAT assessments among samples of students in the USA indicate that when females are either *told* that males perform better on the test, or when they *expect* males to do better (e.g. because of much-publicized SAT results in the media), this reduces the performance of females taking the test (Spencer *et al.*, 1999).

Fogliati and Bussey (2013) investigated stereotype threat among a sample of 54 women and 30 men (average age 21.6) in a large Australian university and found that 'the effect of stereotype threat on women's mathematical performance is potentially compounded by its capacity to reduce motivation to improve' (p. 310).

Hyde and Kling (2001) set out a combination of three factors which they suggest are likely to hinder the performance of those very (gifted) women who should be acting as role models:

> First, individuals do not have to believe that a given negative stereotype is true for it to influence their behaviour... Second, stereotype threat sets up a mutually reinforcing system that will be difficult to disrupt... Third, the current conditions in many academic settings are likely to foster stereotype threat. For example, being the only woman in the group.
>
> (p. 375)

Image of scientists

Two main studies stand out as starting points for examining young people's images of scientists: 1) the Mead and Métraux (1957) study, which looked at US high school students' images of scientists and 2) the Chambers (1983) study which was based on elementary school children's data drawn from Canada, the USA and Australia. Chambers examined a) the influence of factors such as socio-economic class, intelligence, sex and culture on the perception of high school students' images of scientists; b) the age at which children begin to develop a distinctive image of a scientist; c) any variations of the stereotype which might result in social and psychological attitudes towards science and technology; and d) the first indications of any mythic images of scientists.

In both of the above studies, seven stereotypic features often associated with scientists (see Figure 9.1) were evident from Grade 2-aged children onwards. Moreover, these stereotypical features became more evident with increasing age, and were more frequent in children from high-income families (ibid.). Interestingly, in the Chambers study, the only images drawn of female scientists were all produced by girls. Ten years later, in a survey of US college students (biology and liberal arts studies majors), Rosenthal (1993) reported that few participants drew female scientists.

⫸ Lab coat
⫸ Eyeglasses
⫸ Facial growth of hair (including beards, moustaches, etc.)
⫸ Symbols of research: scientific instruments and laboratory equipment
⫸ Symbols of knowledge: principally books and filing cabinets
⫸ Technology: the process of science
⫸ Relevant captions: formulae, taxonomic classification, the 'Eureka' syndrome

Figure 9.1 The seven features chosen in the Chambers study (1983) as being indicators of the standard image of a scientist

Another study in 1993, conducted by Odell *et al.*, looked at a sample of participants ranging in age from elementary school through to junior high school, as well as university students. Using the same Draw-a-Scientist Test used by Chambers (1983), they found that girls in their sample had poorer self-images with respect to science than boys did.

Farenga and Joyce's (1998) study, which sampled 111 high-ability nine- to 13-year-olds (evenly divided by gender), investigated the relationship between boys' and girls' science-related attitudes and their selection of science courses. They assessed science-related attitudes using the Test of Science-Related Attitudes (TOSRA) (Fraser, 1981), which was designed to measure seven distinct attitudes among middle and high school students. They found that, among high-ability girls, three variables were significantly related to the number of science courses selected. These three attitudes were:

- 'Normality of scientists' (i.e. assessing a participant's belief about a scientist's lifestyle, e.g. 'If you met a scientist, he would probably look like anyone else you might meet')
- 'Enjoyment of science lessons' (i.e. evaluating a participant's level of enjoyment of classroom science lessons, e.g. 'Science lessons are fun')
- 'Leisure interest in science' (i.e. evaluating a participant's desire to partake in out-of-school science-related activities, e.g. 'I would like to be given a science book or a piece of scientific equipment as a present').

Collectively, these three variables explained 43 per cent of the variance in the total number of science courses selected by females. The 'Normality of scientists' variable is particularly relevant for stereotyped gender roles, since science is perceived as a dominantly male field. Moreover, the majority of the images of scientists in the press and in the visual media are men and resources like textbooks, cartoons and films express an acceptance of the role of the scientist as

Figure 9.2 A male scientist with lab coat, with glasses, studying in a lab with test tubes and chemicals (7th grade, age 13)

male (LaFollette, 1981, 1988, 1990; Nelkin, 1987; Fursich and Lester, 1996; Steinke and Long, 1996; Camci, 2008). This evidence seems to point to females' selection of requisite science courses being negatively affected by the accepted gender role of scientists – females might well believe that science is not a viable career option for them. To counter such opinions, it has been suggested that more intervention studies would be needed, as well as studies examining the effects of programmes such as the six-part Public Broadcasting Service (PBS, 1995) series *Discovering Women* – a series designed to transform the way middle school children viewed science and to improve the public's understanding of contributions made by women scientists (Steinke, 1997).

Camci-Erdoğan's (2013) study of 7th and 8th graders (n = 11) in Turkey, investigating these students' attitudes to and images of gifted female scientists, showed that the majority of gifted females in the study had positive attitudes and mostly wanted a career in science. However, most of them imagined a scientist with lab coat, with glasses and studying in a lab with test tubes and chemicals (see Figure 9.2). The gifted females in the sample drew mostly (n = 8) smiling female scientists (see Figures 9.3 and 9.4). Encouragingly, according to the a semi-structured questionnaire administered to this sample, more than half of the participants stated that they identified with the drawing and wanted to be scientists in the future.

Perhaps the most striking point about the study was that most (n = 9) of the gifted females wanted to be scientists, but unfortunately expressed the view that

Figure 9.3 A female scientist studying in a lab with test tubes and chemicals (8th grade, age 14)

they had no female scientist role models to follow in their society (ibid.). Thus, it is apparent that gifted females need true role models – mentors who are professionals in their career fields and who can encourage them to enjoy doing science. Gifted women need to be linked to mentors in their field in order to achieve high status and similar success to their male counterparts (Kerr and Kurpius, 2004). Mentoring and internship appointments provide opportunities to experience

Figure 9.4 Male and female scientist working in a group (7th grade, age 13)

collaborative work in structured programmes for gifted females. In science, working with a mentor is a basic necessity for gifted students; an efficient mentor raises and supports curiosity, self-esteem, interest and motivation for gifted students (Esprivalo-Harrell *et al.*, 2004; Miller, 2002; Tsuji and Ziegler, 1990). With true mentors, gifted females can both realize and use their talents in solving real-world problems and laboratory activities in science (Subrahmanyan and Bozonie, 1996). When the mentor is a female, she can also serve as a role model, showing a bright young woman the possibility of fulfilment of potential.

In addition to working with mentors, teachers, counsellors and parents should help a gifted woman to recognize her talents and to know how to use her talent in order to be successful in science. Thus, to encourage gifted females in science, 1) efficient mentors should be provided from early ages (middle school) throughout high school and into college and 2) teachers, counsellors and parents should give support whenever possible.

Being challenged with open-ended real world problems taps gifted students' curiosity and motivation in science and creates both pleasure and positive attitudes towards science (Watters and Diezmann, 2003). In school science, it is important that gifted females consider themselves as part of communities of enquiry in which knowledge, practice, resources and discoveries are shaped (Watters, 2004). Also these activities can be reinforced at home with informal science activities or museum/science centre visits. By helping their children to recognize science in everyday activities, parents can heighten science-related awareness and interest and encourage positive attitudes (Farenga and Joyce, 1998).

Conclusion: the future for girls gifted in science

As we have seen in the various studies discussed in this chapter, gender differences among gifted children are a major factor that emerges within the first years of life in a family. These differences tend to increase with age as students interact with teachers and social groups at school, peaking in puberty. It has been demonstrated by researchers that females in some national contexts frequently hide their abilities (especially in the subjects of science and mathematics) in order to meet the expectations of their friendship groups and in order to obey/meet cultural and societal norms – messages from their families relating to the role of 'the typical woman' affect females dramatically.

As males tend to take more risks than females, and are encouraged by society to do so, they seem to be more successful than females in subjects requiring trial and error, especially in science and mathematics. Although gifted females may often have highly positive attitudes towards science and may *desire* to pursue a career in the sciences, we do not see women *participating* in science as men do. Hence, it may be necessary to instate interventions and guidance for gifted females from their early education through to their later college years. To this end, some suggestions can be made to increase the interest of gifted females in science, and to make their interest in science persist throughout the stage of choosing a career and beyond.

Teachers should:

- be informed about the characteristics of gifted females and why they need to 'mask' themselves
- make sufficient differentiation for the needs of gifted females, i.e. provide a differentiated process with hands-on and enquiry-based science activities, especially laboratory activities connected with everyday science, in order to make gifted females perceive science as an enjoyable, understandable experience
- encourage gifted females to attend science fairs or project competitions
- encourage risk-taking and contributing in class
- expose gifted females to different major areas and to professionals working in these areas (especially women professionals)
- support gifted females' motivation and progress
- provide gifted females with biographies covering the contribution of females to science
- invite female professionals to talk about different topics and females in science
- provide access to counselling service where needed.

Parents should:

- have the same expectations for their daughters as they have for their sons
- make non-sexist choices for toys, games, clothes etc.
- encourage independence of gifted females and avoid over-protectiveness
- provide informal science activities for exposure to different interesting topics and experiences, e.g. certain TV programmes, documentaries, periodicals, zoo visits, science centre, museum visits, botanical gardens, etc.

Career guidance staff/counsellors should:

- talk about the importance of science and mathematics for future career planning by giving real-life examples
- give examples of successful women in gender roles which are not traditional or stereotyped
- provide mentoring from women who are content with their careers
- encourage gifted females to value what they really are and to believe in their abilities, rather than be swayed by what others expect them to be
- encourage gifted females to apply for scholarships in science
- arrange opportunities for females to see examples of women in science – alone, with family, with children, etc.

References

AAUW (Greenberg-Lake, the Analysis Group) (1991). *Shortchanging Girls, Shortchanging America* (A poll). Washington, DC: American Association of University Women (AAUW).

Adams, C.M. (1996). Gifted girls and science: revisiting the issues. *Prufrock Journal*, 7(4), 447–58. http://doi.org/10.1177/1932202X9600700404

Baram-Tsabari, A., Sethi, R.J., Bry, L., and Yarden, A. (2006). Using questions sent to an Ask-A-Scientist site to identify children's interests in science. *Science Education*, 90(6), 1050–72. http://doi.org/10.1002/sce.20163

Benbow, C.P., and Stanley, J.C. (1980). Sex differences in mathematical ability: fact or artifact? *Science*, 210(4475), 1262–4.

Benbow, C.P., Lubinski, D., Shea, D.L., and Eftekhari-Sanjani, H. (2000). Sex differences in mathematical reasoning ability at age 13: their status 20 years later. *Psychological Science*, 11, 474–80. http://doi.org/10.1111/1467-9280.00291

Betz, N.E., and Hackett, G. (1981). The relationship of career-related self-efficacy expectations to perceived career options in college women and men. *Journal of Counseling Psychology*, 28(5), 399–410. http://doi.org/10.1037/0022-0167.28.5.399

Blickenstaff, J. C. (2005). Women and science careers: leaky pipeline or gender filter? *Gender and Education*, 17(4), 369–86.

Brown, L.M., and Gilligan, C. (1992). Meeting at the crossroads: women's psychology and girls' development. *British Journal of Educational Psychology*, 63, 362–4.

Brown, R.P., and Josephs, R.A. (1999). A burden of proof: stereotype relevance and gender differences in math performance. *Journal of Personality and Social Psychology*, 76, 246–57.

Buescher, T.M., Olszewski, P., and Higham, S. (1987). Influences on strategies adolescents use to cope with their own recognized talents. Retrieved from http://eric.ed.gov/?id=ED288285

Caleon, I.S., and Subramaniam, R. (2008). Attitudes towards science of intellectually gifted and mainstream upper primary students in Singapore. *Journal of Research in Science Teaching*, 45(8), 940–54. http://doi.org/10.1002/tea.20250

Callahan, C.M., Adams, C.M., Bland, L.C., Moon, T.R., Moore, S.D., Peri, M., and McIntyre, J.A. (1996). Factors influencing recruitment, enrollment, and retention of students in special schools of mathematics, science, and technology. In K. Arnold, K.D. Noble and R.F. Subotnik (Eds), *Remarkable Women: Perspectives on female talent development*. Cresskill, NJ: Hampton Press, pp. 243–60.

Camci, S. (2008). Comparison of students' perceptions and images of science and scientists among those who have participated the science fairs and those who have not (Bilim şenliğine katılan ve katılmayan öğrencilerin bilim ve bilim insanlarına yönelik ilgi ve imajlarının karşılaştırılması). Unpublished master's dissertation, Hacettepe University, Ankara.

Camci, S. (2011). Gender differences among gifted students. (Üstün zekali ve yeteneklilerde cinsiyet farklılığı). *Journal of Hasan Ali Yucel Faculty of Education*, 16(2), 105–17.

Camci-Erdogan, S. (2013). Gifted female students' scientific attitudes and images of scientists. (Üstün zekali kizların bilime yönelik tutumları ve belim insanı imajları). *Journal of Hasan Ali Yucel Faculty of Education*, 19(1), 125–42.

Campbell, P., and Clewell, A. (1999). *Participation of Females and Women in Math, Science, Engineering, and Technology*. Report to the National Science Foundation Annual Meeting of HRD Project Directors. Arlington: NSF.

Campbell, J.R., and Connolly, C. (1987). Deciphering the effects of socialization. *Journal of Educational Equity and Leadership*, 7(3), 208–22.

Catsambis, S. (1995). Gender, race, ethnicity, and science education in the middle grades. *Journal of Research in Science Teaching*, 32(3), 243–57. http://doi.org/10.1002/tea.3660320305

Chambers, D.W. (1983). Stereotypic images of the scientist: the draw-a-scientist test. *Science Education*, 67(2), 255–65. http://doi.org/10.1002/sce.3730670213

Colangelo, N., Assouline, S.G., Cole, V., Cutrona, C., and Maxey, J.E. (1996). Exceptional academic performance: perfect scores on the PLAN. *Gifted Child Quarterly*, 40(2), 102–10. http://doi.org/10.1177/001698629604000207

Dickens, M.N. (1990). Parental influences on the mathematics self-concept of high achieving adolescent girls. Unpublished doctoral dissertation, University of Virginia, Charlottesville.

Dweck, C.S. (1986). Motivational processes affecting learning. *American Psychologist*, 41(10), 1040–8. http://doi.org/10.1037/0003-066X.41.10.1040

Eccles, J.S. (1987). Gender roles and women's achievement-related decisions. *Psychology of Women Quarterly*, 11, 135–72.

Eccles, J.S. (1994). Understanding women's educational and occupational choices: applying the Eccles *et al.* model of achievement-related choices. *Psychology of Women Quarterly*, 18(4), 585–609. http://doi.org/10.1111/j.1471-6402.1994.tb01049.x

Eccles, J.S. (2011). Understanding women's achievement choices: looking back and looking forward. *Psychology of Women Quarterly*, 35(3), 510–16.

Eccles, J.S., and Harold, R.D. (1992). Gender differences in educational and occupational patterns among the gifted. In N. Colangelo, S.G. Assouline, and D.L. Amronson (Eds), *Talent Development: Proceedings from the 1991 Henry B. and Jocelyn Wallace National Research Symposium on Talent Development*. Unionville, NY: Trillium, pp. 3–29.

Ellison, G., and Swanson, A. (2009). The gender gap in secondary school mathematics at high achievement levels: evidence from the American mathematics competitions (Working Paper No. 15238). National Bureau of Economic Research. Retrieved from http://www.nber.org/papers/w15238

Else-Quest, N.M., Mineo, C.C., and Higgins, A. (2013). Math and science attitudes and achievement at the intersection of gender and ethnicity. *Psychology of Women Quarterly*, 37(3), 293–309.

Esprivalo-Harrell, P., Walker, M., Hildreth-Combes, B., and Tyler-Wood, T. (2004). Mentoring BUGS: an integrated science and technology curriculum. *Journal of Computers in Mathematics and Science Teaching*, 23(4), 367–78.

Farenga, S.J., and Joyce, B.A. (1998). Science-related attitudes and science course selection: a study of high-ability boys and girls. *Roeper Review*, 20(4), 247–51. http://doi.org/10.1080/02783199809553901

Fogliati, V.J., and Bussey, K. (2013). Stereotype threat reduces motivation to improve: effects of stereotype threat and feedback on women's intentions to improve mathematical ability. *Psychology of Women Quarterly*, 37(3), 310–24.

Ford, D.J., Brickhouse, N.W., Lottero-Perdue, P., and Kittleson, J. (2006). Elementary girls' science reading at home and school. *Science Education*, 90(2), 270–88. http://doi.org/10.1002/sce.20139

Fox, M.F., Sonnert, G., and Nikiforova, I. (2011). Programs for undergraduate women in science and engineering issues, problems, and solutions. *Gender and Society*, 25(5), 589–615. http://doi.org/10.1177/0891243211416809

Fraser, B.J. (1981). *Test of Science-Related Attitude (TOSRA)*. Melbourne: Australian Council for Educational Research.

Freeman, J. (2004). Cultural influences on gifted achievement. *High Ability Studies*, 15(1), 7–23.

Fursich, E., and Lester, E.P. (1996). Science journalism under scrutiny: a textual analysis of 'Science Times'. *Critical Studies in Mass Communication*, 13, 24–43.

Goldin, C., Katz, L.F., and Kuziemko, I. (2006). The homecoming of American college women: the reversal of the college gender gap. *Journal of Economic Perspectives*, 20(4), 133–56.

Greene, M. (2003). Gifted adrift? Career counselling of the gifted and talented. *Roeper Review*, 25, 66–72.

Harvey, T.J., and Edwards, P. (1980). Children's expectations and realisations of science. *British Journal of Educational Psychology*, 50, 74–6.

Heilbronner, N.N. (2009). Pathways in STEM: factors affecting the retention and attrition of talented men and women from the STEM pipeline. Master's thesis. Available from ProQuest Dissertations and Theses database (UMI No. 304871257).

Heilbronner, N.N. (2013). The STEM pathway for women: what has changed? *Gifted Child Quarterly*, 57(1), 39–55.

Heller, K.A., and Ziegler, A. (1996). Gender differences in mathematics and the sciences: can attributional retraining improve the performance of gifted females? *Gifted Child Quarterly*, 40(4), 200–10.

Hill, O.W., Pettus, W.C., and Hedin, B.A. (1990). Three studies of factors affecting the attitudes of blacks and females towards the pursuit of science and science-related careers. *Journal of Research in Science Teaching*, 27(4), 289–314.

Holland, D.C., and Eisenhart, M.A. (1990). *Educated in Romance: Women, achievement, and college culture*. Chicago, IL: University of Chicago Press.

Huguet, P., and Regner, I. (2007). Stereotype threat among schoolgirls in quasi-ordinary classroom circumstances. *Journal of Educational Psychology*, 99(3), 545–60.

Hyde, J.S., and Kling, K.C. (2001). Women, motivation, and achievement. *Psychology of Women Quarterly*, 25, 364–78.

Kerr, B., and Kurpius, S.E.R. (2004). Encouraging talented girls in math and science: effects of a guidance intervention. *High Ability Studies*, 15(1), 85–102. http://doi.org/10.1080/1359813042000225357

Kerr, B.A., Vuyk, M.A., and Rea, C. (2012). Gendered practices in the education of gifted girls and boys. *Psychology in the Schools*, 49(7), 647–55. http://doi.org/10.1002/pits.21627

Klein, A.G., and Zehms, D. (1996). Self-concept and gifted girls: a cross sectional study of intellectually gifted females in grades 3, 5, 8. *Roeper Review*, 19, 30–3.

Kramer, L.R. (1991). The social construction of ability perceptions: an ethnographic study of gifted adolescent girls. *Journal of Early Adolescence*, 11, 340–62.

LaFollette, M.C., 1981, Wizards, villains, and other scientists: the science content of television for children. Report presented to Action for Children's Television.

LaFollette, M.C. (1988). Eyes on the stars: images of women scientists in popular magazines. *Science, Technology, and Human Values*, 13, 262–75.

LaFollette, M.C. (1990). *Making Science Our Own: Public images of science*. Chicago: University of Chicago Press.

Lubinski, D., and Benbow, C.P. (1992). Gender differences in abilities and preferences among the gifted: implications for the maths-science pipeline. *Current Directions in Psychological Science*, 1, 60–6.

Luftig, R.L., and Nichols, M.L. (1991). An assessment of the social status and perceived personality and school traits of gifted students by non-gifted peers. *Roeper Review*, 13(3), 148–53.

Lupart, J.L., Cannon, E., and Telfer, J.O. (2004). Gender differences in adolescent academic achievement, interests, values, and life-role expectations. *High Ability Studies*, 15, 25–42.

Maccoby, E.E., and Jacklin, C.N. (1974). *The Psychology of Sex Differences*. Stanford, CA: Stanford University Press.

Manis, J.D., Thomas, N.G., Sloat, B.F., and Davis, C.G. (1989). *An Analysis of Factors Affecting Choice of Majors in Science, Mathematics, and Engineering at the University of Michigan. Research Report #23*. Ann Arbor, MI: University of Michigan Center for Education of Women Research Reports. Retrieved from http://eric.ed.gov/?id=ED356954

Mead, M., and Métraux, R. (1957). Image of the scientist among high-school students a pilot study. *Science*, 126(3270), 384–90. http://doi.org/10.1126/science.126.3270.384

Miller, A.D. (2002). *Mentoring Students and Young People: A handbook of effective practice*. London: Kogan Press.

National Science Board (2000). *Science and Engineering Indicators – 2000* (No. 2000 (NSB-00-1)). Arlington, VA: National Science Foundation.

Nelkin, D. (1987). *Selling Science: How the press covers science and technology*. New York: WH Freeman.

Niederle, M., and Vesterlund, L. (2010). Explaining the gender gap in math test scores: the role of competition. *Journal of Economic Perspectives*, 24(2), 129–44. http://doi.org/10.1257/jep.24.2.129

Odell, M.R.I., Hewitt, P., Bowman, J., and Boone, W.J. (1993). Stereotypical images of scientists: a cross-age study. Presented at the 41st annual national meeting of the National Science Teachers Association, Kansas City, MO.

Olszewski-Kubilius, P.M., and Kulieke, M.J. (1989). Personality dimensions of gifted adolescents. In J. VanTassel-Baska and P. Olszewski-Kubilius (Eds), *Patterns of Influence on Gifted Learners: The home, the self, and the school*. New York: Teachers College Press, pp. 125–45.

Olszewski-Kubilius, P., and Lee, S.-Y. (2011). Gender and other group differences in performance on off-level tests: changes in the 21st century. *Gifted Child Quarterly*, 55(1), 54–73. http://doi.org/10.1177/0016986210382574

Ormerod, M.B., and Wood, C. (1983). A comparative study of three methods of measuring the attitude to science of 10 to 11 year-old pupils. *European Journal of Science Education*, 5(1), 77–86.

Parsons, J.E., Ruble, D.N., Hodges, K.L., and Small, A.W. (1976). Cognitive-developmental factors in emerging sex differences in achievement-related expectancies. *Journal of Social Issues*, 32(3), 47–62. http://doi.org/10.1111/j.1540-4560.1976.tb02596.x

PBS (1995). Discovering women in science. *Discovering Women*. Public Broadcasting Service.

Perry, M.J. (2013). 2013 SAT test results show that a huge math gender gap persists with a 32-point advantage for high school boys, 26 September. Retrieved from https://www.aei.org/publication/2013-sat-test-results-show-that-a-huge-math-gender-gap-persists-with-a-32-point-advantage-for-high-school-boys/

Phillips, D.A. (1987). Socialization of perceived academic competence among highly competent children. *Child Development*, 58(5), 1308–20. http://doi.org/10.2307/1130623

Preckel, F., Goetz, T., Pekrun, R., and Kleine, M. (2008). Gender differences in gifted and average-ability students: comparing girls' and boys' achievement, self-concept, interest, and motivation in mathematics. *Gifted Child Quarterly*, 52(2), 146–59.

Rebhorn, L.S., and Miles, D.D. (1999). High-stakes testing: barrier to gifted girls in mathematics and science? *School Science and Mathematics*, 99(6), 313–19. http://doi.org/10.1111/j.1949-8594.1999.tb17490.x

Reis, S.M. (1987). We can't change what we don't recognize: understanding the special needs of gifted females. *Gifted Child Quarterly*, 31(2), 83–9.

Reis, S.M. (1995). Talent ignored, talent diverted: the cultural context underlying giftedness in females. *Gifted Child Quarterly*, 39(3), 162–70. http://doi.org/10.1177/001698629503900306

Reis, S.M., and Hebert, T.P. (2008). Gender and giftedness. In S. Pfeiffer (Ed.), *Handbook of Giftedness in Children*. New York: Springer, pp. 271–93.

Rosenthal, D.B. (1993). Images of scientists: a comparison of biology and liberal studies majors. *School Science and Mathematics*, 93(4), 212–16.

Roznowski, M., Reith, J., and Hong, S. (2000). A further look at youth intellectual giftedness and its correlates: values, interests, performance, and behaviour. *Intelligence*, 28, 87–113.

Ryan, J.J. (1999). Behind the mask: exploring the need for specialized counselling for gifted females. *Gifted Child Today Magazine*, 22(5), 14–17.

Sart, G. (2014). Gender differences in choice of careers in science, technology, engineering, and mathematics (STEM): a case of Turkey. Presented at the 8th International Technology, Education and Development Conference (INTED2014), Valencia, Spain. Retrieved from http://library.iated.org/view/SART2014GEN

Schober, B., Reinmann, R., and Wagner, P. (2004). Is research on gender-specific underachievement in gifted girls an obsolete topic? *High Ability Studies*, 15, 43–62.

Shymansky, J.A., and Kyle, W.C. (1988). Learning and the learner. *Science Education*, 72(3), 293–304.

Silverman, L.K. (1986). What happens in the gifted girl? In C.J. Maker (Ed.), *Critical Issues in Gifted Education: Defensible programs for the gifted*. Rockville, MD: Aspen, pp. 43–89.

Silverman, L.K. (1993). Social development, leadership, and gender. In L.K. Silverman (Ed.), *Counselling the Gifted and Talented*. Denver: Love, pp. 291–327.

Simpson, R.D., and Oliver, J.S. (1990). A summary of major influences on attitude toward and achievement in science among adolescent students. *Science Education*, 74(1), 1–18. http://doi.org/10.1002/sce.3730740102

Smutny, J.F., and Von Fremd, S.E. (2004). *Differentiating for the Young Child: Teaching strategies across the content areas, PreK-3*. Thousand Oaks, CA: Corwin.

Spencer, S.J., Steele, C.M., and Quinn, D.M. (1999). Stereotype threat and women's math performance. *Journal of Experimental Social Psychology*, 35, 4–28.

Stake, J.E., and Nickens, S.D. (2005). Adolescent girls' and boys' science peer relationships and perceptions of the possible self as scientist. *Sex Roles*, 52(1/2), 1–11. http://doi.org/10.1007/s11199-005-1189-4

Steele, C.M. (1997). A threat in the air: how stereotypes shape intellectual identity and performance. *American Psychologist*, 52, 613–29.

Steinke, J. (1997). A portrait of a woman as a scientist: breaking down barriers created by gender-role stereotypes. *Public Understand Science*, 6, 409–28.

Steinke, J., and Long, M. (1996). A lab of her own? Portrayals of female characters on children's educational science programs. *Science Communication*, 18(2), 91–115.

Subrahmanyan, L., and Bozonie, H. (1996). Gender equity in middle school science teaching: being 'equitable' should be the goal. *Middle School Journal*, 27(5), 3–10.

Summers, L.H. (2005). Remarks at NBER conference on diversifying the science and engineering workforce. Speech presented at the National Bureau of Economic Research (NBER) conference, January. Cambridge, MA. Retrieved from http://www.harvard.edu/president/speeches/summers_2005/nber.php

Taber, K.S. (1991). Gender differences in science preferences on starting secondary school. *Research in Science and Technological Education*, 9(2), 245–51. http://doi.org/10.1080/0263514910090210

Taber, K.S. (1992). Science-relatedness and gender-appropriateness of careers: some pupil perceptions. *Research in Science and Technological Education*, 10(1), 105–15. http://doi.org/10.1080/0263514920100109

Taber, K.S. (Ed.). (2007). *Science Education for Gifted Learners*. London: Routledge.

Tsuji, G., and Ziegler, S. (1990). What research says about increasing the numbers of female students taking math and science in secondary school. *Scope*, 4(4), 1–5.

Walsh, M., Hickey, C., and Duffy, J. (1999). Influence of item content and stereotype situation on gender differences in mathematical problem solving. *Sex Roles*, 41, 219–40.

Watters, J.J. (2004). In pursuit of excellence in science. *Australasian Journal of Gifted Education*, 13(2), 41–53.

Watters, J.J., and Diezmann, C.M. (2003). The gifted student in science: fulfilling potential. *Australian Science Teachers Journal*, 49(3), 46–53.

Weinburgh, M. (1995). Gender differences in student attitudes toward science: a meta-analysis of the literature from 1970 to 1991. *Journal of Research in Science Teaching*, 32(4), 387–98. http://doi.org/10.1002/tea.3660320407

Wigfield, A., and Eccles, J.S. (2000). Expectancy-value theory of achievement motivation. *Contemporary Educational Psychology*, 25, 68–81.

Xie, Y., and Shauman, K.A. (2003). *Women in Science: Career processes and outcomes*. Cambridge, MA: Harvard University Press.

10 Scientific giftedness in Japanese society

Manabu Sumida

Introduction

When we use the term 'gifted', the noun that immediately comes to mind is 'children'. The term 'gifted' includes innate characteristics; however, during the school education stage, it refers to those special children who show signs of high achievement capability compared to other children of the same age and experience. However, the phrase 'gifted adults' will be used to refer to individuals who attain recognition in adulthood for superior performance in a particular talent area. This recognition of giftedness in adults is generally based not on standardized tests and IQ tests but on peer acknowledgement of contributions made to a specific field (Housand, 2009). We should also take into account that, as Moltzen (2009) pointed out, the process of talent development in eminent adults is unique to each individual. Thus, a very talented person may never get to the point where they receive public recognition for their work and may not even have the chance to pursue that work to the end if they do not happen to be in the right conditions for such success. The potential of many gifted adults may, thus, go unused, which results in a loss to society.

There are many science-specific programmes for gifted children in and out of school from early childhood to high school (e.g. Brandwein and Passow, 1988; Johnsen and Kendrick, 2005; McGinnis and Stefanich, 2007; Taber, 2007a, 2007b; Sumida and Ohashi, 2015; Sumida, 2015). For instance, in the 1990s, the Centre for Gifted Education at the College of William and Mary developed original problem-based learning (PBL) science units for high-ability learners from Grade 1 to Grade 8 (e.g. Centre for Gifted Education, 2007). A longitudinal assessment of the PBL science curriculum suggested that gifted children's learning in school science had been enhanced at significant and important levels in terms of scientific experimental research design skills through the implementation of the curriculum (Feng *et al.*, 2005). Boyce *et al.* (1997) showed the positive effects of the problem-based science curriculum on teachers as well as students. Science learning seems to be an appropriate context for children to reveal, and for teachers to identify, giftedness in a practical context, although the criteria for gifted identification are usually domain-independent, such as IQ, creativity and leadership.

In contrast to gifted children, gifted adults are identified not through success in advanced educational programmes but through peer recognition of their extraordinary achievement; sometimes this peer recognition takes the form of awards. In science, the most famous such award, the Nobel Prize, is awarded by the Royal Swedish Academy of Sciences. One of the reasons why the Nobel Prize is one of the most prestigious awards is that this was the first international science award (Larsson, 2001). Shavinina (2009) summarized four extra-cognitive abilities of Nobel Laureates in science: 1) specific intellectually creative feelings, 2) specific intellectually creative beliefs and intentions, 3) specific preferences and intellectual values and 4) intuitive processes. The specific intellectually creative feelings category includes feelings of direction, harmony, beauty, and style, including senses of 'important problems', 'good' ideas, 'correct' theories, elegant solutions and feelings of 'being right, being wrong, or having come across something important'. Sumida and Ohashi (2015) analysed 163 Laureates in Chemistry from 1901 to 2012 and proposed that the twenty-first-century style of scientific research is 'interdisciplinary', 'international' and 'collaborative'. An eminent scientist in the twenty-first century is not an independent genius but a person who has succeeded in creating something new collaboratively, crossing disciplinary fields, cultures and nations. These characteristics of eminent scientists and scientific studies in the twenty-first century have not been reflected enough in science education. Perhaps more importantly, too little thought has been given to the social affordances – that is, the set of institutionally and culturally structured circumstances that allow talent to be realized (Keating, 2009).

The Japanese government has emphasized science and technology and has proposed initiatives in science education. Japan has a history of superior performance in science education and the sciences. For example, in the First International Science Study that was conducted in 1970 by the International Association for the Evaluation of Educational Achievement (IEA), Japanese primary school and secondary school students had the highest science achievement among the participating primary schools (16 countries) and secondary schools (18 countries). Moreover, the rapid scientific progress and qualitative social and life improvements that Japan achieved in the latter half of the twentieth century won the attention of the entire world. However, the country currently has no formal system for educating gifted children (Sumida, 2013); neither does it have a way of identifying gifted adults. This chapter tries to expand the concept of scientific giftedness to adults in the Japanese society. Sumida (2010) developed an original checklist to identify gifted characteristics specific to science learning in Japan. Using the checklist, revised for adults, this chapter describes the giftedness that adults might demonstrate and considers the relationship between their scientific giftedness, what value they see in science learning and annual income.

Giftedness in science and its development over a lifespan

An extensive variety of methods which go beyond the traditional IQ test are now being promoted as ways of identifying gifted children (Johnsen, 2004).

The standards for determining eligibility for gifted education programmes in schools are readily comprehensible as a series of definitions. However, the criteria for determining whether a child is 'gifted' may change over time, depending on assumptions about the need for special programming and the perceived benefits. In the USA, the criteria for 'giftedness' typically include 'mental abilities', 'ability to commit to tasks and to express oneself', 'achievements', 'creativity' and 'leadership' (NAGC, 2007).

As far as screening for gifted and talented programmes is concerned, assessment in one specific domain only (for example, science) is not commonplace. There are a number of widely known and reputable screening tools for gifted children, such as the Scale for Identifying Gifted Students (SIGS) (2004) and the Screening Assessment for Gifted Elementary and Middle School Students, K-8-Second Edition (SAGES-2) (Johnsen and Corn, 2001), which cover a limited number of items related to science. Some proposed behavioural characteristics of children who are gifted in science include 'is imaginative', 'uses numbers often when expressing ideas', 'displays curiosity by asking relevant questions' and 'goes beyond obvious answers' (e.g. Cooper *et al.*, 2005; Matthews, 2006; Alderman, 2008).

In his study, Taber (2007a) discussed gifted education in the context of formal secondary school-level science education in the UK. He proposed four clusters of characteristics of what he termed 'able science learners': 'scientific curiosity', 'cognitive abilities', 'metacognitive abilities' and 'leadership'. More recently, Sumida (2010) developed an original behaviour checklist that can be used for Japanese primary-school children, who study in non-western science classrooms, and which includes 60 items such as 'reports clearly the result of an observation and experiment' and 'tries to do things in his/her own way, not according to the instructions given'. As a result of his analysis, three gifted science styles were identified: 'spontaneous style', 'expert style' and 'solid style'.

There are also a number of longitudinal studies of students who have won science contests or participated in a special science curriculum. For example, Subotnik and Steiner (1994) conducted a longitudinal study of the Westinghouse Science Talent Search Winners. They showed that 49 men and 25 women out of a total of 94 winners went on to become involved in science and recognized the need to impress the research community of which they formed part. Furthermore, many learned to master the political games played in their respective laboratories. In a more recent study, Nokelainen *et al.* (2007) analysed the academic Olympians (mathematics, physics and chemistry) in three age cohorts (16–22 years, 23–9 years and 30–54 years) and found that a conducive home atmosphere is necessary for long-term academic productivity, even for Olympians. Jones *et al.* (2010) interviewed 37 scientists and engineers about their experiences and who may have influenced their career, and noted that socio-cultural factors, such as informal advising and mentoring by a teacher or family members, is important for career decisions in science and engineering. Wai *et al.* (2010) assessed participation in various educational opportunities such as academic competitions, research apprenticeships, academic clubs, summer programmes and accelerated classes among 1,467 individuals who had been identified as gifted in mathematics at age 13. They found that those who had been involved in more of these educational opportunities (i.e. a higher 'science, technology, engineering and mathematics (STEM) dose') had, at age 33, a higher rate of notable accomplishments in STEM, such as earning a PhD, writing publications, obtaining patents, or securing an academic career.

Winner (1996) pointed out that most gifted children never develop to their full potential and some even burn out. She proposed four possible relationships between childhood giftedness and future life which were 'gifted children who drop out', 'gifted children who become experts', 'gifted children who become adult creators' and 'late bloomers'. Sumida (2005) investigated the lifespan development of scientific understanding from kindergartners up to 88-year-old senior citizens and identified some age stages in the developmental change. Baltes (1987) also theorized two kinds of intelligence in lifespan cognitive development: one is the crystallized intelligence that is maintained even in senior citizens and another is the fluid intelligence that declines with age. There may also be some differences between children and adults in terms of scientific giftedness.

Methodology

Subjects and Methods

This study targeted a total of 800 adults aged 40–9 years old in Japan. The subjects were divided into five groups of 160 adults according to different occupational fields: 'general affairs/supervision', 'production/judicial affairs', 'management/planning', 'sales/marketing' and 'research/development'. All subjects were full-time employees and 706 of the 800 adults were male and 94 were female.

The survey was conducted online through the internet using the Yahoo! JAPAN database. The database includes about 250,000 registered members and reliability of sampling was ensured through verification of each respondent's identity. Problems associated with internet research, such as multiple responses and impersonation, were avoided by having all registered monitors establish blank accounts as a means of confirming personal identity. At the same time, highly representative sampling was ensured because monitor bias was reduced by means of recruitment on Yahoo! JAPAN, a website accessed by 80 per cent of the internet users in Japan. The collection rate of requested data from the adults was about 50 per cent. A high response rate in this survey for adults was obtained through careful database maintenance of the respondent monitors.

Questionnaire

Sternberg (2007) pointed out that the process for identifying gifted children often ignored the cultural context in which the child grew up. In non-western countries there are few studies on behavioural characteristics indicating science talent (Phillipson and McCann, 2007). Sumida (2010) developed a checklist for identifying gifted learning characteristics of Japanese primary-school children specific to science, and verified the validity and reliability of the items in the checklist. In this study, the checklist was revised for adults in order to ask about their behavioural characteristics at primary-school age.

Checklist items were broadly organized under the four assessment criteria used in Japanese school science ('interest, motivation and attitude towards natural phenomena', 'scientific thinking', 'skills and expression in observation and experiment' and 'knowledge and understanding of natural phenomena'). On the gifted behaviour checklist, each of the 60 items was given as one of the following scores: 1) frequently; 2) sometimes; 3) seldom; or 4) never.

This survey also asked about the values of science learning and the subject's annual income. Items for the values of science learning included: 1) 'Science learning is useful for work'; 2) 'Science learning develops my potential'; 3) 'Science learning is needed to enter into a good high school/university and to get a good job'; 4) 'Science learning is encouraged by my parents'; 5) 'Science learning satisfies my intellectual curiosity'; 6) 'Science learning provides reliable common knowledge'; 7) 'Science learning develops logical and creative thinking'; 8) 'Science learning helps to make good friends and to develop good habits of mind'; 9: 'Science learning develops problem-solving methods'; and 10) 'Science learning brings pleasure to my life'. Subjects were asked to rate their opinion of each item as: 1) strongly agree; 2) agree; 3) disagree; or 4) strongly disagree.

At the end of the questionnaire, the subjects were asked about their annual income in increments of 1 million Japanese yen (about US$10,000). The distribution of subjects' annual income is shown in Figure 10.1.

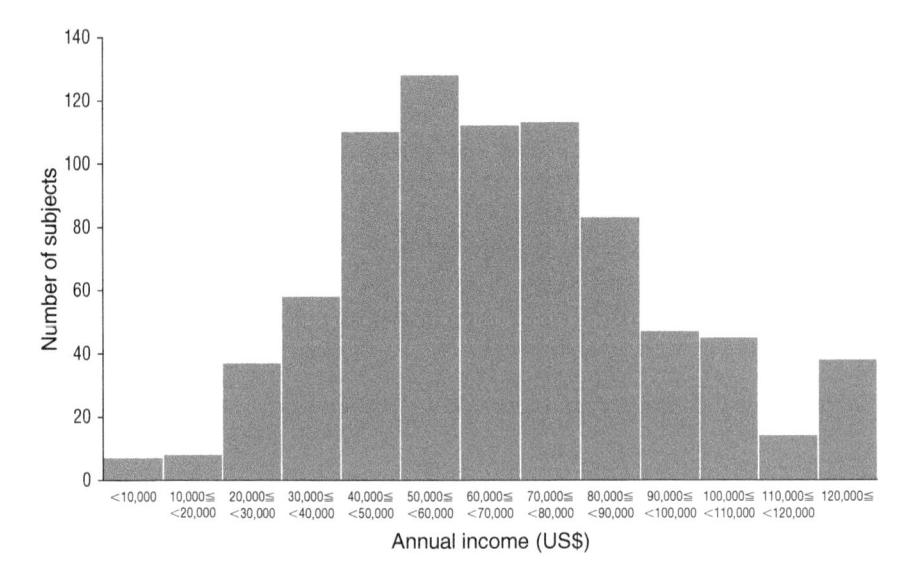

Figure 10.1 The distribution of annual income of subjects in this survey

Results

Factor analysis of the behaviour checklist for giftedness in science

Factor analysis was performed for the questionnaires collected. Four factors were extracted through principal factor analysis. A Promax rotation was then conducted. Items with low factor loadings (absolute value < 0.40) were removed, and another factor analysis was performed. The results are shown in Table 10.1.

Factor I was loaded on items such as 'Solved problems in various ways' and 'Reflected on my own thought process' and was therefore labelled 'strategic competence in science'. Factor II was loaded on items such as 'Knew many scientific terms' and 'Was confident about my knowledge and understanding of science' and was labelled 'competence in knowledge acquisition in science'. Factor III was loaded on items such as 'Was willing to care for and nurture living things' and

Table 10.1 Results of factor analysis of behaviour scales for giftedness in science (factor patterns following Promax rotation)

Items	Loading
Factor I: Strategic competence	
Solved problems in various ways	0.769
Reflected on my own thought process	0.729
Tested out my ideas logically	0.724
Tried to do things in my own way, not by the instruction	0.691
Reasoned deductively and logically	0.677
Reasoned persuasively	0.649
Factor II: Competence in knowledge acquisition	
Knew many scientific terms	0.945
Was confident about my knowledge and understanding of science	0.854
Understood quickly the content of science classes	0.795
Had a concept of what 'science' was	0.793
Was knowledgeable about up-to-date scientific topics	0.777
Retained things studied in science classes for a long time	0.717
Factor III: Competence in environmental awareness	
Was willing to care for and nurture living things	0.717
Took care of animals or grew plants with regard to their ecology	0.716
Liked to collect animals, plants or rocks	0.707
Skilfully collected animals, plants or rocks	0.689
Classified animals, plants or rocks by their characteristics	0.605
Showed understanding of natural phenomena in my daily life	0.539
Factor IV: Competence in information processing	
Drew accurate sketches of observations and experiments	0.661
Expressed my own ideas effectively in diagrams and drawings	0.620
Summarized the results of an observation and experiment appropriately in tables and figures	0.607
Reported clearly the result of an observation and experiment	0.471
Applied scientific ideas creatively when making models	0.431
Used computers adeptly	0.417

Note: Six items with higher factor loading in each of the factors

'Took care of animals or grows plants with regard to their ecology' and was labelled 'competence in environmental awareness'. Factor IV was loaded on items such as 'Drew accurate sketches of observations and experiments' and 'Expressed my own ideas effectively in diagrams and drawings' and was labelled 'competence in information processing in science'.

Mean values for the six items on each of the four factors in Table 10.1 were then calculated and labelled as 'strategic competence in science' subscale scores, 'competence in knowledge acquisition', 'competence in environmental awareness' subscale scores, and 'competence in information processing in science' subscale scores. To investigate the internal consistency of the scores, Cronbach's alpha coefficients were calculated, yielding $\alpha = 0.885$ for Factor I, $\alpha = 0.931$ for Factor II, $\alpha = 0.873$ for Factor III and $\alpha = 0.889$ for Factor IV, respectively. Therefore, a high level of reliability of the internal consistency was obtained for all factors.

Classification of science-gifted styles of adults

Cluster analysis was performed with the cluster method 'within groups linkage' using the subscale scores for strategic competence in science, competence in knowledge acquisition in science, competence in environmental awareness and competence in information processing in science. On the basis of 'Rescaled Distance Cluster Combine Dendrogram' in the hierarchical cluster analysis, two clusters were yielded, with 366 adults in Cluster I, 434 adults in Cluster II. SPSS-PASW Statistics ver.17.0 was used for the analysis.

Analysis of variance was then conducted using the identified two clusters as the independent variables, and the four factors – strategic competence in science, competence in knowledge acquisition, competence in environmental awareness and competence in information processing in science – as dependent variables. Significant differences were found in all cases. Therefore, multiple comparisons based on Tukey's HSD test were performed. The results showed Cluster I < Cluster II for all four competencies in science (alpha level 1 per cent). The mean values of each subscale score for these two cluster groups are given in Figure 10.2. There appear to be two clearly different levels of science-giftedness in Japan.

Science-gifted styles and values of science learning for adults

Figure 10.3 shows the scores of commitment to the values of science learning from Cluster I and Cluster II. The prevalence of each group of the two levels of science-giftedness in the ten items about values of science learning was analysed by ANOVA test, and significant differences in the main effect were found between the groups of two different levels. The higher level of science-gifted group showed the higher commitment to science learning and the lower group showed the lower commitment to all of the values. Interaction effect was also significant. The results of repeated measurement for Cluster I and Cluster II are shown in Table 10.2 and Table 10.3, respectively.

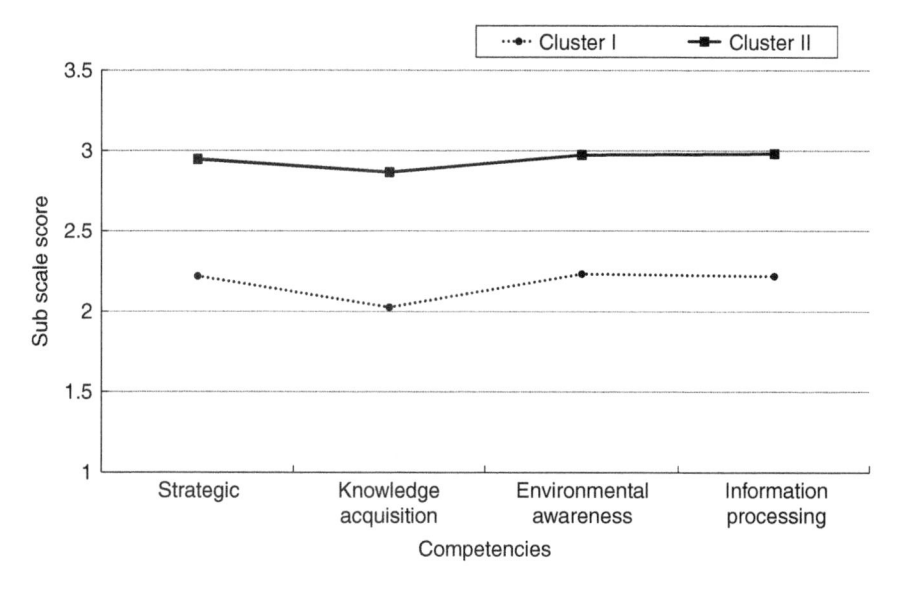

Figure 10.2 Two different levels of scientific giftedness

As is evident from Figure 10.3, Table 10.2 and Table 10.3, adults' response patterns do not differ with the difference in the levels of scientific giftedness. Both of the two cluster groups committed the highest to 'Values_5 (Science learning satisfies my intellectual curiosity)' and gave lower commitment to 'Values_3

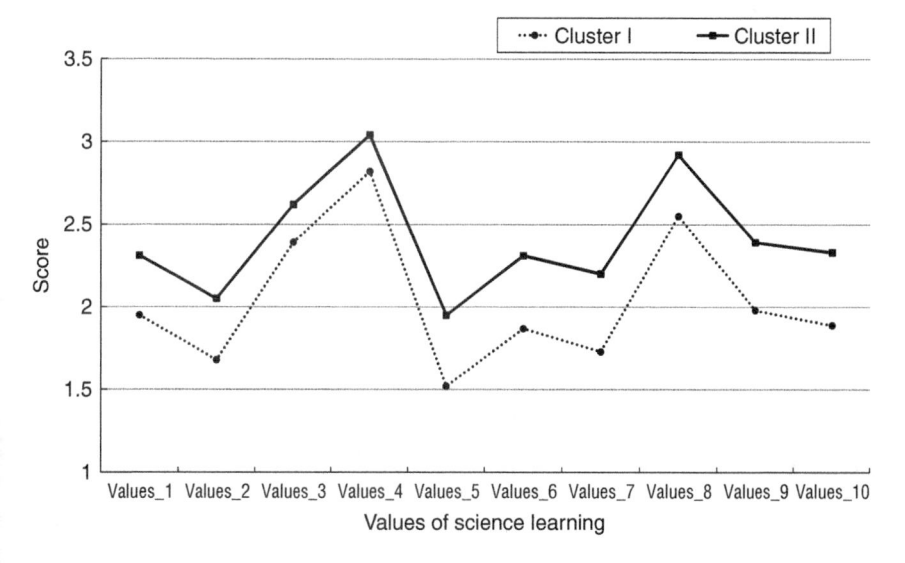

Figure 10.3 Two different levels of commitment to science learning

Table 10.2 The results of repeated measurement between the values of science learning in Cluster I group

	Values_1	Values_2	Values_3	Values_4	Values_5	Values_6	Values_7	Values_8	Values_9	Values_10
Values_1		—	++	++	—		—	++		
Values_2			++	++	—	++		++	++	++
Values_3					—	—	—	++	—	—
Values_4					—	—	—	—	—	—
Values_5						++	++	++	++	++
Values_6							—	++		
Values_7								++	++	++
Values_8									—	—
Values_9										
Values_10										

++: << (p<.01); —: >> (p.<.01)

Table 10.3 The results of repeated measurement between the values of science learning in Cluster II group

	Values_1	Values_2	Values_3	Values_4	Values_5	Values_6	Values_7	Values_8	Values_9	Values_10
Values_1		—	++	++	—			++		
Values_2			++	++		++	++	++	++	++
Values_3				++	—	—	—	++	—	—
Values_4					—	—	—	—	—	—
Values_5						++	++	++	++	++
Values_6							—	++		
Values_7								++	++	+
Values_8									—	—
Values_9										
Values_10										

++: << (p<.01); —: >> (p.<.01); +: < (p.<.05); –: > (p.<.05)

(Science learning is needed to enter into a good high school/university and to get a good job)', 'Values_4 (Science learning is encouraged by my parents)' and 'Values_8 (Science learning helps to make good friends and to develop good habits of mind)'.

Science-gifted styles and occupational fields of adults

Table 10.4 is a matrix of the two cluster groups of science-giftedness and their occupational fields. The prevalence of each group of the two levels of the science-giftedness in the five occupational fields was analysed by the $\chi 2$ test, and significant differences in the two cluster groups were found between the five occupational fields ($\chi 2$ [4] = 13.82, p < .01). Residual analysis showed that the lower level of the science-giftedness (Cluster II) had a greater number of adults in the 'general affairs/supervision' field compare to Cluster I. Cluster I seemed to include a greater number of adults in the 'research/development' field, though no significant difference was found between the two clusters in the field.

Science-gifted styles and annual income

Based on Table 10.1, the subjects were categorized into three income groups: '1) Less than US$40,000', '2) From $40,000 to $80,000' and '3) More than $80,000'. Table 10.5 is a matrix of the two groups of the science-gifted style and three annual income groups.

The prevalence of each group of the two levels of the science-giftedness in the three income groups was analysed by the $\chi 2$ test, and significant differences in gifted style were found between the three income groups ($\chi 2$ [2] = 10.95, p < .01). Residual analysis showed that the highest income group (US$80,000) had a greater number of adults in the higher level of the science-giftedness (Cluster I), and the lowest income group (< US$40,000) had a smaller number. No significant difference was found between the clusters in the middle income group.

Discussion

In this study, 'strategic', 'knowledge acquisition', 'environmental awareness' and 'information processing' learning competencies were extracted from among adults aged 40–9. The gifted behavioural checklist used in this survey was a revised version of the checklist for primary-school children (Sumida, 2010). Sumida used this checklist with Japanese primary-school children and extracted three science learning competencies: 'general competence in science', 'competence in science regarding natural things' and 'creative competence in science' based on the results of factor analysis. Differences between competencies in science learning in primary school and the wider adult society are only to be expected. The results reported in this chapter suggest that science education most suitable for developing gifts in adults might be somewhat different from that for success at primary school.

Table 10.4 The two cluster groups of scientific giftedness and five occupational fields

	Occupational fields					
		General affairs/ supervision N = 160	Production/judicial affairs N = 160	Management/ planning N = 160	Sales/marketing N = 160	Research/ development N = 160
Groups	Cluster I N = 366	55 (15.0)	83 (22.7)	69 (18.9)	76 (20.8)	83 (22.7)
	Cluster II N = 434	105 (24.2)	77 (17.7)	91 (21.0)	84 (19.7)	77 (17.7)

( ):%

Table 10.5 The two cluster groups of scientific giftedness and three annual income groups

	Annual income			
		< US$ 40,000	40,000 ≤ <80,000	80,000 ≤
Groups	Cluster I N = 366	39 (10.7)	205 (56.0)	122 (33.3)
	Cluster II N = 434	71 (16.4)	258 (59.4)	105 (24.2)

( ):%

In some countries, identification of gifted children is conducted at an early stage, often at kindergarten level. Common criteria are used for this identification from primary to high school. Subotnik *et al.* (2011) develop a model of performance trajectories crossing various domains and show that only a few specific domains (i.e. boy soprano) show a peak of ability at a young age. Walberg *et al.* (1981) investigated 221 eminent men in different fields and concluded that childhood traits and conditions are possible clues to or indications of adult eminence rather than certain predictors. Jacobsen (1999) observed that gifted adults are not always provided with opportunities to express the qualities that they possess. It is recommended that guidelines for developing gifted science education should be informed by considering the nature of giftedness in science found among general members of society and to reconsider the significance of identifying or screening for gifted children at a very early stage. Previous research points to gains that may be achieved by interventions with mature and older adults, not only to maintain their capacities, but also to expand them (Birren, 2009). This study attempted to reveal the social structure of the scientifically gifted using a behavioural checklist specific to science. The results showed that one type of scientific giftedness is stereotypical in Japan and two common profiles of science-giftedness exist in Japanese society. The social class of the scientifically gifted appears to be characterized by commitment to science learning, specific occupational fields and high living standards. Vialle (1994) noted a high correlation between the level of giftedness in the subjects of Genetic Studies of Genius and the occupational status of their fathers (mothers were not included). Science education should reflect the socio-cultural context and the fact that children are the citizens of the future, as well as being age and individual appropriate.

The percentage of immigrants in the population has doubled in Japan in the last few decades. The Japanese have gone from looking outward for trade and tourism to seeing parts of their own nation 'internationalized'. That is, Japan is transforming from an asserted homogeneity into a multicultural society that not only acknowledges, but also upholds and celebrates its cultural diversity and even the complex political situation that results (Graburn *et al.*, 2008). As DeCoker and Bjork (2013) note, the theme of diversity has been pre-eminent among the 'new' trends in discussion about Japanese education, wherein 'new' lenses of social reproduction, stratification, multiculturalism, class and disability are being given the opportunity to work their demythologizing magic. At the same time, the rise of new forms of social inequality in Japan has raised new questions about how education should respond to this development while maintaining strong elements of continuity and standardization.

The results of this study imply that scientific competencies among adults play a very important role for all people in Japanese society. The significance and importance of high-quality science education are steadily growing for everyone, especially in terms of the need for fundamental scientific literacy in a technoscience society. Science education for the gifted in the post-modern age should not function for the social selection of the elite or the social exploitation of the intelligent, but instead to encourage science-literate citizens in a healthy, balanced society and foster creative and sustainable development.

References

Alderman, T. (2008). *Meeting the Needs of Your Most Able Pupils: Science*. London: Routledge.

Baltes, P.B. (1987). Theoretical propositions of life-span developmental psychology: on the dynamics between growth and decline. *Developmental Psychology*, 23(5), 611–26.

Birren, J.E. (2009). Gifts and talents of elderly people: the persimmon's promise. In F.D. Horowitz, R.F. Subotnik and D.J. Matthews (Eds), *The Development of Giftedness and Talent Across the Life Span*. Washington, DC: American Psychological Association, pp. 171–85.

Boyce, K.L., VanTassel-Baska, J., Burruss, J.D., Sher, B.T., and Johnson, D.T. (1997). A problem-based curriculum: parallel learning opportunities for students and teachers. *Journal for the Education of the Gifted*, 20, 363–79.

Brandwein, P.F., and Passow, A.H. (Eds) (1988). *Gifted Young in Science: Potential through performance*. Washington, DC: National Science Teachers Association.

Centre for Gifted Education (2007). *Acid, Acid Everywhere: Exploring chemical ecological, and transportation systems* (2nd edn). Dubuque, IA: Kendall/Hunt.

Cooper, C.R., Baum, S.M., and Neu, T.W. (2005). Developing scientific talent in students with special needs. In K. Johnsen, and J. Kendrick (Eds), *Science Education for Gifted Students*. Waco, TX: Prufrock Press, pp. 63–78.

DeCoker, G., and Bjork, C. (Eds) (2013). *Japanese Education in an Era of Globalization*. New York: Teachers College Press.

Feng, A.X., VanTassel-Baska, J., Quek, C., Bai, W., and O'Neill, B. (2005). A longitudinal assessment of gifted students' learning using the integrated curriculum model (ICM): impacts and perceptions of the William and Mary language arts and science curriculum. *Roeper Review*, 27(2), 78–83.

Graburn, N.H.H., Ertl, J., and Tierney, R.K. (Eds) (2008). *Multiculturalism in the New Japan*. New York: Berghahn.

Housand, A.M. (2009). Adult, gifted. In B. Kerr (Ed.), *Encyclopedia of Giftedness, Creativity, and Talent*. London: Sage, pp. 28–31.

Jacobsen, M.-E. (1999). *The Gifted Adult: A revolutionary guide for liberating everyday genius*. New York: Random House.

Johnsen, K. (Ed.) (2004). *Identifying Gifted Students*. Waco, TX: Prufrock Press.

Johnsen, K., and Corn, A. (2001). *SAGES-2* (Screening assessment for gifted elementary and middle school students, 2nd edn). Austin, TX: Pro-Ed.

Johnsen, K., and Kendrick, J. (Eds) (2005). *Science Education for Gifted Students*. Waco, TX: Prufrock Press.

Jones, G., Taylor, A., and Forrester, J.H. (2010). Developing a scientist: a retrospective look. *International Journal of Science Education*, 33(12), 1653–73.

Keating, D.P. (2009). Developmental science and giftedness: An integrated life-span framework. In F.D. Horowitz, R.F. Subotnik and D.J. Matthews (Eds), *The Development of Giftedness and Talent Across the Life Span*. Washington, DC: American Psychological Association, pp. 189–208.

Larsson, U. (2001). *Culture of Creativity: The centennial exhibition of the Nobel Prize*. Cambridge: Science History.

Matthews, M.S. (2006). *Encouraging Your Child's Science Talent*. Waco, TX: Profrock Press.

McGinnis, J.R., and Stefanich, G.P. (2007). Special needs and talents in science learning. In S.K. Abell and N.G. Lederman (Eds), *Handbook of Research on Science Education*. New Jersey: Lawrence Erlbaum Association, pp. 287–317.

Moltzen, R. (2009). Talent development across the lifespan. In L.V. Shavinina (Ed.), *International Handbook on Giftedness.* New York: Springer, pp. 353–79.

NAGC (National Association for Gifted Children) (2007). *State of the States in Gifted Education 2006–2007.* Washington, DC: National Association for Gifted Children.

Nokelainen, P., Tirri, K., Campbell, J.R., and Walberg, H. (2007). Factors that contribute to or hinder academic productivity: comparing two groups of most and least successful Olympians. *Research and Educational Evaluation,* 13 (6), 483–500.

Phillipson, S.N., and McCann, M. (Eds) (2007). *Conceptions of Giftedness: Sociocultural perspectives.* Newq Jersey: Lawrence Erlbaum Associates.

Shavinina, L.V. (2009). Scientific talent: the case of Nobel Laureates. In L.V. Shavinina (Ed.), *International Handbook on Giftedness.* New York: Springer, pp. 649–69.

SIGS (Scales for Identifying Gifted Students) (2004). Waco, TX: Prufrock Press.

Sternberg, R.J. (2007). Cultural dimensions of giftedness and talent. *Roeper Review,* 29(3), 160–5.

Subotnik, R.F., and Steiner, C.L. (1994). Adult manifestations of adolescent talent in science: a longitudinal study of 1983 Westinghouse Science Talent Search winners. In R.F. Subotnik and K.D. Arnold (Eds), *Beyond Terman: Contemporary longitudinal studies of giftedness and talent.* New Jersey: Ablex, pp. 52–76.

Subotnik, R.F., Olszewski-Kubilius, P., and Worrell, F.C. (2011). Rethinking giftedness and gifted education: a proposed direction forward based on psychological science. *Psychological Science in the Public Interest,* 12(1), 3–54.

Sumida, M. (2005). The public understanding of pendulum motion: from 5 to 88 years. In M.R. Matthews, C.F. Gauld and A. Stinner (Eds), *The Pendulum: Scientific, historical, philosophical and educational perspectives.* Dordrecht: Springer, pp. 465–84.

Sumida, M. (2010). Identifying twice-exceptional children and three gifted styles in the Japanese primary science classroom. *International Journal of Science Education,* 32(15), 2097–111.

Sumida, M. (2013). Emerging trends in Japan in education of the gifted: a focus on science education. *Journal for the Education of the Gifted,* 36(3), 277–89.

Sumida, M. (2015). Kids science academy: talent development in STEM from the early childhood years. In M.S. Khine (Ed.), *Science Education in East Asia: Pedagogical innovations and research-informed practices.* Switzerland: Springer, pp. 269–95.

Sumida, M., and Ohashi, A. (2015). Chemistry education for gifted learners. In J. Garcia-Martinez and E. Serrano-Torregrosa (Eds), *Chemistry Education: Best practices, opportunities and trends.* Weinheim: Wiley-VCH, pp. 469–87.

Taber, K.S. (2007a). *Enriching School Science for the Gifted Learner.* London: Gatsby Science Enhancement Programme.

Taber, K.S. (Ed.) (2007b). *Science Education for Gifted Learners.* London: Routledge.

Vialle, W. (1994). 'Termanal' science? The work of Lewis Terman revised. *Roeper Review,* 17(1), 32–8.

Wai, J., Lubinski, D., Benbow, C.P., and Steiger, J.H. (2010). Accomplishment in science, technology, engineering, and mathematics (STEM) and its relation to STEM educational dose: a 25-year longitudinal study. *Journal of Educational Psychology,* 104(4), 860–71.

Walberg, H.J., Tsai, S.-L., Weinstein, T., Gabriel, C.L., Rasher, S.P., Rosecrans, T., Rovai, E., Ide., J., Trujillo, M., and Vukosavich, P. (1981). Childhood traits and environmental conditions of highly eminent adults. *Gifted Child Quarterly,* 25(3), 103–7.

Winner, E. (1996). *Gifted Children: Myths and realities.* New York: Basic Books.

11 Creating a space and place for diverse learners in multifarious contexts

Niamh Stack, Margaret Sutherland, Thomas Aneurin Smith and Frida D. Tungaraza

> Over the life course, human development takes place through processes of progressively more complex reciprocal interaction between an active, evolving biopsychological human organism and the persons, objects and symbols in its immediate external environment.
>
> Bronfenbrenner, 2005, p. 6

As teachers, educators, psychologists, policy-makers and researchers we are all interested in how development occurs, the role education may play within this and what contribution we can each make within this process to help support learners – and, more specifically in the case of this text, gifted learners in science. In trying to address the question of what makes human beings human, Bronfenbrenner, within his bioecological model emphasizes, 'the action in the interaction' (Weisner, 2008, p. 260). This emphasis on dynamic interactions permeated our thinking in writing this chapter and provided the framework for the perspectives taken within it. In this chapter we will argue that learning, including for gifted learners, does not take place in a vacuum and that, rather, it is based on the transactional relationship between learners, educators, parents, communities, the immediate and wider cultural and geographical contexts and the histories in which they are situated. There are two key challenges in taking an international perspective on science education for the gifted. First, the apparent lack of interaction and integration between the fields of science education and gifted education and, second, the lack of attention to considering the multifarious contexts in which gifted science students may find themselves. This book provides a necessary and timely response to these issues. In this chapter we will focus more specifically on addressing the second of these challenges. We will draw upon Bronfenbrenner's arguments, including his belief that development must be considered 'across successive generations and through historical time, both past and present' (2005, p. 3) and we will look at science education for the gifted through the lens of the global South (the nations of Africa, Central and Latin America and most of Asia are collectively known as the global South) to demonstrate how temporal and historical influences can greatly impact upon the opportunities available for creating a space and place for gifted science students internationally.

These discussions will demonstrate that even within one country – for example, Tanzania – there are significant contextual differences, such as between urban and rural regions, which influence educational approaches, opportunities and aspirations. In arguing for the need to acknowledge cultural diversity in educational systems we are not suggesting that the contexts are too different to inform each other, quite the opposite. We will argue that comparison, exploration, scrutiny and critical judgement are necessary if we are to take a meaningful international perspective on the complexity of providing appropriate challenge for gifted science students and that these discussions will enhance understanding in our local contexts within a globalized world. We will argue for an inclusive, culturally and contextually relevant approach to the provision of science education for gifted students, provision in which all learners are challenged, including gifted learners, without social or economic barriers to access and provision in which all gifts are valued and recognized. We will not argue that any of this is easy or without challenges to be overcome, but we will argue that it is an important perspective to consider.

Science education for gifted students in developing countries

'Giftedness' and pedagogies built around the diversities of individual learning styles and needs are constituted around discursive narratives of educational development that primarily originate in the global North, and these have begun to be imported into countries of the global South (Bailey *et al.*, 2012). For example, the belief that all learners should be given a chance to develop their gifts and talents is evidenced in Tanzania in a number of policy documents. In 1995 the Tanzanian Ministry for Education and Culture published an Education and Training Policy that includes an action regarding screening for talented children:

> There is evidence also that some children are exceptionally gifted and that this manifests at different ages: quite early for some, late for others and very late for a few more. It is known that Tanzanian schools and most school systems in the world are not designed to accommodate and assist such children. Yet it is a desirable educational practice to tap and nurture such talents for the benefit of the children themselves and the society. Therefore: Government shall evolve a machinery to identify and develop gifted and talented children.
>
> (p. 21)

This statement demonstrates a clear awareness of the diversities of individual learning needs but also an acknowledgement that a solution for gifted pupils is not yet evident in most school systems in the world and so cannot be easily imported. In 2009 Tanzania developed a *National Strategy on Inclusive Education 2009–2017* that had at its core two key objectives: first, that teaching and learning should respond to the diverse needs of learners and, second, that educational support should be available to all learners (p. 3). However, in spite of these policy objectives, with notable exceptions (Manyowa and Ncube, 2013; Ngara, 2002; Ngara and Porath, 2004, 2007) there is a paucity of research that considers the particular needs and conceptualization of gifted pupils in the context of developing countries within the field of gifted education generally, let alone within specific subject areas such as science. This means it is difficult to assess how successfully these policies have been implemented or what conceptualizations of giftedness they employ in practice. There are studies that consider ethnic groups within western societies who are under-represented on gifted programmes (Chan, 2004; Ford, 2005), but these still have their roots in a Euro-American culture.

Within both science and development education a tension has developed about the importance of local or indigenous knowledge in what is a predominantly western scientifically constructed world (Storey, 2000). Within western research, scientific knowledge is seen as representing that which is replicable, dispassionate, methodical and scientific (Ellen and Harris, 2000) and, thus, indigenous or local knowledge is often viewed as old fashioned and out-dated. These polarized views of science and local knowledges have been unhelpful and McFarlane argues that as long as knowledge remains something that is exported to the global South then we must seek a:

> conception of learning that must be critically reflexive of the power relations between different groups, and that must be able to imagine the possibilities of learning between different contexts in ways that do not conform to historical patterns of colonisation or to contemporary tendencies of aid-based conditionality.
>
> (2006, p. 1416)

This call resonates with gifted science education if cultural diversity is to be celebrated and the needs of gifted learners are to be meaningfully and appropriately met.

The importance of history, time and context

The colonization of Africa has left a legacy for national education systems that has important implications for contemporary accounts of pedagogies associated with high ability and differentiated individual learning needs. Although the spread of formal European-style education to the African colonies began in earnest during the 'scramble for Africa' in the late nineteenth century, much earlier, in the sixteenth century, missionaries took it upon themselves, particularly in British Africa, to introduce western-style education alongside Christian preaching (Bolt and Bezemer, 2009). When competition between European powers intensified, particularly between Britain and France in the late nineteenth and early twentieth centuries, formal education was utilized as a tool in empire building.

While the transfer and import of European-style education systems was typical across the African continent, the experience was neither singular nor monolithic between, or even within, national contexts. Across the sub-Saharan African countries, there have been considerable variations in access and educational investment, making it impossible to universalize across the region (Lewin, 2009). Although the British were typically more active in providing basic primary education than the French, British pragmatism towards running their colonies, or 'indirect rule', left many traditional structures and institutions in place, and local customs, including local forms of education, were somewhat tolerated. Yet, alongside this the British wanted to avoid the emergence of an indigenous educated elite, and thus discouraged education beyond primary level. Evidence has suggested that these early experiences have had an enduring effect on postcolonial education systems (Bolt and Bezemer, 2009), not only in terms of access to schooling, but also on perceptions of childhood development, on what constitutes ability, on what knowledge and skills are valued and, indeed, on what constitutes effective pedagogic practice (Punch and Tisdall, 2012).

The effect of this on the development of gifted learners is not well documented, but in countries where elitism has been encouraged for some but eschewed for others it seems reasonable to assume that being indigenous and gifted (particularly in 'non-academic' areas) might be mutually exclusive positions and significantly reduce the likelihood of identification and consequently appropriate provision. While indigenous and local forms of education existed way before, and alongside, colonial education systems, the expansion of formal universal education across the global South has tended to extend pedagogies that privilege subjects, skills and aspirations which may hold little relation to local realities or potential future employment opportunities, particularly in rural areas (Jeffrey, 2010; Punch, 2004; Smith, 2013). Pedagogies that are associated with the individualization of learning, and predicated on helping an individual's progress into white-collar, skilled work, are associated with contemporary postcolonial education systems in the global South, and have their roots in western educational constructs and in narrow conceptualizations of what it means to be gifted and talented. This emphasis on academic abilities and education leading to white-collar work and the perception of local knowledge and work as antiquated is problematic in numerous ways and has in part contributed to the crisis in land management and food production in some parts of the global South (Ellison, 2014).

Colonial education was, for the most part, very successful in spreading 'western' forms of education, and many contemporary education systems across the African continent still bear the hallmarks of the colonial era in that they are typically highly selective and elitist (for example, the transition from primary to secondary education in Tanzania), follow particular patterns of development and, importantly, often bear little relevance to local realities and knowledge (Crossley and Tikly, 2004). Given these characteristics, it might be assumed that the African continent serves its gifted population well if such an approach to selection successfully identifies and works with 'the best and the brightest'. However, in this approach lies a particular conceptualization of 'the gifted' that gives little credence to the place of local knowledges or 'other' conceptualizations of 'gifted'.

In the global North the identification and conceptualization of gifted individuals historically has been associated with high IQ. Indeed, school systems have been structured around the normative curve distribution and this still dominates in the global North today (Smith, 2006). Problematic and often controversial, the development of IQ can be traced back to the start of the twentieth century. Terman (1916) claimed the scale could ascertain exact intellectual endowment and that a single number could represent the level of intelligence that an individual possessed. Giftedness, in accordance with this perspective, was clearly and easily evidenced by a score at the top end of the scale. More insidious historical uses of this test were related to race, and contemporary writing at the time indicates that views about intelligence and race were acceptable within the discourse, 'among Spanish-Indian and Mexican families of the Southwest and also among Negroes. Their dullness seems to be racial, or at least inherent in the family stocks from which they come' (Terman, 1916, pp. 6–7).

These overt statements about race are part of the IQ legacy, but contemporary gifted education in the global North is still criticized for the lack of representation of children of colour, minority ethnicities and from low socio-economic backgrounds (Worrell, 2009) with identification procedures, societal racism and inequalities being blamed for the phenomenon. These arguments raise two important points: first, that the 'solution' to gifted education has not been found and gifted provision is not perfectly articulated anywhere in the world and, second, given this it would be misguided to blindly import any of these sometimes useful, but often inherently imperfect, perspectives without giving due attention to whether they enhanced or confounded provision.

Participatory, grassroots development and science education

Contemporary thinking in development theory and practice has tended to prioritize participatory approaches that emerge from the grassroots level and from local knowledge (Smith, 2011). In terms of differentiated learning, including the teaching of gifted and talented pupils, prioritization of local knowledge and practices might lead us to question how these concepts are perceived locally (Ngara and Porath, 2004, 2007), and to what extent differentiated learning might prepare young people for local and national realities. It would be a mistake to assume that local knowledge-focused and participatory practices do not already exist in Tanzania. As Barrett (2007) illustrates, some elements of the primary curriculum in Tanzania incorporate knowledge that would be relevant to local future careers, including working out maths problems for local traders and science teaching focusing on nutrition and disease prevention, and local teachers are often keen to equip children with skills relevant to their present context. The Tanzanian science curriculum for primary schools mandates that a topic on 'Health and prevention of diseases, both communicable and infectious' be taught from standard four to standard seven. A topic on 'Food hygiene and quality' is taught in standard six. The objectives for this topic are to enable pupils to appreciate the value of proper nutrition and to explain the effects of poor nutrition.

However, whether these 'local tweaks' to core subjects such as science and maths (which are ultimately formally examined) represent 'local' forms of educational knowledge and provide sufficient challenge to gifted students is debatable. Equally, while some authors have argued that educational systems and pedagogies must attempt to represent or embody local 'culture' (Lindsay, 1989), defining 'culture' in this sense can be highly problematic. One of the key criticisms of the indigenous/local knowledges movement has been that early proponents tended to essentialize and homogenize local/national culture – for example, by referring to 'Tanzanian' or even 'African' forms of education and pedagogy. Tanzania is a country of more than 120 tribes, which may each have distinct notions of education, and therefore of 'giftedness' and 'talent'. The disparity in livelihoods between wealthy urban Tanzanians and those living in rural areas are considerable, and there may be divisions along these lines, wealth or ethnicity, as to what is considered appropriate 'local' pedagogy. For example, in Rukwa region in western Tanzania, those of the Sukuma and Fipa tribes, who co-habit in some villages, can have distinct definitions of what represent valuable skills and practices to be taught to children. The Sukuma are a tribe with a history of pastoralism, they practice polygamy and have extensive families, and are recent migrants to the region, typically making up to around 30 per cent of the population in some villages. The Fipa are the dominant tribe in the Rukwa region in terms of overall population, and are largely agriculturalists, tend to be less wealthy as a result and typically have much smaller families. In Sukuma families, skills associated with pastoralism and cattle tending are highly valued, and young men are typically engaged in tending cattle from a very early age. In Fipa families, there is a much greater diversity of practices that are valued, with more emphasis on agriculture (Smith, 2012). Therefore, for historical, economic and sociocultural reasons, these ethnic groups have different conceptions of what they might regard as valuable 'talents' in a young person. Arguments for 'local' education might also be considered too relativist in outlook, as they ignore the fact that even relatively remote groups live in a globalized world in which a multitude of international influences play out on schools and an individual's broader education. For instance, while not all people in Tanzania have access to a TV/radio or internet, those with access may learn about particular 'talents' from other parts of the world. This is particularly true in the field of music and performing arts, where Tanzanians – especially young adults – have emulated and developed some of the latest styles in pop music – for example, Bongo Flava. Bongo Flava combines aspects of the global hip hop scene with additional influences from reggae, R&B, afrobeat, dancehall and traditional Tanzanian styles such as taarab and dansi to form a unique style of music that is both globally influenced and locally embedded.

Postcolonial literature in education goes some way to help resolve these frictions by working towards 'critical multiculturalism' (Crossley and Tikly, 2004), which might suggest that it is important to avoid simple notions of Tanzanian 'local' conceptions of differentiated learning and what being gifted and talented means; indeed, identifying what precisely is 'local' in a globalized world might itself be very difficult (Smith, 2013). Young people in Tanzanian contexts can have competing and parallel notions of valuable gifts and talents. While many dismiss school knowledge as too 'theoretical' and, therefore, might not value a young person's talent for this kind of learning, and associated pedagogic practices, there is also a recognition that, in the rare circumstances that they might be able to reach education beyond the locality (e.g. if they obtain a scholarship to attend school, or are sponsored by a wealthy relative), then such talents would be highly valuable (Smith, 2013, 2014). While this might seem contradictory, there is recognition that pedagogies and notions of giftedness in particular practices must be appropriate for the context in which the young person will find themselves in their likely future.

Local participation in determining appropriate education and pedagogy has also been at the forefront of recent developments. However, participation must too be regarded critically. In terms of schooling, patterns of participation across sub-Saharan Africa are closely related to household income (Lewin, 2009); similarly patterns of participation in grassroots schemes are also determined (although not necessarily in a linear fashion) along income lines (Mercer, 1999, 2002). Participation by young people in both curricular and extracurricular activities is, therefore, also likely to be strongly determined by household income in Tanzania, which has important implications for involvement in programmes which are aimed at different learners, including those deemed 'gifted and talented'. Children from poor families in Tanzania are inhibited by their circumstances as to the extent to which they can participate in extracurricular activities, such as sports, to develop their talents. Some children, when they return home from school, are needed for household activities, such as farming, cattle raising, fishing, etc. This, in itself, is another form of participation in extracurricular activity, although it is not generally viewed in this way. Developing an understanding of how local conceptualizations of involvement, ability at school and learner development intersect may, therefore, be highly significant for the broader international gifted and talented agenda.

Responding globally to the diverse needs of gifted science learners

Contemporary developments in educational theory and practice have recognized the necessity to support the needs of a range of learners, including those of high ability; indeed, much of the officialization of this practice into policy and curricula has occurred in the global North, just as research in the area of giftedness has tended to almost exclusively focus on high-income countries (Bailey *et al.*, 2012). Although some of these developments are relatively recent, they continue trends in educational practice throughout anglophonic western countries that began in the 1960s which emphasize the learning needs of the individual and non-overt forms of discipline, both of which have been discursively woven into what is understood as 'good' teaching (Barrett, 2007). Learner-centred techniques, concurrent with Bernstein's competence modes of teaching, are often dichotomously presented as opposed to 'bad' teaching practices in low-income countries that are predominated by 'performance', teacher-centred modes of learning (ibid.).

While contemporary developments in education in sub-Saharan Africa have been heavily framed by an international architecture of expectations and commitments to provide education for all, there is also evidence to suggest that drives towards universal primary education can have transient effects, and may, in fact, diminish the quality of teaching and learning by rapidly driving up class sizes (Lewin, 2009). Lewin (ibid.) suggests that with, at least in official figures, high primary enrolment largely achieved in sub-Saharan Africa, there is a need to focus on meaningful quality in education. In Tanzania, dropout rates from grade to grade and completion rates have stagnated, and indicators of quality have failed to improve in line with increased access (Sifuna, 2007). High levels of enrolment conceal the fact that many children fail to reach acceptable levels of achievement, there are high levels of those repeating grades and who are over-age and, overall, uneven quality of access that undermines the spirit of the Millennium Development Goals and the Dakar Education for All targets (Lewin, 2009; UN, 2000; UNESCO, 2008). Despite the high number of children repeating years in Tanzania, primary school curricula are not purposely multi-graded (all children receive the same curriculum independent, and irrespective, of their cognitive development), which is likely to increase the chance of failure and dropout for those who are over-age or under-achieving, while also not offering those of high ability the chance to be recognized or accelerate or be challenged. Although many of these issues are closely related to resource constraints, there is also evidence that such resource constraints do not necessarily mean that competence pedagogies and differentiated learning is not possible (Barrett, 2007). Indeed, some Tanzanian teachers can be highly flexible in their curriculum delivery, are adept at identifying pupils with different abilities and adapting to their needs, often applying inclusive constructivist principles to whole-class teaching, and draw on what might be understood as distinctly 'Tanzanian' pedagogic traditions (ibid.). For example, teachers in rural, urban and coastal areas of Tanzania use managing the planted area around the school grounds as a method of science teaching which also integrates local skills and knowledge of plants, soil types and agricultural practices (Smith 2012, 2014). In examples of rural schools from Smith's (2012, 2013, 2014) research, school grounds are used extensively by teachers to demonstrate the planting of particular types of fruit crop which are highly relevant to the local agricultural economy, and students learn about the local practices linked to how fruit plants and other trees (which are useful for building materials) will develop under typical soil, climate and weather conditions. Such teaching appears to integrate skills, knowledge and talents, which are inherent to local community practices, and pedagogic traditions, which are also present in the students homes, with more abstracted, 'scientific' or 'theoretical' knowledge of soils, weather and botany. They also recognize different conceptions of talent, which might include talents in 'reading' the capacities and suitability of soil types and the overall planting and cultivating of crops using local techniques.

Current evidence therefore suggests that responding to different abilities, and utilizing competence-mode pedagogies, is entirely possible and practicable in low-income countries. Evidence from the global North also indicates that gifted students can perform just as well in mixed classes, and that pupils of all abilities can benefit from challenging learning opportunities and from social interaction with those of different abilities (Bailey *et al.*, 2012), suggesting that such pedagogic practice in the hands of a skilled and knowledgeable educator can, and does, work within whole-class teaching and under resource constraints. Yet there are still important barriers to cross-cultural communication around diverse-ability teaching and what is deemed to be valued as ability in science education. As the 'gifted' education agenda has predominantly emerged from the global North, concepts of 'giftedness' are embedded within these societies, and tend to be used unproblematically (ibid.). Yet such terms may carry quite different meanings in different cultural and societal contexts, and may, in fact, hamper communication across contexts rather than facilitate it (Sutherland, 2012). Evidence has shown that typical classroom science and environment education in Tanzanian secondary and primary schools commonly comes under criticism from local people because it is based on theoretical models from western science (Smith, 2013). For example, when young people learn about climatic and environmental change within secondary schools, they are identified as talented in the subject by their teachers based on how well they are able to articulate the abstract, theoretical constructs of environmental systems, or articulate the values associated with environmental conservation. These include the systems of how release of carbon dioxide might deplete the ozone layer, or the workings of the water cycle, and how these both might be altered by the processes of deforestation, or how forests and wildlife should be protected (ibid.). Local adults, particularly in rural communities, typically do not value these same conceptions of giftedness. Instead, many local people understand this kind of learning and expression of talent as too 'theoretical', largely because, while broadly speaking the ideas might be relevant to the local environment, they bare little practical relevance (Smith, 2013, 2014). Often, in rural communities, it is the ability to acquire practical skills, or to be able to translate 'theoretical' knowledge into an advantage for agricultural production, trading, or pastoralism, which is valued more highly. Therefore, while a student might be identified as 'gifted' in the context of a classroom by teachers, unless there is a strong possibility that a family can afford to invest in that student's further education to utilize these more 'abstracted' talents in science (doubtful for most in rural families), it is unlikely that such talents will be regarded highly in the community. In extreme cases, the values taught to students through science in schools, such as preventing forest destruction or reducing reliance on fishing, may conflict with necessary community livelihood practices (Smith, 2014). As such, in the context of Tanzania, the teaching of vocational skills for likely future livelihoods will be valued more highly, and giftedness and talent will be measured in the individual's ongoing success in agriculture, pastoralism, or other local businesses (Smith, 2013, 2014).

Therefore, there is just as strong an argument for a paradigmatic shift in thinking in the international gifted and talented agenda to accommodate other possible definitions and pedagogic practices, as there is for educators and policy-makers in the global South to begin to formally adopt competence-mode pedagogies adapted to different learning needs. There is an important need to consider scale here, as understandings of these concepts may be variegated, but also interconnected, across regional, national and local geographies. Equally, a spotlight on differentiated learning and ability challenges instrumentalist monitoring of education at the international level. As Al-Samarrai and Reilly (2008) demonstrate, it is much more difficult to quantitatively and empirically capture 'ability' factors than enrolment, yet, at present, international bodies such as the UN rely considerably on measuring national educational 'progress' on simple enrolment measures.

Conclusions and implications for practice in science education for the gifted

> In order to develop – intellectually, emotionally, socially and morally, a child requires, for all of these, the same thing: participation in progressively more complex activities.
>
> (Bronfenbrenner, 2005, p. 9)

In Bronfenbrenner's bioecological model of human development 'complex activities' are not limited to the formal education contexts but rather they emphasize and value all forms of informal education within the home and community as well. In order to support learners in advancing to 'progressively more complex activities' we must first understand what knowledge, skills and experiences they have already mastered. Acknowledging the differences learners bring to the learning context and developing a pedagogy that supports them has to be a priority in science education for the gifted. This is true both in terms of their differences in abilities and their differences in knowledge, experience and context. A pedagogical approach to gifted science education that fails to take into account local knowledges and cultures, and thus fails to value the abilities young people may have in these local practices, may subsequently fail to provide them with opportunities to advance these skills and practise them within their communities.

The evidence from Smith's research in Tanzanian schools (2012, 2013, 2014) suggests, in line with these pedagogies which value knowledge-in-practice, that gifts and talents may be spatial and material practices, expressed in skilled knowing rather than abstracted knowledge. It is also significant that the learning of these skills takes place as much in the home as it does in the space of the school, such that, in the Tanzanian context, it is a constellation of family, local adults and teaching in schools which contributes to the development of talents in local agricultural practices, not just pedagogies which are rehearsed in schools.

However, what is interesting about the Tanzanian case is that, presently, the integration of these practice-based local pedagogies, and the teaching of science and in particular environmental issues, is done in spite of the current Tanzanian nation curriculum, which neither calls for these kinds of activities specifically (Smith, 2012), nor recognizes the skill-based talents which are expressed. Local scientific knowledge informs decisions about all aspects of daily life and, as such, appears to offer developing communities agency in areas that directly affect them (Chambers, 2001). However, local scientific knowledge is not any more monolithic than western science and, in essence, neither western scientific knowledge nor local knowledge holds the answer independently. To return to Bronfenbrenner's argument 'the action is in the interaction'.

It is important to understand the context in which education for gifted learners must be negotiated and how, even within the national space, local scientific knowledge which learners encounter will vary considerably, as do local cultures of children's voice and empowerment, within and between divergent communities. We would argue that it is as much local context and learners' own agency and autonomy as it is the nature and implementation of any formal gifted science education programme that may structure gifted learners' experiences of learning. The new sociology of childhood studies in the 1990s asserted the importance of understanding young people as social actors who do not merely assimilate knowledge and skills, but also who have agency and autonomy in the educational choices they make and identities they choose (Konstantoni, 2012; Punch and Tisdall, 2012). Young people are capable of rapidly adapting their identities (Van Blerk, 2005) and may strategically claim and perform different identities to meet the expectations and norms placed on them in different spaces and places (Holloway *et al.*, 2000; Smith, 2014). We must remember, therefore, that gifted science students are not just passive recipients of labels given to them in schools, they also can actively subvert these by performing different identities – for example, by withholding or expressing knowledge, in different environments. But, equally, some of this 'choice' of expression might be associated with the cultural norms of their environment, thus intertwining the structures acting on young people with their autonomous agency.

Therefore, science education that aims to address the needs of gifted learners has to take account of such issues, especially if it is to address the global challenges of the twenty-first century. Continuing to offer gifted programmes rooted in a narrow conceptualization of 'giftedness' along with a curriculum and pedagogical practices that are rooted in the global North has the potential to produce a particular kind of 'gifted' scientist that may well overlook the rich heritage and information that local scientific knowledge communities hold and which may, in turn, hold solutions for our global problems, such as food security. Barrett (2007) finds that, in Tanzanian school classroom practice, there is a strong tradition of using debate as a tool for learning, which has its roots in distinctly Tanzanian cultural traditions. These traditions of debate may be linked to notions of communal or group learning, which equally might value talents associated with social cooperation and negotiation, rather than the notion of 'individual' talent. If applied critically to science learning, these traditions of debate may allow Tanzanian pupils to collaboratively and critically debate the socio-economic consequences of implementing ideas from science (for example, various forms of environmental conservation) for local community livelihoods. This is what Bailey *et al.* (2012) describe as 'social thinking', the development of social skills which enable the translation of knowledge into local social realities. Such pedagogic traditions already exist in Tanzania, and would be highly valuable for the integration of local pedagogies with other 'western' forms of science learning and knowledge. They would also provide challenging educational opportunities for gifted pupils in science education and give them a valuable sense of autonomy and agency in their own learning. This provides just one example of how local pedagogies and traditions may be used to address the key issues and challenges of science education for gifted pupils in developing countries and the value of extending our understanding of gifted education beyond western and northern contexts.

References

Al-Samarrai, S., and Reilly, B. (2008). Education, employment and earnings of secondary school and university leavers in Tanzania: evidence from a tracer study. *Journal of International Development*, 44(2), 258–88.

Bailey, R., Pearce, G., Smith, C., Sutherland, M., Stack, N., Winstanley, C., and Dickenson, M. (2012). Improving the educational achievement of gifted and talented students: a systematic review. *Talent Development and Excellence*, 4(1), 33–48.

Barrett, A.M. (2007). Beyond the polarisation of pedagogies: models of classroom practice in Tanzanian primary schools. *Comparative Education*, 43(2), 273–94.

Bolt, J., and Bezemer, D. (2009). Understanding long-run African growth: colonial institutions or colonial education? *The Journal of Development Studies*, 45(1), 24–54.

Bronfenbrenner, U. (2005) *Making Human Beings Human: Bioecological perspectives on human development*. London: Sage.

Chan, D.W. (2004). Multiple intelligences of Chinese gifted students in Hong Kong: perspectives from students, parents, teachers and peers. *Roeper Review*, 27, 18–24.

Chambers, R. (2001). The World Development Report: concepts, content and chapter 12. *Journal of International Devlopment*, 13, 299–306.

Crossley, M., and Tikley, L. (2004). Postcolonial perspectives and comparative and international research in education: a critical introduction, *Comparative Education*, 40(2), 147–56.

Ellen, R., and Harris, H. (2000). Introduction. In R. Ellen, P. Parkes and A. Bicker (Eds), *Indigenous Environmental Knowledge and Its Transformations*, Amsterdam: Harwood Academic.

Ellison, M. (2014). Can a reality show really deliver aid to Africa? *The Toronto Star*, 20 January. Retrieved from: http://www.thestar.com

Ford, D. (2005). Intelligence testing and cultural diversity: pitfalls and promises. *National Research Center on the Gifted and Talented News Letter*, Winter, 3–9.

Holloway, S.J., Valentine, G., and Bingham, N. (2000). Institutionalising technologies: masculinities, femininities, and the heterosexual economy of the IT classroom. *Environment and Planning A*, 32, 617–33.

Jeffrey, C. (2010). Timepass: youth, class, and time among unemployed young men in India. *American Ethnologist*, 37(3), 465–81.

Konstantoni, K. (2012). Children's peer relationships and social identities: exploring cases of young children's agency and complex interdependencies from the minority world. *Children's Geographies*, 10(3), 337–46.

Lewin, K.M. (2009). Access to education in sub-Saharan Africa: patterns, problems and possibilities, *Comparative Education*, 45(2), 151–74.

Lindsay, B. (1989). Redefining the educational and cultural milieu of Tanzanian teachers: a case study in development or dependency? *Comparative Education*, 25(1), 87–96.

Manyowa, A.F., and Ncube, M.V. (2013). A consideration of education programs for gifted primary school pupils in Masvingo, Zimbabwe. *International Journal of Development and Sustainability*, 2(2), 617–28.

McFarlane, C. (2006). Crossing borders: development, learning and the north–south divide. *Third World Quarterly*, 27(8), 1413–37.

Mercer, C. (1999). Reconceptualizing state-society relations in Tanzania: are NGOs 'making a difference'?, *Area*, 31(3), 247–58.

Mercer, C. (2002). The discourse of *Maendeleo* and the politics of women's participation on Mount Kilimanjaro. *Development and Change*, 33, 101–27.

Ministry of Education and Culture (1995). *The Education and Training Policy*. United Republic of Tanzania, Ministry of Education and Vocational Training.

Ministry of Education and Vocational Training (2009). *National Strategy on Inclusive Education 2009–2017*. United Republic of Tanzania, Ministry of Education and Vocational Training.

Ngara, C. (2002). Teachers' perceptions of giftedness and talent among primary school children, *Zimbabwe Journal of Educational Research*, 14, 217–27.

Ngara, C., and Porath, M. (2004). Shona culture of Zimbabwe's views of giftedness. *High Ability Studies*, 15, 189–209.

Ngara, C., and Porath, M. (2007). Ndebele culture of Zimbabwe's views of giftedness. *High Ability Studies*, 18(2), 191–208.

Punch, S. (2004). The impact of primary education on school-to-work transitions for young people in rural Bolivia. *Youth and Society*, 36(2), 163–82.

Punch, S., and Tisdall, E.K.M. (2012). Exploring children and young people's relationships across majority and minority worlds. *Children's Geographies*, 10(3), 241–8.

Sifuna, D.N. (2007). The challenge of increasing access and improving quality: an analysis of universal primary education interventions in Kenya and Tanzania since the 1970s. *International Review of Education*, 53(5–6), 687–99.

Smith, C.M.M. (2006). *Including the Gifted and Talented: Making inclusion work for more gifted and able learners* London: Routledge.

Smith, T.A. (2011). Local knowledge in development (geography), *Geography Compass*, 5(8), 595–609.

Smith, T.A. (2012). At the crux of development? Local knowledge, participation, empowerment and environmental education in Tanzania. Unpublished PhD Thesis, University of Glasgow.

Smith, T.A. (2013). The dominant/marginal lives of young Tanzanians: spaces of knowing at the intersection of children's geographies and development geographies. *Geoforum*, 48, 10–23.

Smith, T.A. (2014). The student is not the fisherman: temporal displacement of young people's identities in Tanzania. *Social and Cultural Geography*, doi: 10.1080/14649365.2014.926562

Storey, A. (2000). Post-development theory: romanticism and Pontius Pilate politics. *Development*, 43(4), 40–6.

Sutherland, M. (2012). Paradigmatic shift or tinkering at the edges? *High Ability Studies*, 23(1), 109–11.

Terman, L.M. (1916). *The Measurement of Intelligence: An explanation of and a complete guide for the use of the Stanford revision and extension of the Binet-Simon Intelligence Scale*. Boston: Houghton Mifflin.

UN (2000). *Millenium Summit Declaration*. New York: United Nations.

UNESCO (2008). *EFA Global Monitoring Report*. Oxford: Oxford University Press.

Van Blerk, L. (2005). Negotiating spatial identities: mobile perspectives on street life in Uganda. *Children's Geographies*, 3(1), 5–21.

Weisner, T.S. (2008). The Urie Bronfenbrenner top 19: looking back at his bioecological perspective, *Mind, Culture and Activity*, 15(3), 258–62. doi: 10.1080/10749030802186785

Worrell, F.C. (2009). What does gifted mean? Personal and social identity perspectives on giftedness in adolescence. In F.D. Horowitz, R.F. Subotnik and D.J. Matthews (Eds), *The Development of Giftedness and Talent Across the Lifespan*. Washington, DC: American Psychological Association. doi: 10.1037/11867-008, pp. 131–52.

12 Extending the gifted science student

What the teacher needs to do during enquiry-based teaching

Gillian Kidman

Introduction

Most science teachers would agree that investigative science is a highly effective way to teach science. Students build their scientific understanding and investigative skills through scientific enquiry processes where they make connections between their prior knowledge and new ideas and evidence. Scientific enquiry, especially open enquiry, has long been espoused for extending the gifted student in science (Park and Oliver, 2009; Yuen-Yan *et al.*, 2010). Windschitl (2003) described four types of scientific enquiry: 1) confirmation experiences or 'cook book labs' that are used to verify a fact, 2) structured enquiry through which students are given a question and procedure to discover an unknown answer, 3) guided enquiry through which teachers allow students to investigate a prescribed problem using their own methods and 4) open enquiry through which students form their own questions and conduct independent investigations (p. 114) – but what role does the teacher play in this? And does the teacher alter this role when undertaking enquiry-based teaching of gifted students?

Rarely do teachers have the time to consult educational research journals for classroom guidance. Instead, teachers often base their decisions about what to do in the classroom on the experiences of other teachers (Asay and Orgill, 2010) and from short professional development presentations. Asay and Orgill cite a long list of authors indicating there is a need for descriptions of actual enquiry-based lessons in everyday classrooms which would benefit both pre-service and in-service teachers. The goal then, for this chapter, is to examine the international literature relating to enquiry classrooms, and to use this literature to form a theoretical model that is then examined and modified based on actual classroom observations, and on teacher interviews. Only literature which has explicitly discussed the teacher's role and behaviour is considered.

Specifically, the chapter develops, then refines, two pedagogical models that explore components of the theoretical model based on observations from nine classrooms and interviews with nine teachers. The focus is specifically upon the role of the teacher using enquiry-based teaching pedagogies with gifted students in mainstream classrooms.

Background information for the theoretical model

Science education research journals, policy documents and books were considered so as to establish a consensus of what enquiry-based teaching entails, with the aim of developing a theoretical model of teacher roles and enquiry-based pedagogies. According to Finkel and his colleagues (Finkel *et al.*, 2009), the teacher employs enquiry-based pedagogies to:

- involve students in initial exploration before ideas are introduced and explanations developed;
- incorporate students' own questions;
- involve an open-ended investigation as part of the sequence; use activities to explore and develop ideas rather than simply demonstrate previously presented ideas; and
- support students to develop new knowledge.

But how does the teacher do this? What is the role of the teacher in each of these pedagogies? There was scant literature that responded to these questions. Only four papers provided clear literature analyses and descriptions of the roles of the teacher employing enquiry-based pedagogies similar to those outlined above by Finkel *et al.* However, none of these papers were directed towards the teacher of the gifted student.

Wells (2001) describes the enquiry process as three separate activities the students need to complete – research, interpret and present. A little more detail is provided in the Asay and Orgill (2010) research. They suggest the student needs to initially participate in two concurrent activities – to question and to find evidence. Once evidence has been found, Asay and Orgill state the student needs to then analyse it, making connections between the pieces. Similar to Wells's 'present' activity, the student then needs to communicate their enquiry project and findings. Both the Wells and the Asay and Orgill descriptions of the enquiry process are similar to that of Zubrowski (2007), who describes the enquiry process as three phases – exploratory, evidence gathering and sense-making, plus two transitional phases. Interestingly, Zubrowski does not consider the communication of the enquiry project a necessary component, whereas Wells, and Asay and Orgill, do. Poon *et al.* (2012) present us with a pedagogical framework that introduces 'the pattern of PIE (P for "prepare to investigate," I for "investigate," and E for "explain") [that] were clearly evident in all of the lessons observed' (p. 318). Like Zubrowski, the PIE framework ends with 'explain' where students explain their findings and the teacher leads a discussion relating to the concepts involved. Communication of the enquiry beyond the classroom is not a component of the framework.

A theoretical model (see Figure 12.1) was formed from the rich descriptions found in the Wells (2001), Zubrowski (2007), Asay and Orgill (2010), Poon *et al.* (2012) papers. The model shows five components: basically, three cycles (exploratory, evidence gathering and sense-making), which Wells, Zubrowski,

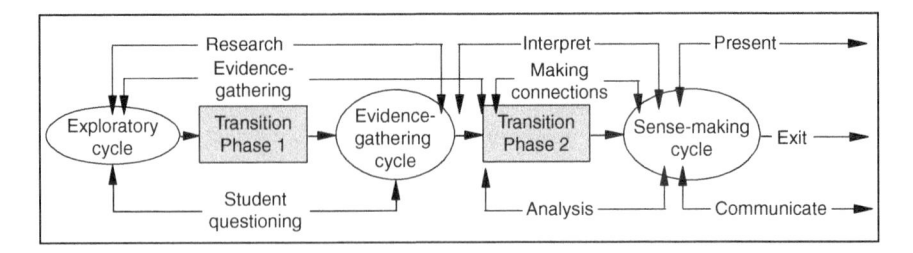

Figure 12.1 Theoretical model for enquiry-based teaching

Asay and Orgill, and Poon *et al.* all consider critical to the teaching of enquiry lessons, but which will not be fully influential on student learning without the two transitional phases emphasized by Zubrowski. The five components are sequential, but link together via student-generated questions, the gathering of evidence and the all-important, but often forgotten, trio of analysis, making connections and communicating findings.

This theoretical model was then considered in terms of the classroom practices of nine teachers, all experienced in delivering guided and open enquiry-based learning opportunities. From the descriptions found in the literature, combined with classroom observations and teacher interviews, pedagogical models have been created for each of the five components of the theoretical model, of which two are presented in the remainder of this chapter. These two models relate to the two transition phases seen as shaded areas in the theoretical model of Figure 12.1. It is here that the teachers all needed to modify their teaching for the gifted student.

Background information for the classroom data

The classroom data consists of teacher interviews, observations and videotaped recordings of enquiry-based lessons. The lessons are from nine different science classes in three schools in Queensland, Australia. Each class had three consecutive enquiry lessons videotaped on three separate occasions during a school year (resulting in 81 videotaped lessons). These videotapes were analysed for determining teacher roles and enquiry-based pedagogies, and then used for stimulated recall in teacher interviews. Stigler *et al.* (2000) claim that using video analysis to study teaching and learning enables the detailed examination of complex activities, and samples of lessons provide information about teaching and learning across a range of conditions, classes, ages and topics that can be then subjected to analysis. Pirie (1996) argues that video-stimulated recall is the least intrusive and yet the most inclusive way to study classroom events. It allows the teacher to experience again an episode of teaching by providing, in retrospect, an accurate account of his/her thought processes and actions (Calderhead, 1981). Details of the participating classrooms are shown in Table 12.1.

Table 12.1 Participating classrooms

School	Class	Science topics explored
primary school 1	3 x Year 6 (11 years old)	insects, friction, sound
high school 1	3 x Year 9 (General Sci) (14 years old)	flight, digestion, catalysts
high school 2	3 x Year 11 (Biology) (16 years old)	osmosis, DNA, physiology

All classes had students that were considered as 'gifted' either by their schools, or by formal testing. In Australia it is rare for gifted students to be segregated from non-gifted students. Teachers nominated a three-lesson sequence in each of Terms 1, 2 and 3 of the school year. For each of the three lesson sequences, the following occurred: 1) pre-interview with teacher to determine the intentions of the lesson sequence (20–30 minutes), 2) the videotaping of the lesson sequence (lesson length varied but was approximately one hour in each instance), 3) post-lesson debriefing (ten minutes) to determine immediate lesson reactions, 4) video analysis of roles and enquiry-based pedagogies (actions of teacher mapped against theoretical operational model), 5) teacher interview involving stimulated recall of aspects of videotaped lesson/s (one to two hours), 6) reconsideration of the theoretical operational model.

Revealing the transition phase pedagogical models

The classroom observations and teacher interviews complemented the theoretical model in that the five components – exploratory cycle, Transitional Phase 1, evidence-gathering cycle, Transitional Phase 2 and the sense-making cycle – were confirmed.

The exploratory cycle

For all students, this cycle was found to be important for establishing the purpose and process of the enquiry experience. Questioning and exploring the students' prior knowledge engaged the students. In most cases (unless the class was experienced with enquiry learning), the enquiry question was negotiated and developed by the teacher and students alike. Often this discussion was dominated by the gifted students in the Biology classes, but not in the Year 6 and 9 classes. It seems younger gifted students do not want to appear interested or knowledgeable in front of their peers. Although the teachers tried to get the ideas from such students, rarely were they successful. Following the shared experience of constructing the research question, the teacher needed to adopt two simultaneous roles. One involves the creation of groups and allocation of group roles. The second concerns the allocation of materials. All teachers allowed the gifted and above-average learners to select who they worked with – 'I don't have to worry about them. It is the weaker students, either from behaviour or intellect that I need to consider so they do actually do the work.' While the students were working at 'answering' the research question, the teacher needed to keep a check on each group and individual. Instead of circulating and observing groups, the teacher openly interacted with each group, asking questions of the students and probing understandings. There was a clear differentiation of questions and responses between the teacher and the groups with the brighter students. It was through these questioning times that the teachers permitted the gifted students to deviate from the class investigation/s to investigations which were more academically challenging.

For the younger children, the teachers found it necessary to keep updating the class of the successes of other groups as a means of keeping the class on task as a whole – 'I don't think I show up some groups, but just highlighting successes on a fair basis. Strugglers need to know they are contributing just like the brighter kids.' There is a cycle the teacher may follow up to five times per lesson, which involves keeping students on task, the checking of progress and maintaining a watchful eye on the resources and maintaining a tidy workplace. It seems the younger the student, the greater the number of times the teacher needs to repeat the cycle. Older students still need their progress checked, and may need advice on resources and materials, but they are less likely to need the teacher to continuously redirect them back to their tasks. In one case, however, a Year 9 teacher did have a difficult time with a gifted student who was constantly drifting off task as she repeatedly saw influences of variables she was failing to control. 'In her case, I had to keep slowing down her thought patterns. She was building investigations inside of investigations. It was weird, but interesting all the same,' reflected the girl's teacher.

Once the students had gathered their evidence the teacher needed to direct the clearing away of all resources and materials or risk being left with a huge mess. It was the students' responsibility to clear away the work areas – rarely did the teacher do this. The gifted students all seemed reluctant to stop their investigations and clear up their work areas as they were highly engaged in their learning. Other students also tried to avoid the clean-up, but more often out of laziness it seemed. The teacher was the director of the process, posing questions to the class as they return materials and clean benches. The clean-up was not a time for students to chat among themselves. The experienced enquiry teacher used the time to pose questions to the class, who responded as they tidied their work areas. For the weaker student, this discussion was very important to consolidate ideas; however, the gifted students did not need the consolidation due to differing motivations. Often the clean-up time was at the end of the lesson, so it was important for the teacher to use the time to establish discussion within the classroom, and then to continue with it once the class has been moved away from tidied materials. This practice maintained the thought processes of the students, ensuring the lesson flowed continuously. It was found that the gifted student often refrained from this class discussion. Four of the teachers indicated they didn't mind that the gifted students refrained from these discussions:

> because they have all sorts of information going on in their heads which is often above that of the other students. They don't need me asking easy

questions, so they think of their own evidence and sorting out its meaning. Then later they run ideas by me.

(Year 11 Biology teacher)

Often the teacher would use his or her questioning during the discussion to ease the class into the Transitional Phase 1 by recognizing the need to gather further evidence.

Transition Phase 1

Figure 12.2 provides a pedagogical model of what the teachers needed to do in their classrooms to transition the students from an exploratory look at their project to being able to gather their evidence. The shaded components indicate roles the teacher varied when working specifically with the gifted student.

The interesting aspect of this phase with respect to the gifted student is the development of a question that is able to be probed with the available resources and the nature of the variables being manipulated. Unless the student has a testable question or hypothesis, and understands the nature of manipulating only one variable at a time, the enquiry-based project can easily collapse. The gifted student is a lot more capable of developing a question than their classmates. However, many of these questions were too difficult to be addressed in the school laboratory. The teachers in this study needed to have the complementary science knowledge, as well as equipment, in order to fully utilize the questions posed by the gifted student. An example of such a difficult question emerged in

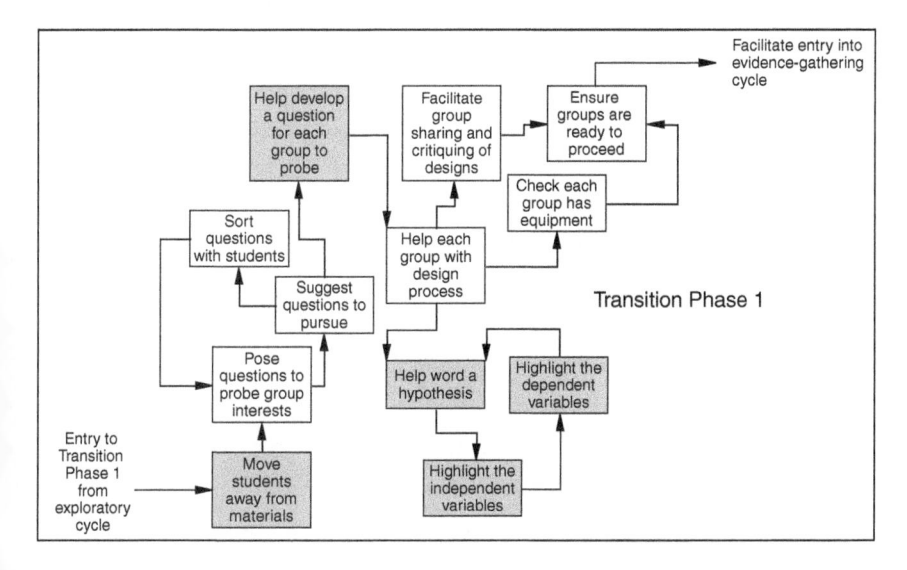

Figure 12.2 Transition Phase 1. Shaded areas are critical for the gifted student.

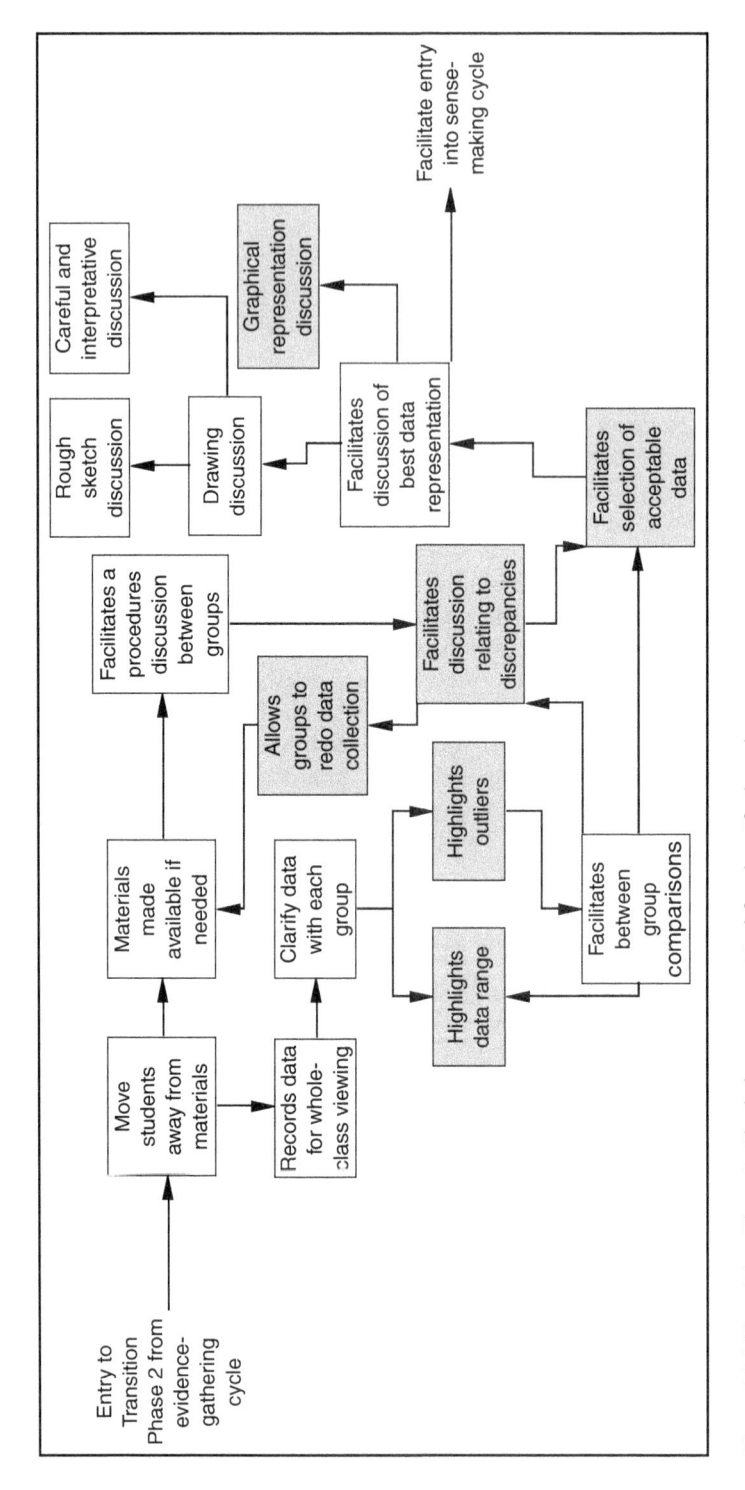

Figure 12.3 Transition Phase 2. Shaded areas are critical for the gifted student.

one of the Year 9 classrooms. The gifted student wanted to test wing strength in birds:

> This boy [teacher points to student during a stimulated recall viewing of a class video recording] wants to explore wing strength in birds. He wrote something like 'That there is a ratio relationship between wing length, wing span and weight of the bird which lets them fly fast'. We worked on the wording to create the hypothesis 'Flight speed is influenced by a set ratio between wing span and body weight in birds'.
>
> (Year 9 teacher)

Unfortunately for the student, access to birds was very limited, so the collection of primary data was not possible. Neither the student nor the teacher could locate the appropriate secondary data on the internet that would have permitted the student to conduct the study. The teachers all conducted whole-class brainstorm sessions involving variables.

Most students struggled with the notions of independent and dependent variables, despite clear differentiations by the teachers. The Year 6 and 9 teachers all introduced the notions of dependent and independent variables in terms of 'One thing I can change' and 'Things I will not change'. This resulted in a widespread confusion by students and with the gifted students using the two terms correctly during the discussions, but, as soon as they had to multi-task in the practical sense, they either stopped using the terms or used them interchangeably. One of the Year 11 Biology teachers, however, had better success with her gifted students by exploring the 'independent variable' notion in terms of it being nominal, ordinal or interval ratio:

> I tell the whole class the three categories. I don't make it an overall focus, but I insist the brighter students use the terms correctly. This way they quickly learn the three types, and then learn that these are the independent variables and then they fly.

All teachers agreed that, with the average student, they need encouragement to get motivated to pose testable questions and to design the investigation with appropriate variable consideration. However, with the gifted student, the teacher has to increase the intellectual demands of the lesson. The gifted student does not like to be confused about the design of their investigation. They need to feel like they are in control of their learning. They are happy to be extended as long as they reconcile their confusion. The average student, however, 'is a lot more dismissive of their learning, and seems content to leave the room and the lesson in a state of soon-to-be-forgotten confusion' (Year 9 teacher):

> Anticipation or frustration? I need to keep a balance with the bright ones. I want everyone to finish the lesson sure their hypothesis or question and variables are correct. So when we come to the next lesson there is an excitement. The gifted student can't wait to get an outcome. Sometimes the

outcome is more eagerly awaited than the act of generating the data. I need to slow them down and to get them to enter the data stage with an open mind and contained enthusiasm.

The evidence-gathering cycle

Clearly, the most enjoyable aspect of open enquiry for the students – and, indeed, for the learning of the teacher – was in gathering the evidence. In all of the classrooms, the teachers needed to clarify the purpose of the task. This reminded the students of what they were doing and why, and enabled the teacher to check the students were familiar with their methodologies. It was interesting to note that the teachers of the Year 9 and 11 classrooms felt the need to repeatedly check the students were recording their evidence – especially with the gifted students, who tended to forget this. An experienced Year 11 Biology teacher explained:

> The clever ones have coasted through past science pracs [i.e. practicals] with an ability to remember their data, or just scribble it down. Now that I have them doing something a little more intellectually appropriate, they struggle to change their ways. But we are getting there. Slowly they record data meaningfully because if they don't they get very frustrated and that's not pretty at all!

The younger students (Year 6) record evidence automatically. This would align with the subtle differences in pedagogies between the primary and high school teachers and perhaps between a mainstream student and a gifted student. The teacher needed to insist the gifted student not rely solely on memory. The primary teachers were more likely to give students control over their project, compared to the high school teachers, who felt the need to continuously guide the students through their projects.

It seems that some high school students expect to be given instructions for everything; they do not think independently to record evidence unless instructed to do so. High school teachers also tended to spend a lot of time with the groups of students who were working well and intellectually engaged. Such groups usually had the gifted student working alongside above-average (but not gifted) peers. When interviewed, one teacher explained 'I found the science of interest as I didn't know the answer... I knew what was happening in other investigations, so they were of less interest beyond safety and facilitating equipment' (Year 9 teacher).

Transition Phase 2

The fourth component of the theoretical model that requires closer examination in terms of the teacher's role and the gifted student is Transition Phase 2. This phase occurs between the evidence-gathering cycle and the sense-making cycle.

The critical aspect of this second transition phase for the gifted student is in the consideration of the data, especially the outliers and the discussion relating to how to include or reject any outliers. The consideration of the outliers and discrepancies in the data is crucial for the students to fully understand the data and to be able to turn this data into evidence in the final phase – the sense-making phase. The occurrence of outliers was a major issue for a pair of gifted Year 11 students. These students attended an elite school for boys and had high aspirations. When their results were significantly different from other groups, they became very defensive: 'We did it as we saw it to be. You must have mixed up your yields or weighed it [DNA] wrong.' When the teacher asked the boys to reconsider their methodology for extracting DNA from a variety of fruits, it was found that the boys had forgotten to tare the weighing scales, and had also not maintained all variables – their initial sample of one fruit was approximately half the mass of what it should have been. Instead of ignoring the erroneous data, or giving the boys access to more reliable data from another group, the teacher modified the task for these students so that their discussion considered the implications of errors in the methodology. In order to appease the students need 'to get it right' the teacher allowed the students to rerun the investigation in their own time. The boys did this, achieved reasonable results and reported on DNA yields and then the importance of care in scientific procedures and possible resultant errors in the methodology. These individuals later went on to win a student science award from the state government for this work.

It was very interesting observing how all the teachers managed the numerical data the students generated. In all cases, the teachers directed the students to share their data where applicable, to find averages and to plot graphs to investigate relationships. The teachers made further suggestions as to how to represent the data to the gifted students. Rather than just plotting the averages, the students were also required to plot their raw data, including all outliers, and to use the resultant scatter and range to assist with making sense of their data:

> It's too much for most kids to get their head around. They have enough trouble plotting averages and making informed comparisons. But the bright kids can take it further and say whether or not two or more averages differ based upon the spread or overlap of the raw data points. We have troubles doing it on an Excel spreadsheet, you know the scatter and a bar graph all in one, so we do it by hand on a computer printout. I'm not interested in the ICT skills, more on the interpretation.
>
> (Year 9 teacher)

The sense-making cycle

There are two critical components to the sense-making cycle: the relating of the evidence back to the question/hypothesis and the communication of the findings to outsiders. Reporting and communication were found to be a challenge for the gifted students. They all had the initiative to deeply research their topics, which resulted in much learning, but also much frustration as they could not condense their findings into the word limit of the task set by the teacher. They also had a deep desire to present findings that were not evidenced-based. The teachers each had to constantly remind the gifted student that for each claim they made they needed to supply at least two pieces of evidence. This is in contrast to the average students who:

> Do what they have to do. Once they have an answer that is it. They stop. It's like they have been trained to get an answer and take it no further. I have to keep prompting them 'Does the answer look realistic? Is it logical?' Totally different from the brighter kids. I have to keep reining them in!!
>
> (Year 11 teacher)

Conclusion

In relation to the research questions, the theoretical model developed from the literature and the observations of lessons and stimulated recall of the lessons by the teacher indicates that questioning by the teacher is critical to all students, but gifted students may actually prefer to initiate their own thinking prior to questioning. It is the ability of the teacher to step back, and allow the gifted student to explore and work with the problem using their own ideas and initiative that will lead to success.

It was possible to develop a theoretical model of enquiry-based teaching pedagogies that represents enquiry teaching in mainstream Australian classrooms. Some aspects of this model are common to mainstream students, but the teacher does need to modify their pedagogies to instruct gifted students in Years 6, 9 and 11. No study was found which investigated the growth of teacher skill and enquiry-based pedagogies relevant to this age span or to the gifted student. Much of the research published describes key aspects of enquiry-based pedagogies in the form of text-based pedagogical frameworks, but this research is not presented diagrammatically in a step-by-step fashion illustrating teacher roles and actions, and the consideration of differentiation for the gifted is not considered. The study described in this chapter, then, contributes significantly to the literature on enquiry-based pedagogies with the gifted student. It attempts to bridge theoretical notions of enquiry, and the practical classroom actions of the teachers from a sample of mainstream Australian schools. In particular, the study highlights the similarities and differences of enquiry-based lesson sequences, with gifted and non-gifted students. Based on my experience in the present study, there is still more work to be done by researchers and teachers to provide a complete and effective pedagogical model depicting enquiry-based pedagogies suitable for all student types.

The study described in the chapter is relevant to the gifted and talented community as it: 1) builds on the research tradition of classroom observation to highlight teacher action; 2) focuses on enquiry-based teaching pedagogies in numerous classrooms – and it contributes to the literature that deals with teacher role, especially in relation to mainstream classes containing both gifted and non-gifted students; and 3) explores enquiry-based teaching which is a global recommendation by science educators for inclusion in science curricula.

References

Asay, L.D., and Orgill, M. (2010). Analysis of essential features of inquiry found in articles published in *The Science Teacher*, 1998–2007. *Journal of Science Teacher Education*, 21, 57–79.

Calderhead, J. (1981). Stimulated recall: a method for research on teaching. *British Journal of Educational Psychology*, 51, 211–17.

Finkel, A., Pentland, P., Hubber, P., Blake, D., and Tytler, R. (2009). STELR: improving science retention rates in Australian secondary schools. *Teaching Science*, 55 (3), 28–33.

Park, S. and Oliver, J.S. (2009). The translation of teachers' understanding of gifted students into instructional strategies for teaching science. *Journal of Science Teacher Education*, 20(4), 333–51.

Pirie, S. (1996). Classroom video-recording: when, why and how does it offer a valuable data source for qualitative research? Paper presented at the Annual Meeting of the North American Chapter of the International Group for Psychology of Mathematics Education, Panama City, Florida. ERIC Reproduction Service No. 401 128.

Poon, C.-L., Lee, Y.-J., Tan, A.L., and Lim, S.S.L. (2012). Knowing inquiry as practice and theory: developing a pedagogical framework with elementary school teachers. *Research in Science Education*, 42 (2), 303–27.

Stigler, J.W., Gallimore, R. and Hiebert, J. (2000). Using video surveys to compare classrooms and teaching across cultures: examples and lessons from the TIMSS video studies. *Educational Psychologist*, 35(2), 87–100.

Wells, G. (2001). Action, talk, and text: learning and teaching through inquiry. Teachers College Press. Available at: http://people.ucsc.edu/~gwells/Files/Papers_Folder/ATT. theory.pdf, accessed June 2015 [article online, based on Chapters 1 and 10 of this book].

Windschitl, M. (2003). Inquiry projects in science teacher education: What can investigative experiences reveal about teacher thinking and eventual classroom practice? *Science Education*, 87 (1), 112–143.

Yuen-Yan C., Hui, D., Dickinson, A.R., Chu, D., Cheng, D.K.-W., Cheung, E., Wing-Hung Ki, Wing-Hong Lau, Wong, J., Lo, E.W.C. and Luk, K.-M. (2010). Engineering Outreach: a successful initiative with gifted students in science and technology in Hong Kong. *IEEE Transactions on Education*. 53(1), 158–71.

Zubrowski, B. (2007). An observational and planning tool for professional development in science education. *Journal of Science Teacher Education*, 18, 861–84.

13 The US Science Olympiad experience

Interplay between competition and cooperation

Lucy Kulbago, Bridget K. Mulvey and Aziz Alamri

Introduction

Early on a Saturday morning, when most adolescents are still sleeping, Science Olympiad students are awake, full of excitement and anticipation as they head to school to take science tests for fun. As students enter the academic competition, they can feel the energy in the air. Students and adults are full of hope and anticipation. Will the last-minute adjustments to the catapult launch the projectile with improved accuracy? Will the new asteroids I added to my study sheet help me score better on the astronomy test? Did I remember my goggles and pH paper? Will I see my friend from the other school today? These students are excited about science – excited to learn about science and test their skills against other students who also love science. They are part of a larger community of like-minded peers, a community where they belong and can display their talents in science, technology, engineering and mathematics (STEM).

In Science Olympiad, students are challenged to study content knowledge to depths that far surpass the standard school science curriculum. Students in general and gifted students in particular need opportunities to develop their talents through solving challenging problems. The added component of peer comparison helps students to gauge their level of understanding and performance relative to others. Academic competitions such as Science Olympiad provide an opportunity for gifted students to obtain new knowledge and apply what they have learned while solving challenging problems and improving their performance at competitions. Science Olympiad, a national academic science competition in the USA, has been offering a competitive environment to gifted science students for over 30 years while also promoting cooperation between team members and fostering friendships between teams.

The interplay between competition and cooperation is fundamental to the Science Olympiad experience and can be viewed through the contexts of interactions between students on the same team and interactions between students on different teams. The students' passion for science can be awakened as they develop STEM talents (Forrester, 2010; McGee-Brown, 2006; Oliver and Venville, 2011; Wirt, 2011). Students also develop social and life skills, which contribute to students pursuing a STEM college major and career (Forrester, 2010; McGee-Brown,

2006; Wirt, 2011). Even students who do not choose a STEM major or career maintain a long-term positive association with STEM disciplines (Forrester, 2010; Wirt, 2011).

Because gifted students represent a large portion of Science Olympiad participants, let us consider what is meant by 'gifted'. When a student is initially identified as 'gifted', it is often linked with future potential. Later, as a student progresses, their performance or production is often compared to that of others who are strong in the same area (Subotnik *et al.*, 2011). Gifted achievement and talent development depend on skills such as exertion of effort and persistence (ibid.). Supporting adults are needed to provide positive feedback and models of the talent to be developed (Bloom and Sosniak, 1981; Ozturck and Debelak, 2008). Gifted students can be motivated by a desire to win, which provides the extra incentive to work hard and, consequently, improve performance (Bloom and Sosniak, 1981; Franken and Brown, 1995; Ozturck and Debelak, 2008; Tassi and Schneider, 1997). Talents can be developed through competitive extracurricular activities that provide an opportunity to compare oneself with others of similar ability (Bicknell, 2008; Bloom and Sosniak, 1981; Tassi and Schneider, 1997; Udvari, 2000). Working together on a team and competing in academic competitions in successive years further supports talent development (Bicknell, 2008).

What is Science Olympiad?

Science Olympiad is an extracurricular academic science competition for students in grades kindergarten (K) through secondary school (K–12) including ages five to 18 in countries around the world. There are even multiple-country International Science Olympiad competitions focused on a specific academic discipline. While the USA competes in these international competitions, they are only for a small group of elite students. Many more US students from all 50 states compete in local, regional, state and national competitions.

The present investigation focuses on the US experience in grades six to 12 (i.e. ages 11–18). At the middle school and high school levels, teams consist of up to 15 students who compete in 23 varied events. These events cover many science disciplines including: life sciences; physical science and chemistry; earth and space science; technology and engineering; and enquiry and nature of science. These events incorporate content knowledge, scientific process, engineering design and/or application. For some events, students need to answer content knowledge-based questions and apply this knowledge to process-based questions. For example, the anatomy event requires body systems knowledge that is used to answer questions identifying parts of a diagram. Other events, such as the experimental design event, are entirely performance-based events. Given a problem statement, students design and conduct an experiment to address the problem and then communicate the results. Engineering events involve students building, testing and refining an apparatus prior to competition that then is tested in the competition. An example is bridge building, where the goal is to maximize the efficiency ratio of weight held to weight of the bridge.

Mathematics and technology integration have been part of US national science standards through time (e.g. National Research Council, 1996), and the most recent US national science standards add a substantial emphasis on engineering and science practices (NGSS Lead States, 2013). These emphases are not yet present in most formal K–12 science courses (Kimmel *et al.*, 2006), yet they are prevalent in Science Olympiad events. All events are aligned with and extend beyond national and state science standards, challenging students to gain understanding and abilities beyond what is required at their given grade level. This can include college-level content and/or topics such as entomology and epidemiology.

Each Science Olympiad team may take up to 15 members to any competition. Team members commonly work with different partners to compete in each of the 23 events. Middle school teams range from grades 6–9 (i.e. ages 11–15) and high school teams range from grades 9–12 (i.e. ages 14–18). Each student usually participates in three or four different events, and commonly pairs with a different student for each event. The partners act together to address event questions or problems; together they can earn ribbons or medals for finishing near the top. Each event performance contributes to an overall team score. Then teams are ranked by their cumulative event scores. Each team is managed by a head coach, who is supported by several additional coaches. Middle school teams are generally supported by many adult coaches who may be science teachers, parents of participating students, past team members, or other community members. These coaches usually work with students on a specific event and help the students learn content as well as study and test-taking strategies. High school teams are generally managed by a few coaches while the students are responsible for learning the content and preparing for the competitions.

The competition-level structure begins with local competitions, organized by local schools and open to any area team. This level is informal, not impacting advancement to the state or national competitions. Each school is assigned to a region, and any team in that region can compete in the regional competition. This is usually held at a local college and run by a regional director not directly affiliated with a team. Each school can take up to two teams. The top-scoring teams at a regional competition advance to the state competition. Only one team per school can advance. The top one or two teams from the state then advance to the US national competition.

Interplay between competition and cooperation

The structure of Science Olympiad depends upon cooperation between team members while competing against other teams. This interplay between cooperation and competition is the framework that supports advanced learning and talent development of gifted learners. Competitive extracurricular activities that showcase a student's talent and provide recognition for their achievements also provide them with a chance to compare their ability level with others of similar ability and to strengthen cooperative learning through teamwork (Bloom and Sosniak, 1981; Udvari, 2000). The combination of and interplay between cooperation and competition are thought to provide a positive experience for the students.

The theory of social interdependence (Johnson and Johnson, 1989) combines within-group cooperation with between-group competition to promote positive student interdependence and a positive experience compared to cooperation or competition alone. Characteristics needed for positive interdependence for cooperation within a group include: personal responsibility to achieve group goals; communication and exchange of resources; intrinsic and extrinsic achievement-based motivation. Between groups, the supportive characteristics include: a belief that there is a chance of winning; event pairs are ranked in comparison to pairs from other teams; and elements of good sportsmanship and fair play are evident (ibid.). Social interdependence is infused throughout students' Science Olympiad experiences, and the theory informed data collection and analysis for the present investigation.

Research

This is an exploratory qualitative investigation to learn about the perceptions of middle school and high school students and supporting adults about the perceived outcomes of participation in the US Science Olympiad programme. The experiences of student participants and supporting adults may help us to better understand the strengths of this programme and the perceived short- and long-term outcomes for students. Based on the emergent themes in this and previous studies, we developed a conceptual model of the US Science Olympiad experience and its outcomes.

The first author had eight years of experience as a middle school Science Olympiad coach and parent prior to this investigation. This personal experience motivated her to explore Science Olympiad from a research perspective. At two northeast Ohio invitational competitions, the first author sought out participants with a range of roles, ages and years of experience in the programme from multiple attending schools. Adult participants were included to provide another perspective on student outcomes. The resulting 26 participants included nine middle school students and six high school students (all self-identified as gifted), two non-coaching parents, four coaches who were also parents, three coaches who were also science teachers and two administrators. Parents of participating students may serve as an event coach or support the team in a non-coaching capacity such as driving students to practices and competitions. Administrators also may support the team and coaches in a number of ways such as through the allocation of funds, space and transportation allocation.

The first author took informal observational notes of student-to-student and student-to-coach interactions during competitions and conducted one approximately 20-minute flexible and responsive semi-structured interview per participant. The observations informed interview questions. At least two researchers independently coded the interview transcripts and observation notes. All researchers discussed initial codes to develop themes, which were then checked against the full data set. Themes were refined and differences were resolved through discussion. These themes then were compared to those of previous studies (Forrester, 2010; McGee-Brown, 2006; Wirt, 2011) to identify commonalities. Finally, we organized these themes in a conceptual model to illustrate the experiences and perceived outcomes of Science Olympiad participation.

Results

We identified the following themes associated with Science Olympiad student participation: cooperation, competition, learning, talent development, social and life skills development and STEM pathways. The competitive aspect of Science Olympiad involves students comparing themselves against students that have prepared for the same event using the same rules and guidelines. These students are then ranked based on their performance, culminating in the highest-performing students being awarded medals and ribbons for their achievements. The cooperative aspect involves students working with partners when preparing and studying for their events, with their individual event performance contributing to the overall team score. Learning new science content and scientific practices is fundamental to the experience, and students speak of an awakening passion for learning science. Science Olympiad provides an outlet for this developing passion that does not limit their thirst for depth of knowledge and challenging problems. These challenges develop students' talents for problem-solving, device design and science content knowledge application. Development of skills associated with scientific practices in a talent domain promotes gifted students' talent development (Udvari, 2000). Social and life skills development includes communication, organization and time management, which are components of twenty-first-century skills essential for all students (McComas, 2014). Overall, through competition and cooperation, Science Olympiad participation provides students with opportunities to deepen science content understanding and develop problem-solving and engineering talents. Students also develop social and life skills that will help them work with others in any context. These experiences can lead students towards a STEM pathway and future STEM career.

Competition and cooperation within team

When a team has more than the maximum number of students allowed to compete at a competition, or more than 15 students, coaches noted that an element of competition within the team can develop, since each team can only send one set of partners into any one event. A coach stated, 'It does upset me sometimes when I see the competition among our own team… I want to stress the importance of sharing your information with other people. I really discourage them from becoming competitive with each other.' This coach counteracted some of the inherent competition within the team by encouraging team cooperation. Students found this competition to motivate them and push them to work harder because they have to earn their place on the team. Even in large teams that can have more internal competition, that competition commonly is situated in a cooperative and supportive team environment.

When students talked about their favourite part of their Science Olympiad experience, they often mentioned having fun with friends and being on a team. The cooperative aspect of working with a partner during an event also often made students more comfortable than competing alone in an event. High school students were more likely to emphasize the role of accountability to the team as a motivation for fulfilling their responsibilities. A female high school student explained, 'I kind of feel I have to keep my part of the bargain up.' Both middle and high school students liked being part of a team and building friendships and memories while learning science.

Competition and cooperation between teams

Students described how they strived to do well in their events. They hoped to be recognized by earning ribbons and medals and/or praise from coaches and parents for their hard work. Competition allowed students to compare their ability with their peers who had been working on the same event, important for gifted learners. A male high school student commented:

> I think the biggest thing is being able to put myself against all of these other students who try just as hard as I do. And I try to show that I can do something at a higher level. It's very rewarding for me when I do well.

Comparison with their own previous performances also motivated students to work harder for the next competition, as seen in this male middle school student's comment: '[Competition] is more about trying to improve yourself and your score.'

During competitions, students and coaches from different teams form friendships that sometimes last for years, and teams can genuinely admire another team's accomplishments. When asked what was motivating about the competitions, a male middle school student remarked, 'The desire to be the best at what I do and the spirit of friendship between teams is more important than anything else I have participated in.' He valued fostering friendships with students from other teams, something largely missing from his experiences in other extracurricular activities. Teams cooperated with each other too during competitions. For example, a team offered supplies and advice to another team. Coaches often communicated between competitions to share ideas and resources. Coaches supported and cooperated with one another to create a positive student experience.

The interplay of competition and cooperation within and between teams provided students with individual outcomes that overlap and influence the other themes. These individual outcomes are categorized as learning, talent development, social and life skills development and STEM career pipeline, described in detail below.

Learning

Students and coaches alike talked about how they loved to learn about science and saw Science Olympiad as an ideal enrichment opportunity for all learners, but especially gifted learners. Events often covered science content above and beyond that commonly covered in school science, and many students welcomed this opportunity. In response to a question about what motivated him to prepare for events, a male middle school student replied, 'My love of knowledge and learning. I really find it interesting, all of the information and reading.' Similarly, a male high school student explained:

> Just a couple days ago I had some of my senior friends who are in [Advanced Placement*] physics who were talking about what they were learning in electrostatics and magnetism. And it was funny because I am not at that level in school, but I knew exactly what they were talking about. I was even giving them a little bit of aid with some things, and it was really kind of surprising to them because there is no reason why I would have learned that stuff within school. But with Science Olympiad, I have pushed up the levels of education that I am more interested in. (*Advanced Placement courses in the US provide high school students with the potential to earn college course credit if they score well enough on the Advanced Placement Exam for that subject.)

This student recognized that what he learned in Science Olympiad was beyond his current grade level science. This supported a growing pride in his unexpectedly advanced content understanding.

Many students were excited to explore engineering and design techniques, scrutinizing their design to improve their performance after each competition. In one competition, middle school students' mousetrap vehicle overshot the target. Students started to consider reasons for missing the target. For the next competition, they prepared the vehicle more carefully, knowing how many times to wind the wheels to achieve the targeted distance. The students improved their performance, and this personal victory fuelled them to push themselves further and make additional improvements for future competitions. Students applied their book learning to real situations. Some students described how their excitement energized those around them during team practice and competitions, making students look forward to spending weekends taking science tests.

Talent development

As students learned and applied science content and practices, they developed STEM talents. Gifted learners commonly looked for ways to compare their talent to their peers in meaningful ways. When students study for a Science Olympiad competition, they know that other students have also prepared for their events, and this provided gifted learners a way to compare their talent and efforts to their peers. A high school male student remarked that the best part of the competitions is the awards: 'You want to see how other schools did; you want to see how you stand.' This comparison with other teams supported students' self-assessment of their talents. When a coach was asked to identify the benefits to students in a competitive situation, he remarked, 'They can measure themselves with other students, and I think there are real benefits in that. Competitions within different layers of Science Olympiad can draw out their interests.'

The level of content knowledge is often much more advanced than what students learn in school science. A middle school teacher and head coach reflected,

> They're just a group of kids who like to learn. It's not necessarily something they are doing in their curriculum.... This is not junior high material that we're dealing with. This is high school material. This is very difficult stuff. So we really see what these kids are made of.

Science Olympiad is seen as providing students with an opportunity to push their limits, going beyond what is expected of them in school, thereby encouraging students' talent development.

Science professionals sometimes acted as coaches or as event supervisors during competitions, influencing students' understanding of what scientists do in different fields. Students also liked the personalized attention from their coaches during event preparation. This attention focused on individual student needs rather than the standard needs of the class. All of these aspects combined to provide students with opportunities to develop their talents in science and engineering and awaken a passion to continue such studies in college.

Social and life skills development

While talent development largely involved peer comparison, social and life skills development largely involved students' social interactions within and between teams. Students developed social skills through working with a partner or in groups. Membership in the team promoted life skills such as organization, time management and responsibility. One parent stated that Science Olympiad participation 'is more than simply learning a subject; it is learning the personal responsibility, studying on your own, dealing with other students and teammates… They have to have good sportsmanship, be honest and willing to help other teams.' Students also recognized the importance of sportsmanship as a way to communicate respect for others. Adult participants noted an increase in student self-confidence in their social and life skills, as well as performance abilities. Some events required students to verbally explain how their device worked or to verbally communicate with the event judges, strengthening their verbal communication skills with peers and adults. Students learned how to deal with disappointments and turn them into self-improvement opportunities. When students did not perform as well as they would have liked, they commonly looked for ways to improve for the next competition. Strengthened social and life skills can prepare students for future STEM interests and careers.

STEM pathways

Many students joined Science Olympiad because of their STEM interests. However, some students identified Science Olympiad participation as awakening a passion for science. One female high school students remarked:

> I would never have realized how much I love [biology]; I would never have realized how much of a passion it was for me. Like it was a way of relating to the world. I don't think I could see the world the same way if I didn't have [Science Olympiad].

Through Science Olympiad, students explored various science and engineering disciplines beyond traditional school science including anatomy, genetics, remote sensing, robotics, epidemiology and engineering. A female high school student explained that 'because of Science Olympiad, now I know I will go into engineering... I started building things and became better and better... I'm in all building events... so it probably picked my career path for me.' Awakening a passion for science steered this female high school student towards a STEM career as well:

> I was actually thinking about becoming a ballet dancer. And this is something I enjoy doing, but definitely since I've been in Science Olympiad, I've realized how fun and engaging science can be. And that's really inspired me. I want to become a chemical engineer now and possibly go to medical school and be a doctor.

A veteran coach reflected on the STEM career pathways taken by his previous students:

> I have a former student that just finished up his degree at Johns Hopkins... getting ready for medical school. Another student went to medical school and is now working at the Museum of Natural History. One of my first students works at the University of California Berkeley. He's an astronomer. I have a couple of NASA engineers and some go to MIT. It is a big [source of] pride.

Science Olympiad participation broadened students' exposure to STEM fields beyond the scope of most middle and high school science. The programme encouraged students to become more serious about STEM at early ages, and even changed some students' ideas of their future careers.

For each of the above themes, student and supporting adult participants emphasized different aspects of the Science Olympiad experience. All students enjoyed earning medals and ribbons for their performance. Middle school students mostly reflected on the fun they had with friends both within and between teams. They enjoyed the challenge of events, being part of a team and competing with a partner during competitions. High school students mentioned exploring science and engineering disciplines with a look to future college major and career paths. These students also talked more about talent development and peer comparison benefits. Adults often reflected on students' development over many years, seeing growth that would impact students' long-term future, including talent development, social skills development, and life skills development.

By combining the perspectives of both students and supporting adults associated with the present investigation with other Science Olympiad research findings (Forrester, 2010; McGee-Brown, 2006; Wirt, 2011), we developed a conceptual model of students' Science Olympiad experience and outcomes (Figure 13.1). Inside the Science Olympiad box is the interplay between competition and cooperation, fundamental to the Science Olympiad experience. This interplay is revealed through the interactions between students on the same team and interactions between students on different teams. The team acts as a support system, encouraging students to challenge their limits. This structure also serves to motivate students, as they are responsible to the team. Further motivation stems from the competition within and between teams. Yet there also can be an element of cooperation between teams. At times, teams share resources at a competition to be sure students can compete. In general, competitions have an air of promoting a positive experience for all students.

The elements of competition and cooperation overlap and influence each other. They promote the perceived outcomes shown in the outside square. The perceived outcomes of learning, talent development, social and life skills development and STEM pathways can support and promote one another. They also can further motivate students to compete and cooperate within and between teams. In fact, the Science Olympiad model components both influence and are influenced by each other.

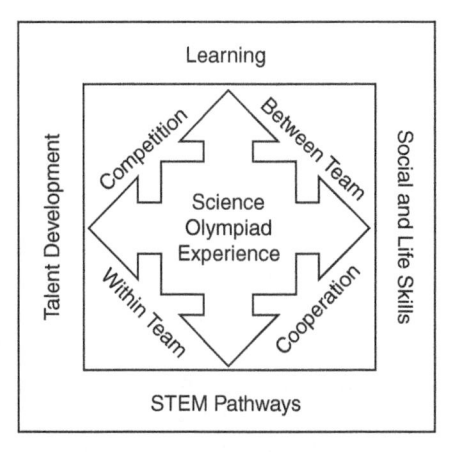

Figure 13.1 Conceptual model of the US Science Olympiad experience and its outcomes

Although initial student motivation to study and prepare for their events can be strongly linked to competition, the outcomes of improving and/or finishing ahead of others continue to fuel motivation to do better. This promotes the development of students' talents. It is also more than that. Students spend time with others who also like science. Working with others, enjoying down time, and making friends builds community, builds motivation to continue and, further, builds interest for science. Students have the opportunity to learn about disciplines new to them. Often they uncover an interest, and Science Olympiad strengthens their experience with and connections to that discipline. In particular, students can develop engineering skills through the design and testing process of their devices. The recent US national science standards (NGSS Lead States, 2013) promote this development of engineering skills. Science Olympiad provides a pathway unavailable in most formal K–12 schooling. Although many Science Olympiad students may study a STEM discipline in college regardless of the programme, Science Olympiad helps many to be more certain of their future plans at an earlier age. Others only discover their interest in STEM and STEM careers through the programme.

Along with content knowledge improvements, students realize that social and life skills are necessary to do well in competitions. The interactions within and between teams provide a framework for students to improve their social and life skills. Communication skills are needed for effective interactions with their coaches, partners and event judges. Good sportsmanship is encouraged within a team through support of teammates as well as between teams during awards presentation. Time management and organization are essential for students to be prepared and have the necessary supplies for competitions. This complex interplay helps to awaken a passion and develops students' STEM talents.

Recommendations

The Science Olympiad programme meets the recommendations for the talent development of gifted students. It can provide another layer of opportunity for gifted students beyond those commonly available in traditional K–12 school environments. The programme harnesses the power of combining competition and cooperation to challenge yet support students. This chapter has reported on the characteristics of the US Science Olympiad programme. Given the potential value of this programme to gifted learners, we would recommend that science educators in countries that do not presently have a similar Science Olympiad programme consider the potential of implementing a similar programme.

The research presented here has implications for student and adult recruitment efforts. As Science Olympiad is a voluntary programme, schools that wish to participate need to recruit both coaches and students. When recruiting adults as coaches, it would be important to highlight the long-term benefits of students' skills development. With students, descriptions of more immediate and short-term experiences and outcomes could entice participation.

We recommend that coaches focus on the teamwork and social aspects of the programme when talking to potential student participants. In addition, high school coaches could persuade students by highlighting exposure to STEM disciplines and problem-solving not included in the school science curriculum. The potential to compare themselves with others within and outside of their school also may encourage high school student participation.

In the words of one Science Olympiad student, 'If this took the place of my fourth period science class, I would love science.' Science Olympiad has the potential to ignite a STEM spark and keep it burning.

References

Bicknell, B. (2008). Gifted students and the role of mathematics competitions. *Australian Primary Mathematics Classroom*, 13(4), 16–20.

Bloom, B., and Sosniak, L. (1981). Talent development vs schooling. *Educational Leadership*, November, 86–94.

Franken, R., and Brown, D. (1995). Why do people like competition? The motivation for winning, putting forth effort, improving one's performance, performing well, being instrumental, and expressing forceful/aggressive behavior. *Personality and Individual Differences*, 19, 175–84.

Forrester, J.H. (2010). Competitive science events: gender, interest, science self-efficacy, and academic major choice. Doctoral dissertation. Retrieved from http://repository. lib.ncsu.edu/ir/bitstream/1840.16/6073/1/etd.pdf

Johnson, D., and Johnson, R. (1989). *Cooperation and Competition: Theory and research*. Edina, MN: Interaction.

Kimmel, H., Carpinelli, J., Burr-Alexander, L., and Rockland, R. (2006). Bringing engineering into K–12 schools: a problem looking for solutions? In Proceedings of the 2006 ASEE Annual Conference, June.

McComas, W.F. (2014). 21st-century skills. In W.F. McComas (Ed.), *The Language of Science Education*. Rotterdam: Sense, p. 1.

McGee-Brown, M. (2006). *Science Olympiad: The role of competition in collaborative science inquiry*. Retrieved from http://www.soinc.org/sites/default/files/uploaded_files/NSFcompres.pdf

National Research Council. (1996). *National Science Education Standards*. Washington, DC: National Academy Press.

NGSS Lead States, Inc. (2013). *Next Generation Science Standards*. Retrieved from http://www.nextgenscience.org/msets1-engineering-design

Oliver, M., and Venville, G. (2011). An exploratory case study of Olympiad students' attitudes toward and passion for science. *International Journal of Science Education*, 33(16), 2295–322.

Ozturk, M. and Debelak, C. (2008). Affective benefits from academic competitions for middle school gifted students. *Gifted Child Today*, 31(2), 48–53.

Subotnik, R.F., Olszewski-Kubilius, P., and Worrell, F.C. (2011). Rethinking giftedness and gifted education: a proposed direction forward based on psychological science. *Psychological Science in the Public Interest*, 12(1), 3–54.

Tassi, F., and Schneider, B. (1997). Task-oriented versus other-referenced competition: differential implications for children's peer relations. *Journal of Applied Social Psychology*, 27, 1557–80.

Udvari, S. (2000). Competition and the adjustment of gifted children: a matter of motivation. *Roeper Review*, 22(4), 212–17.

Wirt, J.L. (2011). An analysis of Science Olympiad participants' perceptions regarding their experience with the science and engineering academic competition. Doctoral dissertation. Retrieved from http://scholarship.shu.edu/cgi/viewcontent.cgi?article=1014&context=dissertations

14 The experiences of Scholarship students

Perceptions of New Zealand physical science Scholarship holders

Jenny Horsley and Azra Moeed

Motivation to learn, and learning, are partners for academic achievement and educational success. Success in learning leads to motivation for further learning and future success. High-achieving learners set challenging goals and work with determination to achieve them. When these high-achieving students experience success, their success communicates to them that they have the requisite capabilities for learning; they become intrinsically motivated (Meece, 1991; Pintrich and Schunk, 2002). Motivation strongly influences learning for deeper understanding, often leading to academic interest in a subject and educational success (Entwhistle, 2005; Moeed, 2015). A balance between ability and level of challenge is considered crucial for intrinsic motivation for high-achieving students (Scager *et al.*, 2014). Evidence suggests that student engagement is dependent upon a number of factors including: challenge offered by the task; work at a more advanced level; the nature and context of content; relevance and meaningfulness; and choice (Sak and Eristi, 2012).

This chapter focuses on gifted and talented New Zealand secondary school science students' views about their motivation to take Scholarship examinations in one or more science disciplines. The New Zealand Qualifications Authority (NZQA) Scholarship examinations are optional and prestigious. If students are successful in these examinations they gain financial reward. These students are most often in Year 13 – their final year of school – but, as this study found, some students are sitting and succeeding in Scholarship exams while in Year 11 or 12. The chapter draws upon two research projects: first, an investigation of the motivational factors, personal qualities and support that participating science students identify as contributors to their success in Scholarship examinations; the second, a longitudinal case study of a gifted student who was accelerated through secondary school between Years 9 and 13. He gained ten Scholarships, including two in mathematics, four in science and four in English and social sciences during his schooling.

Research suggests there is a relationship between attribution for academic success and motivation (McClure *et al.*, 2011). The presented study considered motivational attributions including: ability, effort, persistence, interest and enthusiasm and luck. Weiner (2010) classifies motivational attributions based on three dimensions: locus (personal, internal or external), controllability and stability. For example, ability is internal, uncontrollable and stable, whereas luck is external, uncontrollable and unstable. Effort, interest and persistence can be considered internal, and are controllable by the individual. Applying Weiner's theory to interest and enthusiasm for a subject or task suggests these attributions can be considered as either internal or external and controllable or uncontrollable.

In New Zealand, giftedness is a contextual concept reflected in a range of approaches to meeting the needs of gifted and talented students (Ministry of Education, 2002). Furthermore, stakeholders (parents, teachers, students and school boards of trustees) do not share a common way of defining or identifying gifted and talented students. Consequently, definitions and criteria include a wide range of abilities comprising intellectual ability and academic aptitude, cultural abilities, creative abilities and a range of other abilities pertaining to support, leadership and the arts (Ministry of Education, 2009). Scholars differentiate between giftedness and talents and argue that giftedness relates to natural abilities whereas talents demonstrate systematically developed skills (Gagné, 2005; Horsley, 2010). The qualitative research reported here investigated students' perceptions about the success in Scholarship Science and classroom practices that had a positive impact on this success. Gaining NZQA Scholarship produces an outcome that is evidence of students demonstrating high academic ability.

Acceleration and enrichment programmes for gifted and talented students

Two kinds of programmes are offered to the gifted and talented students in school systems: acceleration and enrichment (Ministry of Education, 2009; Taber, 2007). These students' educational outcomes can be enhanced by placement in acceleration programmes and provision of educational opportunities such as advanced and enrichment programmes (McClarty, 2015). There is considerable research that supports gifted and talented students' acceleration through schooling (Colangelo *et al.*, 2004; Wardman and Hattie, 2012). This acceleration comes in varied forms, including being promoted to complete secondary education in less time than most other students. Acceleration can be in a single subject or across all subjects. Evidence suggests that many New Zealand high schools claim to have 'acceleration' programmes; however, students rarely go to university after only four years at high school and most stay on and take extra subjects even though they may fulfil the requirements for university entrance by the end of Year 12.

A synthesis of over 800 meta-analyses, including 50,000 investigations relating acceleration to academic achievement, is reported to have an effect size of .88, the highest contribution to student achievement where 135 factors were considered (Hattie, 2009). Recently, McClarty (2015) has found that students who were accelerated through their schooling outperformed those in non-accelerated programmes, and that gifted learners benefit most when 'acceleration is coupled with advanced study' (p. 3). There are positive social and emotional outcomes for students who are accelerated (Gross, 2006). No significant negative impact of acceleration was found on students' social and emotional development (McClarty, 2015; Steenburgen-Hu and Moon, 2011). Conversely, boredom and loneliness appear to be common feelings among gifted and talented students who have not been accelerated (Gross, 2006; Wardman and Hattie, 2012). Although previous research indicated that teachers were not in favour of acceleration, recent research suggests that more teachers are in favour of full-year acceleration (Wardman, 2009; Wardman and Hattie, 2012).

Acceleration has a more positive influence on science, technology, engineering, mathematics (STEM) career outcomes for male students (Park *et al.*, 2013), whereas gifted females also benefited from acceleration but tended to take up careers in medicine or law rather than STEM (McClarty, 2015). Acceleration appears to be used in some secondary schools to address the needs of gifted and talented students in New Zealand (Horsley, 2009).

Enrichment programmes have a broader base and are underpinned by the belief that able students need wider experiences, whereas acceleration programmes extend the students beyond their chronological age cohorts. Programmes for gifted and talented students are seldom personalized to specific student abilities and talents (Education Review Office, 2008). Kaul *et al.* (2015) researched the effects of participation in a summer enrichment programme for three or more years on gifted students from low socio-economic backgrounds and found a positive effect on social, emotional and motivational outcomes and better academic achievement and career prospects. However, in Hattie's (2009) meta-analysis, enrichment was 68th out of 135 factors with an effect size of .39, which is considerably lower than for acceleration. Overall, research on gifted and talented students is somewhat limited in New Zealand (Riley *et al.*, 2004).

Although New Zealand schools are expected to address the needs of gifted and talented students, only 19 per cent of primary and 13 per cent of secondary schools, approximately, have provision for these students (Education Review Office, 2008). Students in this study provided evidence of one aspect of giftedness and talent – that of high academic ability, demonstrated through gaining at least one NZQA Scholarship in Science – which placed them within the top 3 per cent of students in the country. Most students would take this examination in their final year (Year 13) but the system allows for gifted students to be accelerated and to take Scholarship exams earlier than Year 13. Some students participating in this study were in Years 11 and 12. The participants were 56 male and 60 female students who gained one or more NZQA Scholarship in Physics, Chemistry, Biology, or Earth and Space Sciences.

New Zealand secondary schools use a range of approaches to identify and meet the needs of their most able students. For example, in some schools students sit a standardized test upon entry and the results, coupled with data from their primary school, are used to identify students who may be offered acceleration or enrichment programmes (the case study school described later exemplifies this). However, this is not a common practice in either primary or secondary schools.

In 2005, the Scholarship Reference Group advised the New Zealand government to establish redesigned NZQA Scholarship Awards. The awards were considered to have a motivational purpose for students to strive for excellence. The target group was approximately 3 per cent of students studying at Level 3 National Certificate of Educational Achievement (NCEA). This proportion was consistent with the level many consider to be 'gifted and talented' learners (Horsley, 2010). In 2014, from a cohort of 8,237 students studying Chemistry, 2.87 per cent (n = 236) attained Scholarship (New Zealand Qualifications Authority, 2015).

Students' views about Scholarship success

Two sources of data are reported here. The first was from an online questionnaire completed by students who were successful in gaining Scholarship in one or more science subject. Students (n = 116) responded by selecting one of four options to identify the perceived influence of each motivational factor. The options were:

- 1 = no influence at all
- 2 = this had a little influence on my successful results
- 3 = this had some influence on my successful results
- 4 = this was a big factor in my successful results.

Students provided written responses to explain their answers to each question. The second source was a case study of one successful Scholarship student who received both enrichment and acceleration in science subjects, and the perspective of the teacher who mentored this student. First, the perceptions of the students completing the questionnaire are presented, then the case study provides an example of school practices that support high academic achievement in science.

Science students' perceptions

Students participating in the online questionnaire attributed their success in Scholarship to ability, effort, persistence, interest and enthusiasm, luck and people who influenced them. Students were asked to consider each of these and any additional factors that influenced their successful Scholarship results. The following graphs show student responses along with illuminating quotes.

Ability: Over 80 per cent students (n = 116) attributed their success to innate ability in the subject and had a strong belief that it was their ability that led to Scholarship success (see Figure 14.1).
  For example, one student said:

> my ability, the nature of the Scholarship exam was that for the largest part it was not things you could study specifically for but rather had to understand what was going on in order to apply it to the situation provided. This is especially true in chemistry and physics, whereas stats could be by and large prepared for, although even history required a broad understanding of people.

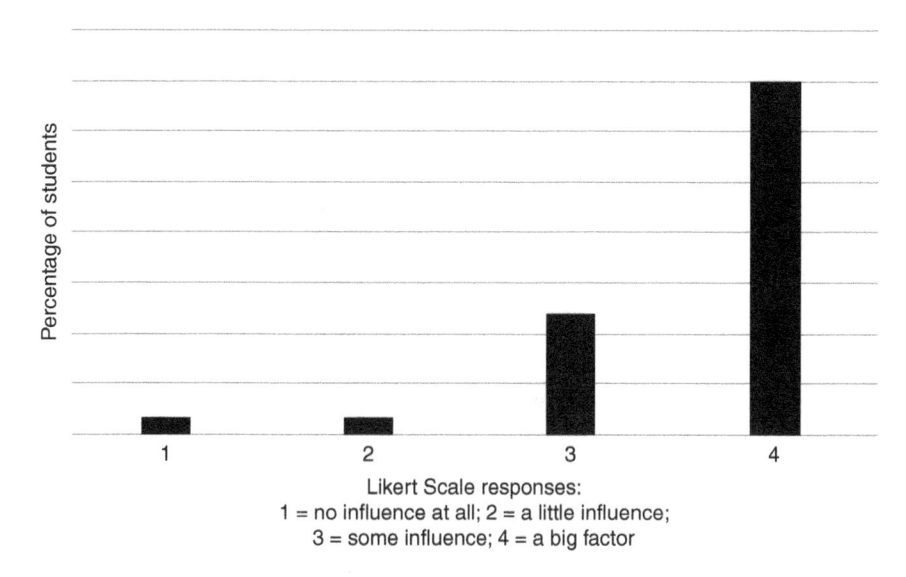

Figure 14.1 My ability in the subject influences my success

Three other students offered their thoughts:

> My ability, because if I didn't get decent marks in the subjects in the years prior to the Scholarship exams I wouldn't have attempted them in the first place.
>
> The skills required to answer the questions came naturally and I found it easy to grasp the concepts.
>
> Ability (duh)… If I can't do well in a subject, there's no point in trying to attain Scholarship, thus I only sat Scholarship for the subjects I did well in throughout the year.

Interestingly, ability has internal locus, is stable and is considered to be uncontrollable. These students were not giving credit to the effort they may well have put into preparation.

Interest: A large number of participants considered interest in the subject as a strong influence on their success (107, n = 116). They provided reasons for their interest in the subject as, for example:

> It was my interest in the subject that really helped me to feel motivated to study… If I wasn't interested and enthusiastic about the subject, the other factors would not matter because I would not be interested enough to make the effort to get the Scholarship or attempt it at all.

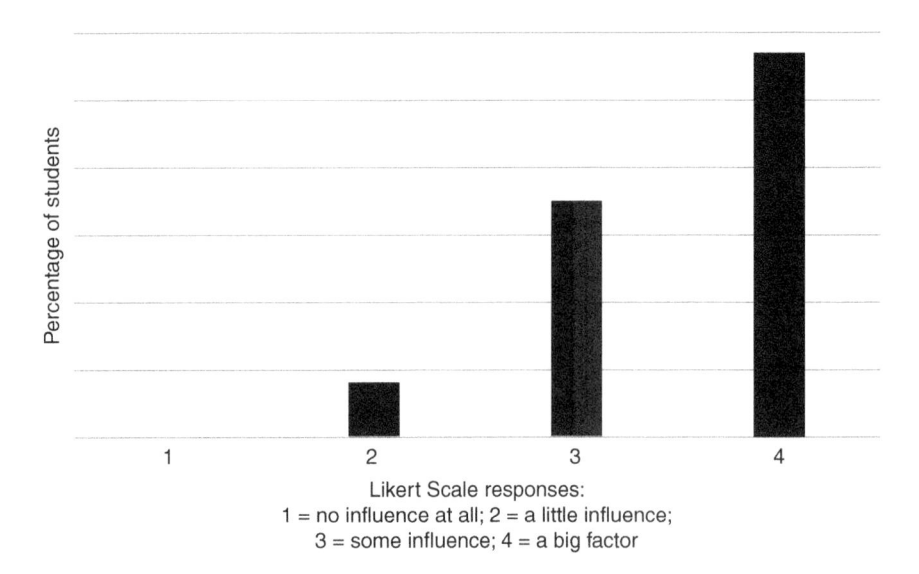

Figure 14.2 My interest and enthusiasm for the subject influenced my success

> Being interested in a subject means I was intrinsically motivated to do well. This made it easier to look beyond the limited NCEA curriculum into the deeper underlying concepts of what I had learned in class.

Effort: Over half the participants (63, n = 116) attributed the effort that they put into preparation to success in Scholarship (see Figure 14.2).

Interestingly, students who believed that effort was influential in their success talked about the effort put in over a longer period of preparation time (see Figure 14.3).

For example, one student said:

> it would be the cumulative effort of all my years of high school that built up the skill required to undertake the Scholarship exams successfully. It wasn't necessarily the amount of effort I put into the Scholarship exams themselves, as I left preparation for those till rather late in the year, and focused more on my Cambridge exams.

Perhaps this student was prioritizing their Cambridge examinations; however, they did not think that the preparation for those examinations would have helped with Scholarship. Conversely, this student attributed his success to the preparation he had made for the NCEA examination: 'I put very little effort/ preparation into Scholarship. I believe my successful results were due to a thorough and deep knowledge of the NCEA Level 3 content, which I was able to apply to Scholarship.' And this student's response shows their belief that ability

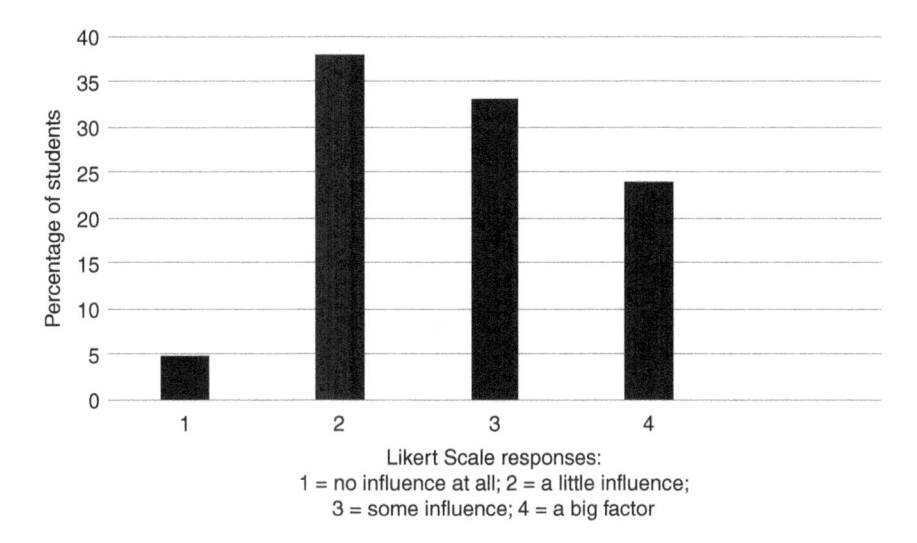

Figure 14.3 The effort I put into studying influenced my success

can be enhanced: 'Effort: I worked very hard all throughout the year to increase my initial ability in the subjects.'

Persistence: Nearly 75 per cent of the students (n = 116) believed that their ability to carry on when faced with challenges was the key to their success (see Figure 14.4). This student attributed his success to persistence and personal

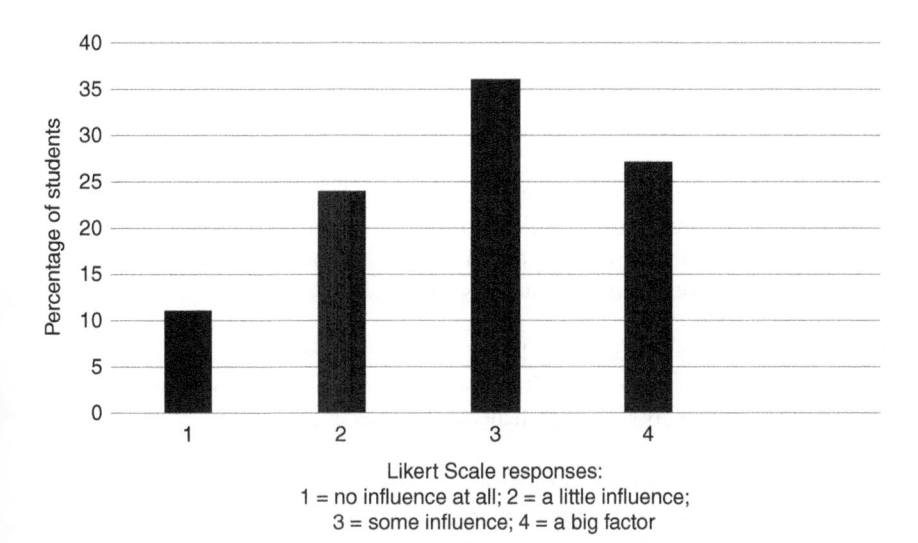

Figure 14.4 My persistence played a part in my success

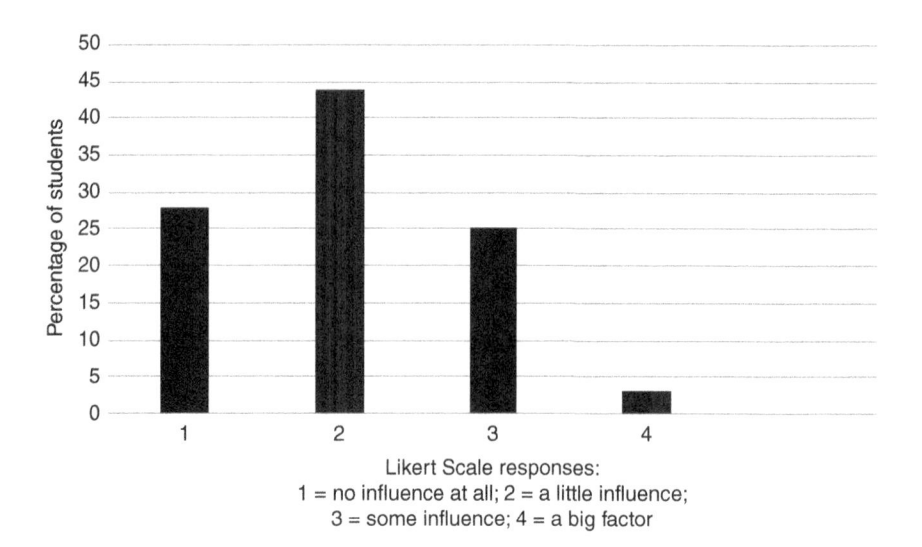

Figure 14.5 Luck played a part in my success

decision-making: 'Persistence... my personal decision that I wanted to succeed in the Scholarship examinations was first and foremost the greatest influencing factor, as all work and study from that decision was my own personal choice.' For another student, it was a combination of factors: 'My persistence, working hard to make the most of my natural ability.'

Luck: Most of the high-achieving students did not attribute their success to luck. Only three students thought that luck was a big factor that influenced their success and 33 (n = 116) thought it had some influence. The remaining 83 (n = 116) did not consider it to be a major influence on their Scholarship results (see Figure 14.5).

Time spent on Scholarship preparation: More than half the participants said that they spent about five hours a week specifically in preparation for the Scholarship examination. About 30 (n = 116) put in between five and ten hours and a minor ity of nine said more than 20 hours (see Figure 14.6).

Influential people: Students believed that their teacher's interest in the subject, enthusiasm for teaching it and support helped them to succeed in Schol- arship. They talked about being challenged, for example:

> My biology teacher was the factor that had the greatest overall influence on my Scholarship results. She was very supportive and pushed me to try my best, and was positive with praise and constructive with criticism in order to help my learning.

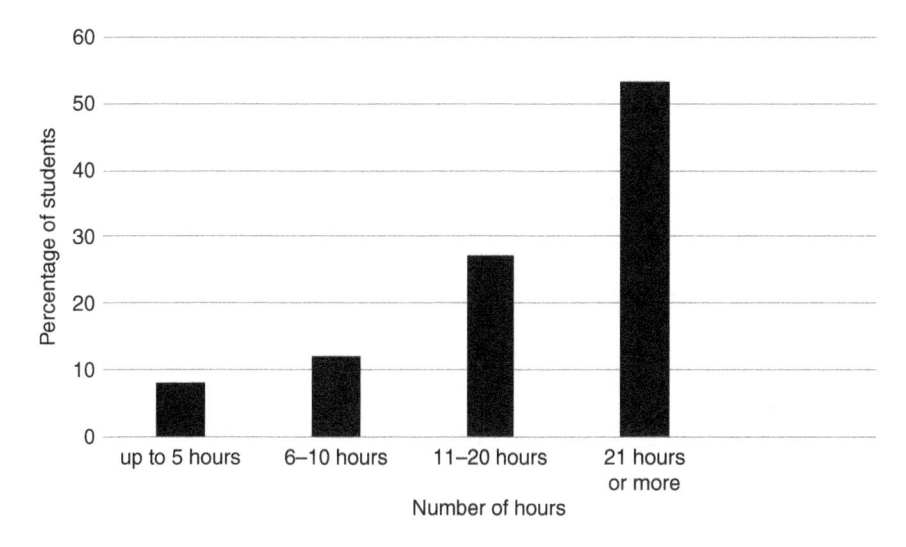

Figure 14.6 Hours per week spent preparing for Scholarship

Teachers were the most important factor in my success because without their extra effort and attention outside of normal class hours for Scholarship I know I would not have done as well as I did.

Some students mentioned the support from family and friends and the school environment that challenged them to try hard and to do their best. One student said that his competitors motivated him to want to do better than them. Others mentioned personal motivation, pride, self-belief and even the associated financial gain:

Pride, I believed I could do it, I told people I could do so, so I made damn sure I would pass.

To be really honest, I think the prize money was the key factor for me (and I think many others will feel the same actually).

The last words go to this student: 'The greatest overall influence is yourself and your own attitude towards the subject. No one else is gonna do it for you.'

It would appear that these highly motivated and confident students are aware of their ability to succeed. Generally, their perceptions of why they were successful align with the findings of McClure *et al.* (2011) who believed in 'Doing my best', rather than 'Doing just enough'; the latter was unlikely to lead to success. A number of students reported being accelerated beyond their peer group. Some were critical of the 'enrichment' offered:

Sometimes I was given research work to do... enriching work that I just did not want to do. One time I got to do researching on oil spills so they got me to do an experiment with a can of oil and a boat. I did not know where to get oil from or how to make a boat or anything. So I just didn't do that.

Teacher expectations were cited as motivational:

It is physics and students who come through are usually doing quite well academically. But the teacher has this idea that all the kids in his class will get excellence every time… he has confidence in us… he uses a lot of excellence type questions because that is what he expects we will get.

One further aspect of these students' preparation for Scholarship relates to their involvement in extracurricular activity. Most students (82 per cent) reported continued involvement in athletic activity throughout their final three years at high school and 58 per cent reported involvement in performance clubs (e.g. choirs) and 71 per cent reported holding part-time jobs. Clearly, aiming to attain NZQA Scholarship was not perceived as a barrier to student participation in additional out-of-class activities.

A case study: Andrew and Sarah's story

The research reported took place over five years. The data were gathered from yearly (audio-recorded) interviews with Andrew and his mentor teacher Sarah (both pseudonyms) at the beginning and at the end of each academic year. The research was approved by the school board and participants gave informed consent which was renewed each year.

Andrew started secondary school in Form 3 (Year 9, age 13) in a large urban coeducational school in a middle to high socio-economic community in New Zealand. He was an only child of educated parents and was placed in the *accelerated learning class* in the school. Andrew had experienced acceleration from a young age, already having passed the national Scholarship examination for mathematics in Year 8, rather than Year 13. He was identified as a gifted student by the school and placed in the accelerated learning programme, and Sarah was appointed his mentor. During his five years at secondary school, he sat the national Scholarship examination for Year 13 (age 17/18) in ten subjects and was awarded Scholarships in all of them. The quotations used here are from the audio-recorded interviews with Sarah and Andrew.

Andrew started his first year very much a loner. He was not included by other students, some of whom had been to the same primary school and did not 'like' him because he was 'brainy' and others because he was well behaved. At the end of the year he had completed Scholarship Mathematics with Calculus and had taken up every opportunity, participating in competitions including a science fair, future problem-solving and science, mathematics and English national competitions. He was proud of his achievements but aware that he did not have

friends. Sarah had taken up the challenge of developing an enrichment programme with the following considerations:

> The Principal has appointed me the teacher director of this new programme.
> I am excited but anxious as well... I would like the programme to enrich the
> learning experiences of these students not just get them to do the work at
> the next level up... my main concern is Andrew, who by all accounts is a
> gifted student who has already got Scholarship in Mathematics with
> Statistics and he is going to be in Form 3! So, even at this early stage I have
> a dilemma, within this enrichment programme I have to include acceleration
> for Andrew. (Sarah)

During the year, Andrew participated in an enrichment programme offered by
the school along with being accelerated in Mathematics with Calculus. He said
that he enjoyed Horticulture 'because he grew cacti for interest'. Sarah was
pleased with his progress during the first year and considered that he was getting
on well with other students. She allowed him to spend the lunch times in the
laboratory and, by the end of the year, he invited a friend to come and play chess
with him. Andrew enjoyed his involvement in the enrichment class, identifying
that he loved Horticulture because:

> It is the forest conservation project, it is so good to grow plants and plant
> them in the forest. You know, we are restoring the forest... it was a dying
> forest with no new seedlings... now we are collecting seeds from there, for
> genetic purity, then growing them and planting them back. The teacher also
> got me to do the school certificate examination for horticulture.

The following year, Sarah reported that Andrew had grown in confidence to
participate in extracurricular school activities. She was impressed that although
he was very capable, he still worked hard:

> He is such a good role model for the others.... Oh, and this year he not only
> played the piano for the musical but also participated in the stage challenge.
> He decided not to sit any Scholarship examinations this year.
>
> (Sarah)

In Year 11, Andrew chose not to sit Scholarship exams but to focus on new
subjects (Accounting and Economics) and achieved the highest marks in School
Certificate Horticulture, competed in a chess championship and worked with
two other students on a science fair project:

> We had to design and make the maze three times because the rats kept getting
> bigger, the judge said it was good that we kept solving problems and completed
> the project. Peter had kept all our notes in the journal. We won first prize.
>
> (Andrew)

For Sarah, the fourth year was mostly about consolidation and refining the programme. Sarah was comfortable in her role and had three different year groups working their way through accelerated learning programmes. She built excellent relationships with students and form teachers of these classes. She organized a full-day professional development programme for the staff teaching the accelerated learning classes. The first group of students in this programme did their Bursary (equivalent to A level) examinations and some, including Andrew, did Scholarship examinations. Andrew had a very busy year and reported:

> I need a holiday! I just wanted to do everything and it was so busy. Space camp in Australia was so much fun and I made lots of friends.... I also did Scholarship exams in Biology and Accounting this year.... Another highlight was Shakespeare Day, we could choose the play we wanted to perform and then we had costumes and even prepared food from that era.... I am going to be a school prefect next year and will also be involved in the peer support programme.
>
> (Andrew)

According to Sarah, in the fifth year, the final year of the research project, she felt as though 'her performance was going to be measured'! The first enrichment group sat their Bursary examinations and ten students, a third of the class, sat Scholarship in one or more subjects: 'Andrew is doing six Scholarship exams this year… let's see how he goes' (Sarah).

Andrew said he found school work challenging, but he liked that. He summed up the highlights of his final year:

> I was elected as the student representative on the school board... good experience as I got to attend the interview for the new Principal... We did a major planting in the forest... our whole class helped with the fourth form camp that was fun. And then there was the college magazine, sometimes it was tricky to get everyone on the committee together but we just got them printed and they look great.

In the final interview, Andrew said that although he had thought about engineering, he had decided to go to university and do his first degree in Mathematics, Science and Accounting. He reflected on his time at school:

> I know I have grown up, but I guess that is expected. I made friends in my accelerated learning class, James, and Tony and Emma are friends I still have... I think being in that class and the teacher being very helpful and encouraging... I have had so many opportunities... all my teachers have been great. The hands-on science summer course helped me make up my mind that engineering is not what I really wanted to do. Before that I was making a career choice based on what I think it was about, then I got to

experience it.... and the environment project... that was great... I think this is a great school, no one said that I could not take subjects I wanted to try... they made it possible for me to pick both Accounting and Economics. I have finished school this year with Physics, Chemistry, Biology and Maths, and I did Horticulture because it was fun.

The final comment he made was:

> The best comment on my school leaving report was... is socially well adjusted, works well with his peers and has given time to the school community... this school has taught me to get on with others and I am grateful.

During his time at the secondary school, Andrew was accelerated through the programme, enabling him to access individual subjects at the next level. Consequently, he completed ten Scholarship subjects in a combination of science and arts options. The survey results demonstrate that students perceived interest, effort and persistence to be important factors in their success, which is consistent with research findings that motivation is critical to academic success (Meece, 1991). Students reported a strong belief that their ability was also crucial to gaining Scholarship. These students did not take a surface approach to learning and said that understanding and being able to apply what they knew helped with Scholarship, which is consistent with a deeper approach to learning (Entwhistle, 2005). As can be expected, most relied on effort, preparation, practice and support, but not luck. When the task did not offer challenge, the students refused to do it, which is consistent with Taber (2015), who argues that a lack of challenge is problematic and may affect the motivation of gifted learners.

The case study highlighted several interesting factors including hard work and being accelerated, which allowed Andrew to gain ten Scholarships. The case for acceleration finds strong support in literature (Gross, 2006; Wardman and Hattie, 2012). It appears that Sarah initially believed that enrichment was better than acceleration. However, she focused on Andrew's need for challenge, which the acceleration offered. Having the choice to take on more or less cognitive challenge by deciding on the number of Scholarships he attempted allowed Andrew emotional security and assisted his social development, which is in congruence with Taber (2015). Interestingly, both the surveyed students and Andrew reported strong involvement in extracurricular activities, suggesting that these students although very gifted academically, were able to experience activities that enabled them to develop their talents, contribute to school life and experience success in other areas.

Finally, all schools and teachers worldwide have a responsibility to ensure that high-achieving students are capable of, one day, contributing to their country. To enable this to happen, these students need to be provided with learning experiences commensurate with a level of challenge that empowers them to perform to their potential.

References

Colangelo, N., Assouline, S., and Gross, M.U.M. (Eds) (2004). *A Nation Deceived: How schools hold back America's students: The Templeton national report on acceleration*, Vols 1, 2. Iowa City: Belin-Blank Center.

Education Review Office (2008). *Schools' Provision for Gifted and Talented Students*. Retrieved from www.ero.govt.nz

Entwistle, N. (2005). *Learning and Studying: Contrasts and influences*. Retrieved 8 September 2005, from http://www.newhorizons.org/future/Creating_the_Future/crfut_entwi9stle.html

Gagné, F. (2005). From gifts to talents: the DMGT as a developmental model. In R.J. Sternberg and J.E. Davidson (Eds), *Conceptions of Giftedness* (2nd edn). New York: Cambridge University Press, pp. 93–112.

Gross, M.U.M. (2006). Exceptionally gifted children: long-term outcomes of academic acceleration and nonacceleration. *Journal for the Education of the Gifted*, 29(4), 404–32.

Hattie, J. (2009). *Visible Learning: A synthesis of meta-analyses relating to achievement*. Oxford: Routledge.

Horsley, J.M. (2009). Out-of-level-achievement. The case for acceleration in New Zealand secondary schools. In M. Sinclair (Ed.), *A Journey of Discovery: Facilitating the initiation and application of schooling research*. Plymouth: Cognition Institute.

Horsley, J. (2010). How high ability students perceived the practice of influential teachers. *New Zealand Annual Review of Education 2009*, 19, 114–29.

Kaul, C.R., Johnsen, S K., Witte, M.M., and Saxon, T.F. (2015). Critical components of a summer enrichment program for urban low-income gifted students. *Gifted Child Today*, 38(1), 32–40.

McClarty, K.L. (2015). Life in the fast lane: effects of early grade acceleration on high school and college outcomes. *Gifted Child Quarterly*, 59(1), 3–13. doi.org/10.1177/0016986214559595

McClure, J., Meyer, L.H., Garisch, J., Fischer, R., Weir, K.F., and Walkey, F.H. (2011). Students' attributions for their best and worst marks: do they relate to achievement? *Contemporary Educational Psychology*, 36(2), 71–81. doi.org/10.1016/j.cedpsych.2010.11.001

Meece, J.L. (1991). The classroom context and students' motivational goals. In M.L. Maehr and P.R. Pintrich (Eds), *Advances in Motivation and Achievement: A research annual: Vol. 7*. Greenwhich, CT: JAI Press.

Ministry of Education (2002). *Initiatives in Gifted and Talented Education*. Wellington: Learning Media.

Ministry of Education (2009). *Gifted and Talented Students: Meeting their needs in New Zealand schools*. Wellington: Learning Media.

Moeed, A. (2015). *Science Investigation: Student views about learning, motivation and assessment*. Singapore: Springer.

New Zealand Qualifications Authority (2015). Overall New Zealand scholarship results. Retrieved from http://www.nzqa.govt.nz/qualifications-standards/awards/new-zealand-scholarship/scholarship-results/overall-scholarship-results-2014/

Park, G., Lubinski, D., and Benbow, C.P. (2013). When less is more: effects of grade skipping on adult STEM productivity among mathematically precocious adolescents. *Journal of Educational Psychology*, 105(1), 176.

Pintrich, P.R., and Schunk, D.H. (2002). *Motivation in Education: Theory, research and applications* (2nd edn). Columbus, OH: Merrill Prentice Hall.

Riley, T., Bevan-Brown, J., Bicknell, B., Carroll-Lind, J., and Kearney, A. (2004). *The Extent, Nature and Effectiveness of Planned Approaches in New Zealand Schools for Providing for Gifted and Talented Students.* Retrieved from http://www.mined.govt. nz/goto/gifted

Sak, U., and Eristi, B. (2012). Think less – talk more or talk less – think more: a comparison of gifted students' engagement behaviors in regular and gifted science classrooms. *Asia-Pacific Journal of Gifted and Talented Education*, 4(1), 1–11.

Scager, K., Akkerman, S.F., Pilot, A., and Wubbels, T. (2014). Challenging high-ability students. *Studies in Higher Education*, 39(4), 659–79, http://dx.doi.org/10.1080/03075079.2012.743117

Steenburgen-Hu, S., and Moon, S.M. (2011). The effects of acceleration on high-ability learners: a meta-analysis. *Gifted Child Quarterly*, 55, 39–53. doi:10.1177/0016986210383155

Taber, K.S. (2007). *Enriching School Science for the Gifted Learner. The ASCEND Project: Able Scientists Collectively Experiencing New Demands*, London: Gatsby Science Enhancement Programme.

Taber, K.S. (2015). Affect and meeting the needs of the gifted chemistry learner: providing intellectual challenge to engage students in enjoyable learning. In Murat Kahveci and MaryKay Orgill (Eds), *Affective Dimensions in Chemistry Education*. Berlin: Springer, pp. 133–58.

Wardman, J. (2009). Secondary teachers', student teachers' and education students' attitudes to full year acceleration for gifted students. *Gifted and Talented (UK)*, 12 and 13, 43–58.

Wardman, J., and Hattie, J. (2012). Administrators' perceptions of full-year acceleration at high school [online]. *Australasian Journal of Gifted Education*, 21(1), 32–41.

Weiner, B. (2010). The development of an attribution-based theory of motivation: a history of ideas. *Educational Psychologist*, 45(1), 28–36. doi.org/10.1080/00461520903433596

15 Neuroscience research on science-talented learners

Ching-Chih Kuo, Ching-Po Lin and Hsiao-Lan Sharon Wang

Introduction

Although numerous psychological reports describe the characteristics of giftedness, few studies have investigated gifted students from a neurological perspective. However, researchers have recently begun to explore the relationship between the brain structure (grey matter volume) and IQ (Frangou *et al.*, 2004; Narr *et al.*, 2007; O'Boyle, 2005; O'Boyle *et al.*, 2005; Wilke *et al.*, 2003; Singh and O'Boyle, 2004). Neuroimaging studies have revealed that the grey matter densities of the orbitofrontal cortex, cingulated gyrus, cerebellum, thalamus and posterior temporal cortices were positively related to IQ (Frangou *et al.*, 2004; Narr *et al.*, 2007; Wilke *et al.*, 2003). By contrast, the grey matter density of the caudate nucleus was negatively correlated with IQ (Frangou *et al.*, 2004). However, few studies have focused on the brains of gifted persons or have analysed the brain function of mathematically talented students (Singh and O'Boyle, 2004; O'Boyle, 2005; O'Boyle *et al.*, 2005; Prescott *et al.*, 2010; Kuo *et al.*, 2012). Desco and colleagues (2011) suggested that the greater ability of maths-gifted adolescents for complex mathematical reasoning may be related to more bilateral patterns of activation and increased activations in the parietal and frontal regions, which are associated with enhanced skills in visuospatial processing and logical reasoning. Zhang *et al.* (2015) indicated that the dynamically reconfigured network architecture in a maths-gifted brain enhances both global and local information processing in reasoning processes, which can be considered neural correlations with the superior problem-solving ability of maths-gifted adolescents for logical reasoning.

Although numerous physical characteristics such as the brain structure and function of maths talents are known to academia, few neuropsychological studies have investigated science-talented students. Compared to the psychological traits of giftedness and talents, the characteristics of science-gifted brains remain unclear to educators and psychologists.

This chapter presents the neuroscientific findings on science-talented students in Taiwan. A series of studies from 2006–14 have been completed (Table 15.1), including those comparing differences in brain activity during numerical reasoning, figural reasoning and emotional tasks between science-talented students and their typically developing peers.

Table 15.1 Brain research studies of science-talented students, 2006–14

Year	Subjects	Variables	Researchers
2006–9	36 ST and 37 TD senior high school students	Brain volume differences and sex differences between groups	Kuo, Lin, Chang, Chang, Chou, Lin and Chen
2009–10	46 ST and 53 TD high school students	Functional differences during maths reasoning and the emotional tasks	Kuo, Lin, Chang, Chou, Tseng, Chang and Lin
2010–14	24 STHIQ, 17 STAIQ, 29 TD and 14 ASD college students	Functional differences in neuropsychological mechanism and training of thinking and social skills	Kuo, Liang, Su, Soong and Gau

The finding that some science-talented students exhibited lower activation of brain areas when viewing emotional pictures suggested to the author studying the social adjustment of these talented students further. This study, therefore, focused on comparing the differences in social adjustment and neuropsychological mechanisms among science-talented students with various IQ levels and students with Asperger syndrome (Kuo *et al.*, 2014). The knowledge generated by this research has significantly advanced the understanding of their social and neuropsychological characteristics.

Participants

The participants were recruited from northern Taiwan. All participating science-talented students studied in science-talented classes; the typically developing students were recruited from non-gifted programmes. Students in Taiwan identified as science-talented students had to take achievement or aptitude tests in both mathematics and science, and these students generally outperformed other students in these two academic domains.

Research instruments

Functional magnetic resonance imaging: technical details

In this study, 3T magnetic resonance imaging (MRI) equipped with a 12-channel head coil (Siemens Medical Systems, Erlangen, Germany) at National Yang Ming University was used. A single-shot T2-weighted gradient echo-planar imaging (EPI) sequence (TR = 2500ms, TE = 30ms, flip angle = 90°, resolution = 64 × 64, slice thickness = 3.4mm) was used for BOLD MRI.

Functional imaging data were analysed using SPM 8 software (Wellcome Department of Imaging Neuroscience, London, UK) running in Matlab (Math-Works, Natick, MA, USA). All images were slice-timing corrected before motion correction and spatially normalized to MNI space (Montreal Neurological

Institute) by using an EPI template. The data were smoothed with a 6mm FWHM Gaussian kernel. The analysis of each participant was performed by computing linear t contrasts (easy, intermediate, or difficult figural reasoning items versus fixation).

Analysis of variance was used to determine the differences between the groups (ST versus TD) and genders (male versus female).

Numerical reasoning task

The stimuli were 24 items in a numerical reasoning task designed by Cheng-ching Tseng, who is a maths teacher at Taipei Municipal Jianguo High School. These items were visually presented on a goggle display system. Twenty four items were divided into three difficulty levels according to the rates of correct answers: easy (70–100 per cent), intermediate (39–69 per cent) and difficult (0–38 per cent). The items were presented in a block manner. Each block contained one item that was presented for 17.5 seconds, and after the thinking time was over, a red fixation was presented for 2.5 seconds, followed by a 10-second fixation cross. When the subjects saw the red fixation, they had to press the button to indicate which of the four possible answers was correct.

Figural reasoning task

The stimuli were 24 items in a figural reasoning task designed by Robert J. Stern-berg (1986, pp. 142, 146–56). These items were visually presented on a goggle display system. Twenty-four items were presented to the senior and junior groups each and were divided into three difficulty levels according to the rates of correct answers in each group: easy (70–100 per cent), intermediate (39–69 per cent) and difficult (0–38 per cent). The items were presented in a block manner. Each block contained one item that was presented for 17.5 seconds. After the thinking time was over, a red fixation was presented for 2.5 seconds, followed by a 10-second fixation cross. When the subjects saw the red fixation, they had to press the button to indicate which of the four possible answers was correct.

International Affective Picture System

The emotional pictures were chosen from the International Affective Picture System (IAPS) (Lang *et al.*, 1995, 1999, 2001, 2005) and visually presented on a goggle display system. Our design consisted of three affective valences: positive, negative and neutral. Each affective valence had 30 pictures, thus providing a total of 90 pictures. Each valence consisted of 15 high-arousal and 15 low-arousal pictures to control the effect of arousal.

Our design consisted of two sessions, each of which included 45 pictures. The pictures were presented in a block manner. Each block consisted of five pictures of the same affective valence. Each picture was presented for 5 seconds and each block was presented for 25 seconds, followed by a 12.5-second fixation cross.

Self-assessment Manikin

After the scanning period of viewing emotional pictures, self-assessment Manikin (SAM) (Bradley and Lang, 1994) was used to measure the valence and arousal of 18 pictures. The subjects were asked to assign a rating of 1 to 9 to each dimension of valence and arousal. The valence scale ranged from pleasant to unpleasant; the arousal was the intensity of emotion ranging from calm to excite.

Results and discussion

How does the brain structure differ between science-talented students and their typically developing peers?

For the period from 2006–9, the brain structure differences between science-talented students and their typically developing peers were compared. The main instruments used were the Chinese version of the Otis-Lennon School Ability Test 8 (Chen and Chen, 2006; Chian *et al.*, 2008), MRI scan and voxel-based morphometry of statistical parametric mapping. Different regions of brain tissue are commonly referred to as Brodmann areas (BA) following the work of the German anatomist Korbinian Brodmann.

In total, 36 science-talented senior high school students (16 male and 20 female) and 37 typically developing students (20 male and 17 female) in Taipei City were recruited in the study. The science-talented group received significantly higher scores than did the typically developing group on the maths–science achievement and intelligence tests (Kuo *et al.*, 2012). The science-talented group had a higher percentage of grey matter in several regions (cluster size > 10 voxel, $p < 0.05$–$p < 0.0001$) including the (a) precentral gyrus (right BA 44), subgyrus (BA 10), middle frontal gyrus (left BA 8) and bilateral inferior frontal gyri (BA 47) in frontal lobe areas, (b) precuneus (BA 7) and postcentral gyrus (right BA 7 and right BA 43) in parietal lobe areas, (c) fusiform gyrus (BA 37), right superior temporal gyrus (BA 22) and left superior temporal gyrus (BA 41) in the temporal lobe areas, (d) inferior temporal gyrus (BA 19) in occipital lobe areas and (e) other areas such as the bilateral cerebellum and culmen, insula (BA 13), uncus (BA 38) and right anterior cingulate cortex (BA 32). These findings are consistent with those of previous studies (Colom *et al.*, 2006; Frangou *et al.*, 2004; Haier *et al.*, 2004; Reiss *et al.*, 1996) that have generally found that intelligence is related to some areas of the brain such as the bilateral cerebellum, subgyrus (BA 10), bilateral inferior frontal gyri (BA 47), fusiform gyrus (BA 37), postcentral gyrus (right BA 7 and right BA 43), precuneus (BA 7) and anterior cingulate cortex (BA 32). Mathematical ability is found to be related to the fusiform gyrus (Hanakawa *et al.*, 2002).

Compared with the science-talented group, the typically developing group had a higher percentage of grey matter in several regions including the precentral gyrus (bilateral BA 4 and left BA 6) and middle frontal gyrus (right BA 6 and right BA 8) in frontal lobe areas and the inferior parietal lobule (bilateral BA 40) and temporal parietal junction (right BA 40). The precentral gyrus is most functionally related to motor perception, whereas the inferior parietal lobule is most functionally related to somatosensory, empathetic and interpersonal perception (Morrison *et al.*, 2006; Cheng *et al.*, 2009, 2006, 2008).

The results drew our attention to the interpretation that a gifted brain undergoes unbalanced growth. The science-talented group possessed a higher grey matter density than that of their typically developing peers mostly in the cortical regions of the left hemisphere, which are related to intelligence and mathematics; however, they had a lower grey matter volume in the motor- and somatosensory-related regions. Because the inferior parietal lobule is essential for emotion recognition and contagion, the question remained whether science-talented students are less empathetic than their TD peers?

Which grey matter volumes are correlated with mathematics and science achievement?

Our study on the brain volume indicates that the maths achievement scores were positively correlated with left temporal lobe, particularly the left temporal insula and left superior temporal gyrus (BA 22). The insula was known to be associated with visceral functions and the integration of autonomic information and syntactical processing involving the left superior temporal gyrus. This study revealed a positive correlation between mathematical ability and the left hemisphere of the brain.

Regarding the science achievement scores, no positive relationship was observed between the science scores and grey matter volumes. By contrast, a negative correlation was observed between grey matter and science scores including those pertaining to the left parietal postcentral gyrus (BA 2 and 3), left frontal precentral and postcentral gyrus, left frontal paracenreal lobule, left limbic cingulated gyrus (BA 31), right frontal precentral gyrus (BA 4) and right inferior parietal lobule. These areas are mainly located in the left hemisphere and are involved in primary sensory motor and motor functions (BA 2, 3 and 4) (May, 1991), spatial attention, multimodal sensory integration and oculomotor control (inferior parietal lobule) (Clower *et al.*, 2001). Higher grey matter volumes were observed in the left frontal and parietal regions, and the participants obtained lower science scores; however, which grey matter volumes were closely related to scientific ability remains unclear, requiring further research.

How does brain activation differ between science-talented students and their typically developing peers during a numerical reasoning task?

Numerical reasoning is the ability to perceive complex arithmetic relations. The processing of numerical reasoning includes working memory, reasoning and arithmetic. The working memory holds and manipulates multiple numbers during numerical reasoning processing, and arithmetic constructs a relationship between those numbers. Reasoning involves the ability to perceive relations between multiple pieces of information. Hanakawa *et al.* (2003) used functional MRI (fMRI) to scan the brains of six experts in abacus operations and eight non-experts while administering mental-operation tasks (numerical, spatial and verbal). Higher activation was observed in the left posterior superior parietal cortex (BA 7) of the experts than in that of the non-experts while administering the numerical mental-operation task and in the right intraparietal sulcus (BA 40) of the experts while administering the spatial mental-operation task. Other findings show that the intraparietal lobule, inferior parietal lobule and prefrontal areas were involved in the processing of mental calculation (Dehaene *et al.*, 1999; Gruber *et al.*, 2001; Menon *et al.*, 2002; Rickard *et al.*, 2000).

The participants in this study were assigned to the four comparison groups according to their classes and grade levels. In total, 47 senior high school students and 43 junior high school students were recruited in this study. They were divided into science-talented senior group (n = 24), typically developing senior group (n = 23), science-talented junior group (n = 23) and typically developing junior group (n = 20); the average ages of the senior and junior groups were 17.9 and 13.8 years, respectively. The stimuli were items in a numerical reasoning task with three levels of accuracy: easy (accuracy $\geq$ 0.7), intermediate (0.38 < accuracy < 0.7) and difficult (accuracy $\leq$ 0.38). The result showed that, when solving the difficult trials, the typically developing senior group exhibited higher activation than the science-talented senior group did in the left frontal lobe (BA 10). The science-talented junior group exhibited higher activation than the typically developing junior group did in the left frontal area (BA 9/46), which is related to calculation, when solving the easy, intermediate and difficult trials. Among the four groups, the science-talented junior group demonstrated the highest activation and the science-talented senior group showed the lowest activation.

The frontoparietal network seems to have played a significant role in the numerical reasoning task. However, increased activation was observed in the science-talented group, especially in the left middle frontal gyrus at the difficult level of the task. By contrast, the typically developing group showed additional activation in the right parietal and temporal lobes at the easiest level of the task compared with the science-talented group.

Our result showed that frontoparietal activation was reduced as the difficulty level of the numerical reasoning task was decreased and was independent of the intelligence level of the subjects. The frontoparietal activation has been known to support numerous cognitive tasks such as shifting attention, working memory and problem-solving (Corbetta *et al.*, 2000; Perfetti *et al.*, 2009). It has been considered an adapting function to task demands or a facilitating system to support specific processing (Duncan, 2001). Perfetti *et al.* (2009) used fMRI to scan the brain of eight high-IQ and ten low-IQ subjects while administering the moderate and complex tasks that were adapted from the Raven Progressive Matrices. They found that when the complexity of problems were increased, the high-IQ subjects showed increased activation in frontal and parietal regions and the low-IQ subjects exhibited decreased activation in the same regions. When solving the moderate problems, the low-IQ subjects exhibited higher activation in the medial and lateral frontal regions. This suggested that different IQ groups differed in their patterns of brain activation.

How does brain activation differ between science-talented students and their typically developing peers during a figural reasoning task?

Prabhakaran *et al.* (1997) used fMRI to scan the brains of seven subjects while the subjects were solving three types of problems from the Raven's Progressive Matrices Test: match problem, figural reasoning and analytic reasoning. The result showed that, compared with the match problem, the analytic reasoning resulted in higher activation in the frontal regions (BA 6, 9, 44, 45, 46 and 10), parietal regions (BA 7, 39 and 40), occipital regions (BA 7, 18 and 19), temporal regions (BA 19, 21 and 37) and anterior cingulate (BA 32). While subjects were solving the figural reasoning problem (compared with the match problem), they found higher activation in the frontal regions (BA 9 and 46), parietal regions (BA 7 and 40), temporal regions (BA 37), occipital regions (BA 7 and 19) and anterior cingulate (BA 32). Compared with the figural reasoning problem, the analytic reasoning problem resulted in higher activation in the frontal (BA 6, 9, 44, 45 and 46), parietal (BA 7, 39 and 40), temporal (BA 37, 21 and 19) and occipital regions (BA 18, 19 and 37). The reports indicated that the functionally related brain areas for various level of reasoning tasks are different.

Participants in this study were classified into four groups: 1) the science-talented senior high school group, 2) the typically developing senior high school group, 3) the science-talented junior high school group and 4) the typically developing junior high school group. In total, 47 senior high school students and 49 junior high school students were recruited in the study and were asked to sign a consent form. The main instruments used in this study were the figural reasoning task and MRI. The participants underwent fMRI scanning while performing the figural reasoning items. The accurate results indicate a significant difference in the figural reasoning ability between the science-talented students and the typically developing students. Our research results were as follows:

1. Interaction effects between classes and grade levels were observed (p < 0.001 uncorrected, cluster size > 30 voxel). The interaction effects were found in left superior frontal gyrus (BA 6) and left lingual gyrus (BA 19) during solving easy items; in left lingual gyrus (BA 19) during solving intermediate items; in right cerebellum, left inferior parietal lobule (BA 40) and left cuneus (BA 17) during solving difficult figure reasoning items.
2. During the easy task, the typically developing senior group exhibited higher brain activation in BA 39 than did the science-talented senior group; the science-talented junior group exhibited higher brain activation in BA 6 and 19 than did the typically developing junior group. During the intermediate

task, the typically developing senior group exhibited higher brain activation than did the science-talented senior group in temporal lobe (BA 22, 41, 39, 20, 38, 21), occipital lobe (BA 19), sublobar (BA 13, thalamus, lentiform nucleus, claustrum), frontal lobe (BA 8, 9), limbic lobe (BA 24, 30, 31, 29, 23), brainstem (midbrain) and parietal lobe (BA 3, 31); the science-talented junior group exhibited higher brain activation than did the typically developing junior group in frontal lobe (BA 6), occipital lobe (BA 19) and parietal lobe (BA 7). During the difficult task, the typically developing senior group exhibited higher brain activation than did the science-talented senior group in occipital lobe (BA 19) and parietal lobe (BA 39); the science-talented junior group exhibited higher brain activation than did the typically developing junior group in parietal lobe (BA 7, 3), frontal lobe (BA 6, 10, 47, 9), occipital lobe (BA 19), limbic lobe (BA 36, 25, 32), cerebellum and temporal lobe (BA 37).

3. The typically developing senior group exhibited higher brain activation in the reasoning- and intelligence-related areas (insula and cerebellum) during solving intermediate items than during solving more difficult items; the typically developing junior group exhibited higher brain activation in the reasoning- and intelligence-related areas (BA 6 and cerebellum) during solving intermediate items than during solving easy (or difficult) items.

4. The science-talented groups recruited the same brain regions to perform the figural reasoning task; no main effect of the difficulty level was observed in the science-talented groups. However, the main effect of difficulty level was found in the typically developing groups. Compared to when solving difficult items, the typically developing senior group exhibited higher brain activation in left insular (BA 13), left superior temporal gyrus (BA 22) and right cerebellum (uvula) during solving intermediate items. Conversely, the typically developing junior group exhibited higher brain activation in right precentral gyrus (BA 6, BA4), right middle frontal gyrus (BA6) and right cerebellum (culmen) during solving the intermediate items.

In this research, we found that the brains of the four groups activated in different regions during performing tasks with variant difficulty. First, the brains of the science-talented senior group and typically developing junior group activated less than the other groups during solving the problems. We wonder if the most items were too simple for science-talented senior group and were too difficult for typically developing junior group. When the task difficulty does not match the participant's ability, it may decrease the motivation to solve problems. Second, during solving the intermediate items, the typically developing group exhibited higher brain activation than solving difficult or easy items. However, the activated regions were different between senior group and junior group. This indicated the task with moderate difficulty aroused the brain activation more than the task with high difficulty or low difficulty. Third, the effect of difficulty level was not observed in both senior and junior science-talented group; this may indicate the discrimination of difficulties was not good. Fourth, we found the brains of science-talented junior group activated higher than their typically developing peers in several brain regions: frontal lobe (BA 6, 10, 47, 9), parietal lobe (BA 7, 3), cerebellum, temporal lobe (BA 37), occipital lobe (BA 19) and limbic lobe (BA 36, 25, 32). Most of these brain regions were found functionally related with solving the figural reasoning problem by Prabhakaran *et al.* (1997), Christoff *et al.* (2001) and Perfetti *et al.* (2009) while solving reasoning problems adapted from the Raven's Progressive Matrices.

How does brain activation differ between science-talented students and typically developing students during an emotional task?

In total, 46 senior high school and 53 junior high school students were recruited in this study. The participants included science-talented senior students ($n = 24$), typically developing senior students ($n = 22$), science-talented junior students ($n = 30$) and typically developing junior students ($n = 23$); the average ages of the senior and junior groups were 17.83 and 13.74 years, respectively. The stimuli were emotional pictures chosen from the IAPS (Lang *et al.*, 1995, 1999, 2001, 2005). The first step involved recruiting participants and administering an IQ test to ensure exceptional competencies. The subjects underwent fMRI scanning while viewing affective pictures chosen from the IAPS and thereafter assigned the SAM (Bradley and Lang, 1994) ratings of 1 to 9 to each dimension of valence and arousal to the pictures.

Unexpectedly, the science-talented senior group did not show as much activation as the typically developing senior group when viewing the positive and negative pictures ($p < 0.001$, cluster size > 10 voxel), and the typically developing senior group demonstrated higher activation than did the science-talented senior group in the limbic (bilateral BA 32), temporal (left BA 20) and frontal lobes (right BA 11, bilateral BA 10) when viewing the positive pictures. The bilateral anterior cingulate (ACC) is a part of the limbic lobe of the brain that is thought to be related to emotional responses (Hutchison *et al.*, 1999; Wicker *et al.*, 2003; Singer *et al.*, 2004). When viewing the negative pictures, the typically developing senior group exhibited higher activity than did the science-talented senior group in the temporal lobe (right BA 20), parietal lobe (bilateral BA 7, right BA 19), occipital lobe (left BA 18), sublobar (right insular, right thalamus) and left cingulate (BA 31), which is thought to be related to pain and episode memory (Becerra *et al.*, 1999; Maddock *et al.*, 2001; Maguire *et al.*, 2001; Kulkarni *et al.*, 2007).

Both the science-talented and typically developing junior groups exhibited empathy-related brain activation when viewing affective pictures. Compared with the typically developing junior group, the science-talented junior group exhibited higher activity in the right inferior parietal lobule (IPL, BA 40), limbic lobe (right BA 19) and frontal lobe (right BA 9) when viewing the positive pictures and in the left caudate head, right IPL (BA 40) and frontal lobe (right BA 43) when viewing the negative pictures ($p < 0.001$, cluster size > 10 voxel). The inferior parietal lobule is responsible for observation and execution of movement.

It consists of the inferior frontal gyrus (BA 44/45) and parietal lobe (BA 40), which are areas related to empathy (Gallese, 2003; Carr *et al.*, 2003; Gallese *et al.*, 2004) and the theory of mind (Gallese and Goldman, 1998; Borghi and Binkofski, 2011). By contrast, the typically developing junior group exhibited higher activation than did the science-talented junior group in the left limbic lobe (ACC, BA 24) when viewing the positive pictures; however, the group did not exhibit higher activation when viewing the negative pictures.

Our research indicated that the typically developing senior group exhibited significantly higher activation in the empathy-related brain areas than did the other three groups. The science-talented senior group demonstrated significantly lower activation than did the other groups. Some inconsistencies were observed in the brain responses to emotional stimuli in the science-talented senior and junior groups, such as the science-talented junior group exhibiting higher activation when viewing affective pictures. We wonder if the left brain thinking styles of science-talented senior group lead them view the pictures in logical way? Or the differences in IQ scores may explain the different patterns of brain activation between the science-talented junior and senior groups when the science-talented junior group (M = 136.10, SD = 9.99) scored higher on the intelligence than did the science-talented senior group (M = 118.63, SD = 8.44); however, this still requires further study.

Are scientific skills related to autism spectrum disorders?

To analyse the association between scientific skills and autism spectrum disorders (ASDs) (Baron-Cohen *et al.*, 2001; Billington *et al.*, 2007), this research examined the cognitive profiles and social adjustment of the science-talented participants (Kuo *et al.*, 2014). The instruments used were the Wechsler Adult Intelligence Scale (WAIS-III), Chinese version of the Autism Diagnostic Interview-Revised, Me Scale II (OE's Scale), Chinese version of the social responsiveness scale and Chinese version of the adult autism spectrum quotient. The behaviour assessment results showed that the science-talented participants with a high IQ (IQ 130 or higher on the WAIS-III) exhibited a balanced development in cognitive and affective aspects. The science-talented participants with an average IQ were weak in perceptual organization and working memory and had problems in social awareness and socialness. The participants with ASD scored lower in performance IQ, particularly in digit symbol coding and symbol search. They also exhibited significantly more severe problems regarding autistic symptoms and reported higher emotional OE and lower empathetic OE. These findings support differential cognitive profiles and social adjustment between the science-talented and ASD participants and the influence of IQ on these manifestations in science-talented participants. However, several special cases reported poor social adjustment among science-talented participants. Two science-talented participants with a high IQ and two with an average IQ presented similar difficulties in social reciprocity as autistic-like traits (Kuo *et al.*, 2014).

Conclusion

This chapter presents key findings from research series. The structural study indicates the different patterns of growth of brains in the science-talented and typically developing groups. An uneven growth of the gifted brain was observed because the science-talented group had higher grey matter densities in the left cortical regions that are related to intelligence and mathematics; however, they had lower densities in the motor- and somatosensory-related regions. Mathematical skills were positively correlated with the left temporal insula and superior temporal gyrus, which are involved in syntactic processing; however, which hemisphere is closely related to scientific ability remains uncertain, requiring further research.

In addition to these structural differences, different brain regions were involved at varying levels of difficulty in numerical reasoning, figural reasoning and emotional tasks. During the numerical reasoning task, increased activation was observed in the science-talented group in the left middle frontal gyrus when solving the difficult trials; however, the typically developing group exhibited additional activation for the easier level of the task in the right parietal and temporal lobes. Frontoparietal activation was reduced with the difficulty of the numerical reasoning task and was independent of the intelligence level of the subject. During solving the figural reasoning task, the brain activated in several brain regions: frontal lobe (BA 6, 10, 47, 9), parietal lobe (BA 7, 3), cerebellum, temporal lobe (BA 37), occipital lobe (BA 19) and limbic lobe (BA 36, 25, 32). The findings were in accordance with the literatures. Besides, our study indicated that the task difficulty may impact brain activation and the motivation to solve problems.

The study of brain response to emotional stimuli indicated that the science-talented senior group showed significantly lower activation than did the other groups; however, the science-talented junior group exhibited higher activation than did the typically developing junior group. When viewing the positive and negative pictures, the science-talented junior group exhibited higher activity in inferior parietal lobule (IPL, BA 40) which is a brain area functionally related to empathy.

When the participants were assigned to different groups according to their IQ levels and a talent in mathematics and science, the science-talented group with a high IQ exhibited a balanced development in cognitive and affective aspects; however, special cases reported their poor social adjustment as autistic-like traits.

Soon, the brain connectivity patterns will be further analysed by our research team to provide a more comprehensive understanding of structural and functional integration in cognitive performance.

Promise of neuroscience for informing educational practice

Currently, neuroscientific studies are basic sciences that have yet to offer direct implications for classroom practice. However, science can now identify statistical differences in the brain structure between science-talented students and other students and between some subgroups within the science-talented group. This area of research is still new; however, it has led to a series of findings that might have seemed impossible only a few years ago.

1. The structural brain imaging findings show that, compared with the typically developing participants, the science-talented learners had more grey matter in areas associated with intelligence and mathematical skills and particular regions of the left hemisphere; however, they had less grey matter in the motor cortex, somatosensory cortical regions and empathy-related brain regions. Future studies can investigate the brain structures of science-talented learners with different educational periods and changes in their brain structure can be followed-up through panel studies.

2. As other chapters in this book discuss, regular classroom activities and tests may often fail to fully engage and challenge the most able students. The studies reported in this chapter found statistically significant differences in brain structure and activity between students categorised as science-talented and those considered typically developing based on educational evaluations. This area of work, therefore, shows that it is possible to find organic correlates of giftedness and talent in science, reinforcing educational arguments that educators and teachers need to differentiate teaching materials and methods for students with diverse abilities.

3. The results of analysing the association between scientific skills and ASDs suggested that the science-talented learners with a high IQ had more empathy and achieved social adjustment more effectively. Apparently, learners with high intelligence have more resources and information available and can thus solve high-level cognitive tasks and demonstrate effective social interaction skills. Nevertheless, a few participants with high intelligence presented more autistic-like traits on the symptom-related scales. More attention should be paid to such gifted learners with autism-like traits. Counselling and providing resources will help them to develop social skills. Educators are recommended to carefully investigate any social interaction problems among students in science talent classes and provide counselling and intervention for those with social reciprocity problems to help them develop appropriate and adequate social skills to improve their interpersonal relationships.

4. Our studies mainly compared groups for statistical differences; however, individual differences in the brain structure or function still exist among them. No matter whether the students have special needs or not; whether they have high IQ or not, successful teaching needs to offer challenging experiences for each student to engage him or her in effective classroom learning.

References

Baron-Cohen, S., Wheelwright, S., Skinner, R., Martin, J., and Clubley, E. (2001). The autism-spectrum quotient (AQ): evidence from Asperger syndrome/high-functioning autism, males and females, scientists and mathematicians. *Journal of Autism and Developmental Disorders*, 31(1), 5–17.

Becerra, L.R., Breiter, H.C., Stojanovic, M., Fishman, S., Edwards, A., Comite, A.R., and Borsook, D. (1999). Human brain activation under controlled thermal stimulation and habituation to noxious heat: an fMRI study. *Magnetic Resonance Medicine*, 41, 1044–157.

Billington, J., Baron-Cohen, S., and Wheelwright, S. (2007). Cognitive style predicts entry into physical sciences and humanities: questionnaire and performance tests of empathy and systemizing. *Learning and Individual Differences*, 17, 260–8.

Borghi, A.M., and Binkofski, F. (2011). S28–04 – Intentionality of movement: mirror neuron system and theory of mind. *European Psychiatry*, 26, 2113.

Bradley, M.M., and Lang, P.J. (1994). Measuring emotion: the self-assessment manikin and the semantic differential. *Journal of Behavior Therapy and Experimental Psychiatry*, 25, 49–59.

Carr, L., Iacoboni, M., Dubeau, M.C., Mazziotta, J.C., and Lenzi, G.L. (2003). Neural mechanisms of empathy in humans: a relay from neural systems for imitation to limbic areas. *Proceedings of the National Academy of Sciences of the United States of America*, 100, 5497–502.

Chen, M.F., and Chen, H.Y. (2006). *Junior High School Ability Test* (revised from the Otis-Lennon School Ability Test, OLSAT 8). Taipei: Chinese Behavioral Science Corporation.

Cheng, Y., Chou, K.-H., Decety, J., Chen, I.-Y., Hung, D., Tzeng, O.T.-L., and Lin, C.-P. (2009). Sex differences in the neuroanatomy of the human mirror-neuron system: a voxel-based morphometric investigation. *Neuroscience*, 158, 713–20.

Cheng, Y., Tzeng, O.J.L., Decety, J., Imada, T., and Hsieh, J.-C. (2006) Gender differences in the human mirror system: a magnetoencephalography study. *Neuro Report*, 17(11), 1115–19.

Cheng, Y., Yang, C.-Y., Lin, C.-P., Lee, P.-L., and Decety, J. (2008). The perception of pain in others suppresses somatosensory oscillations. *NeuroImage*, 40, 1833–40.

Chian, M.F., Ho, R.G., and Kuo, C.C. (2008). *Senior High School Ability Test* (revised from the Otis-Lennon School Ability Test, OLSAT 8). Taipei: Chinese Behavioral Science Society.

Clower, D.M., West, R.A., Lynch, J.C., and Strick, P.L. (2001). The inferior parietal lobule is the target of output from the superior colliculus, hippocampus, and cerebellum. *The Journal of Neuroscience*, 21(16), 6283–91.

Colom, R., Jung, R.E., and Haier, R.J. (2006). Distributed brain sites for the g-factor of intelligence. *NeuroImage*, 31, 1359–65.

Corbetta, M., Kincade, J.M., Ollinger, J.M., McAvoy, M.P., and Shulman, G.L. (2000). Voluntary orienting is dissociated from target detection in human posterior parietal cortex. *Nature Neuroscience*, 3(3), 292–7.

Christoff, K., Prabhakaran, V., Dorfman, J., Zhao, Z., Kroger, J.K., Holyoak, K.J., and Gabrieli, J.E. (2001). Rostrolateral prefrontal cortex involvement in relational integration during reasoning. *NeuroImage*, 14, 1136–49.

Dehaene, S., Spelke, E., Pinel, P., Stanescu, R., and Tsivkin, S. (1999). Sources of mathematical thinking: behavior and brain-imaging evidence. *Science*, 284, 970–4.

Desco, M., Navas-Sanchez, F.J., Sanchez-González, J., Reig, S., Robles, O., Franco, C., Guzmán-De-Villoria, J.A., García-Barreno, P., and Arango, C. (2011). Mathematically gifted adolescents use more extensive and more bilateral areas of the fronto-parietal network than controls during executive functioning and fluid reasoning tasks. *NeuroImage*, 57(1), 281–92.

Duncan, J. (2001). An adaptive coding model of neural function in prefrontal cortex. *Nature Reviews Neuroscience*, 2(11), 820–9.

Frangou, S., Chitins, X., and Williams, S.C.R. (2004). Mapping IQ and gray matter density in healthy young people. *NeuroImage*, 23(3), 800–5.

Gallese, V. (2003). The roots of empathy: the shared manifold hypothesis and the neural basis of intersubjectivity. *Psychopathology*, 36, 171–80.

Gallese, V., and Goldman, A. (1998). Mirror neurons and the simulation theory of mind-reading. *Trends in Cognitive Science*, 2, 493–501.

Gallese, V., Rizzolatti, G., and Keysers, C. (2004). A unifying view of the basis of social cognition. *Trends in Cognitive Science*, 8(9), 396–403.

Gruber, O., Indefrey, P., Steinmetz, H., and Kleinschmidt, A. (2001). Dissociating neural correlates of cognitive components in mental calculation. *Cereb Cortex*, 11, 350–9.

Haier, R.J., Jung, R.E., Yeo, R.A., Head, K., and Alkire, M.T. (2004). Structural brain variation and general intelligence. *NeuroImage*, 23, 425–33.

Hanakawa, T., Honda, M., Sawamoto, N., Okada, T., Yonekura, Y., Fukuyama, H., and Shibasaki, H. (2002). The role of Rostral Brodmann Area 6 in mental operation tasks: an integrative neuroimaging approach. *Cerebral Cortex*, 12, 1157–70.

Hanakawa, T., Honda, M., Okada, T., Fukuyama, H., and Shibasaki, H. (2003). Neural correlates underlying mental calculation in abacus experts: a functional magnetic resonance imaging study. *NeuroImage*, 19, 296–307.

Hutchison, W.D., Davis, K.D., and Lozano, A.M. (1999). Pain-related neurons in the human cingulate cortex. *Nature Neuroscience*, 2, 403–405.

Kulkarni, B., Bentley, D.E., Elliott, R., Julyan, P.J., Boger, E., Watson, A., Boyle, Y., El-Deredy, W., and Jones, A.K. (2007). Arthritic pain is processed in brain areas concerned with emotions and fear. *Arthritis Rheum*, 56, 1345–54.

Kuo, C.C., Chang, H.J., Chang, Y.P., Chou, K.H., Lin, Y.H., Chen, H.C., and Lin, C.P. (2012). Psychological traits and brain structures of mathematically and scientifically senior high school talented students. *Bulletin of Educational Psychology*, 43(2), 805–31.

Kuo, C.C., Liang, K.C., Tseng, C.C., and Gau, S. (2014). Comparison of the cognitive profiles and social adjustment between mathematically and scientifically talented students and students with Asperger's syndrome. *Research in Autism Spectrum Disorders*, 8, 838–50.

Lang, P.J., Bradley, M.M., and Cuthbert, B.N. (1995). *International Affective Picture System (IAPS): Technical manual and affective ratings*. Gainesville: University of Florida, Center for Research in Psychophysiology.

Lang, P.J., Bradley, M.M., and Cuthbert, B.N. (1999). *International Affective Picture System (IAPS): Instruction manual and affective ratings* (Tech. Rep. A-4). Gainesville: University of Florida, Center for Research in Psychophysiology.

Lang, P.J., Bradley, M.M., and Cuthbert, B.N. (2001). International Affective Picture System (IAPS): *Technical manual and affective ratings*. NIMH Center for the Study of Emotion and Attention.

Lang, P.J., Bradley, M.M., and Cuthbert, B.N. (2005) *International Affective Picture System (IAPS): Digitized photographs, instruction manual and affective ratings* (Tech. Rep. A-6). Gainesville: University of Florida, Center for Research in Psychophysiology.

Maddock, R.J., Garrett, A.S., and Buonocore, M.H. (2001). Remembering familiar people: the posterior cingulate cortex and autobiographical memory retrieval. *Neuroscience*, 104, 667–76.

Maguire, E.A., Vargha-Khadem, F., and Mishkin, M. (2001). The effects of bilateral hippocampal damage on fMRI regional activations and interactions during memory retrieval. *Brain*, 124, 1156–70.

May, J.J. (1991). *Neuropsychology*. Taipei: Laureate Press.

Menon, V., Mackenzie, K., Rivera, S.M., and Reiss, A.L. (2002). Prefrontal cortex involvement in processing incorrect arithmetic equations: evidence from event-related fMRI. *Human Brain Mapping*, 16(2), 119–30.

Morrison, I., Peelen, M.V., and Downing, P.E. (2006). The sight of others' pain modulates motor processing in human cingulated cortex. *Cerebral Cortex*, 17, 2214–22.

Narr, K.L., Woods, R.P., Thompson, P.M., Szeszko, P., Robinson, D., Dimtcheva, T., Gurbani, M., Toga, A.W., and Bilder, R.M. (2007). Relationships between IQ and regional cortical gray matter thickness in healthy adults. *Cerebral Cortex*, 17(9), 2163–71.

O'Boyle, M.W. (2005). Some current findings on brain characteristics of the mathematically gifted adolescent. *International Education Journal*, 6(2), 247–51.

O'Boyle, M.W., Cunnington, R., Silk, T., Vaughan, D., Jackson, G., Syngeniotis, A., and Egan, G. (2005). Mathematically gifted male adolescents activate a unique brain network during mental rotation. *Cognitive Brain Research*, 25, 583–7.

Perfetti, B., Saggino, A., Ferretti, A., Caulo, M., Romani, G.L., and Onofri, M. (2009). Differential patterns of cortical activation as a function of fluid reasoning complexity. *Human Brain Mapping*, 30, 497–510.

Prabhakaran, V., Smith, J.A.L., Desmond, J.E., Glover, G.H., and Gabrieli, J.D.E. (1997). Neural substrates of fluid reasoning: an fMRI study of neocortical activation during performance of the Raven's Progressive Matrices Test. *Cognitive Psychology*, 33, 43–63.

Prescott, J., Gavrilescu, M., Cunnington, R, O'Boyle, M.W. and Egan, G.F. (2010). Enhanced brain connectivity in math-gifted adolescents: an fMRI study using mental rotation. *Cognitive Neuroscience*, 1(4), 277–88.

Reiss, A.L., Abrams, M.T., Singer, H.S., Ross, J.L., and Denckla, M.B. (1996). Brain development, gender and IQ in children: a volumetric imaging study. *Brain*, 119(5), 1763–74.

Rickard, T., Romero, S., Basso, G., Wharton, C., Flitman, S., and Grafman, J. (2000). The calculating brain: an fMRI study. *Neuropsychologia*, 38, 325–35.

Singer, T., Seymour, B., O'Doherty, J., Kaube, H., Dolan, R.J., and Frith, C.C. (2004). Empathy for pain involves the affective but not sensory components of pain. *Science*, 303, 1157–61.

Singh, H., and O'Boyle, M.W. (2004). Interhemispheric interaction during visual information processing in mathematically gifted youth, average ability adolescents and college students. *Neuropsychology*, 18(2), 371–7.

Sternberg, R.J. (1986). Toward a unified theory of human reasoning. *Intelligence*, 10(4), 281–314.

Wicker, B., Keysers, C., Plailly, J., Royet, J.P., Gallese, V., and Rizzolatti, G. (2003). Both of us disgusted in my insula: the common neural basis of seeing and feeling disgust. *Neuron*, 40, 655–64.

Wilke, M., Sohn, J.H., Byars, A.W., and Holland, S.K. (2003). Bright spots: correlations of gray matter volume with IQ in a normal pediatric population. *NeuroImage*, 20(1), 202–15.

Zhang, L., Gan, J.Q., and Wang, H. (2015). Mathematically gifted adolescents mobilize enhanced workspace configuration of theta cortical network during deductive reasoning. *Neuroscience*, 289, 334–48.

16 Meeting the needs of twice-exceptional children in the science classroom

Manabu Sumida

Introduction

This chapter focuses on children who are both gifted and simultaneously feel challenged in science education. 'Twice exceptionality' (henceforth referred to as 2E) is used to refer to the phenomenon of gifted or talented individuals who simultaneously have learning difficulties or disabilities (Buttriss and Callander, 2005). Illingworth and Illingworth (1966) analysed 450 eminent adults' childhoods and found that several were underachievers in a specific subject or had learning difficulties. Kumagai (2015) studied Leonardo da Vinci, Isaac Newton, Thomas Alva Edison, Soseki Natsume and Albert Einstein, finding several common characteristics such as 'lonely boyhood'; 'psychological properties similar to autism or attention deficit hyperactivity disorder (ADHD)'; and 'mismatch with school education'. Kumagai noted that such innovative geniuses needed to create their own worlds not equivalent to those of laypersons, which might have engendered characteristics in them similar to those of people with autism or ADHD. This chapter introduces these two sides of the gifted and identifying 2E children in science.

The criteria for gifted identification, such as IQ, creativity and leadership, are usually domain-independent. Importantly, a child might be identified as gifted based on multiple criteria, but may simultaneously have special educational needs (SENs). Alderman (2008) pointed out that children with physical, sensory, emotional, or other SENs may be competent in understanding science, and that specific disorders may mask particular strengths, gifts and talents. For example, the 'odd' behaviour of students with autism spectrum disorders may overshadow their scientific skill. Cooper *et al.* (2005) identified the behavioural characteristics of 2E students and developed Project HIGH HOPES, which included the science domain. Sumida (2010) developed an original gifted behavioural checklist for science and advanced reasons why 2E children are adept at learning science. He also implemented science lessons for 2E primary school children and insisted that science is beneficial for reinforcing children's dominant strengths.

The following recent developments serve to highlight the importance of 2E pedagogy in Japan. Since 2007, special needs education in Japan has expanded to include learning disabilities (LD), ADHD, high-functioning autism (HA) and

Asperger's syndrome, in addition to disabilities previously targeted in special education, such as visual disorders, hearing disorders, intellectual disabilities, physical handicaps, health impairments, speech disorders and emotional disturbances. In 2012, a survey conducted by the Ministry of Education, Culture, Sports, Science and Technology (MEXT) indicated that teaching staff noted pronounced difficulties in learning or behavioural problems in 6.5 per cent of students in public primary schools (MEXT, 2012). Based on responses to each survey item, 4.5 per cent of these students are considered to have LD, 3.1 per cent may have ADHD and 1.1 per cent may have HA (ibid.). These disabilities are especially apparent in arithmetic, mathematics and Japanese language. Some of these students with learning disabilities may be 2E, gifted children. Thus, this chapter also discusses guidelines of practice for 2E children in the science classroom and argues that inclusive science education benefits children both with and without developmental disorders.

'Twice exceptionality' in science education

How is 'twice-exceptional' different from 'gifted'?

Twice exceptionality is beginning to be examined and more specifically categorized using the fields of neurospsychology and cognitive neuroscience across various disabling conditions such as autism spectrum disorder, specific learning disability, sensory processing disorder, attention disorder and dyslexia (Kalbfleisch, 2014). The 2E children may have above grade-level vocabulary with poor spelling skills. They may have an excellent sense of humour, but may not want to engage in a social activity. As Baum and Owen (2004) noted, the term 'learning disability' and 'giftedness' have been at the opposite ends of the learning spectrum for many years, but there are some gifted children who are underachievers and have a poor self-concept. Therefore, it is imperative to clearly understand the two sides of gifted children with learning disabilities.

Weinfeld *et al.* (2006) summarize a comparison of the characteristics of gifted students with and without disabilities. For example, they describe 'keen powers of observation' as a characteristic of gifted students without disabilities while 'strong observation skills, but often have deficits in memory skills' as a characteristic of gifted students with disabilities. Cooper *et al.* (2005) listed the characteristics of gifted students and problems associated with special needs students, and proposed directions for curriculum accommodations. For example, gifted students are producers of new knowledge through innovative products, while 2E students may have difficulties with spelling and handwriting. In this context, Cooper *et al.* (ibid.) propose alternate ways to express ideas and create products for curricular accommodations.

Two sides with eminent scientists

Andreasen (2005) introduced a survey of the relationships between genius and psychosis among artists and scientists of the German-speaking countries in the eighteenth and nineteenth centuries. The results of the 181 eminent scientists showed that 75 per cent did not have any psychosis, but 15 per cent had personality disorders and 4 per cent were manic depressive. Among those scientists who have made their mark on history, quite a few are known to have lived with not only outstanding talent, but also some kind of learning difficulty.

For example, Michael Faraday, who made many great discoveries such as the law of electromagnetic induction, and who is famous for the Royal Institution Christmas lectures for children, seemed to have exhibited several traits that generally fit within the broader definition of learning difficulties (e.g. difficulty with mathematics and an unreliable memory) (West, 1991). Further, he started late, or very late, with continuous and increasingly valuable work throughout his lifetime; this may be an extreme case of 'late bloomer'. In the same research field of electromagnetics, West (ibid.) pointed out that James Clerk Maxwell was very different from Michael Faraday. Maxell was a talent in mathematics and showed an unusual flexibility of mind but was not good at speech and seemed to show some characteristics of dyslexia.

In the context of a modern non-western country, it is pertinent to consider Toshihide Masukawa, who shared the Nobel Prize for Physics in 2008. He is a theoretical physicist and a talent in mathematics and science. However, he has been an underachiever in English. The Nobel Prize Ceremony occasioned his first trip outside Japan, and he delivered his Nobel Lecture in Japanese. He said the reason he stopped studying English when at a schooling age was that he was tone-deaf (Masukawa, 2009). He found a good colleague to share, interpret and express his creative ideas for journal articles.

Why is science education effective for 2E children?

Since children with developmental disorders may suffer setbacks in academic performance in the areas of listening, speaking, reading, writing, calculating and reasoning, the main focus of research on academic instruction in special needs education has been on classroom teaching, to enable such children to overcome learning difficulties in language, arts and mathematics (Japan Association of the Special Educational Needs Specialist, 2007).

Science learning is an appropriate context for children to reveal, and for teachers to identify, giftedness in a practical context. The word science comes from the Latin *scientia*, which means knowledge. The domain-specific, dynamic nature of science, with its encompassing of a wealth of different fields of study, can accommodate 2E children's varied areas of interest.

DeVries (2002) defined 'physical-knowledge activities' as those in which children act on objects and observe their reactions, and pointed out that such activities appeal to children's interests, inspire experimentation and usually involve cooperation. The physical and creative intellectual activity that science offers – the opportunity to observe, experiment and make things – also provides an appropriate environment for teachers to determine the potential of 2E children, and for children to develop their science talent. Hands-on activities in science learning can promote creative ideas and develop a persistence in children that often surpasses their teachers' expectations. Activity-oriented science learning that addresses fewer topics in greater depth can be especially beneficial for children with special needs (Patton, 1995).

The skills of recording observations, interpreting experimental data and making models in science can potentially deepen and extend the learning process into other areas such as Japanese, arithmetic and the arts. As Baum (1990) recognizes, a child who is an expert on insects at age eight, for example, may be able to name and classify over 100 species of insects even though he has difficulty reading. For 2E children, in particular, an integrated scientific approach is beneficial in that their dominant strengths can be reinforced and developed in a broader context.

Science encompasses collaborative learning activities in the laboratory and in the field. Natural science is a team effort, working within self-established norms and sharing basic attitudes and ways of thinking, to build a well-founded system of knowledge that makes sense to the students themselves. Science can help improve social skills through activities in areas that the student excels in and enjoys (Sumida *et al.*, 2007).

The realities of twice-exceptional (2E) children in science

In Sumida's study (2010), 13 out of 86 primary school children in a city in Japan were categorized into the expert style group in science; five of these children had LD/ADHD/HA. The science and homeroom teachers of the four LD/ADHD/HA children in the 'expert gifted style' group were interviewed. The interviews with teachers provided further evidence of traits exhibited by the 2E children that have implications for the science education of 2E science learners.

'Enthusiastic'

In regard to application to science tasks in school science classes, it was found that high interest in and knowledge of science was characteristic. The following teacher comments, which have been translated from the original Japanese for this chapter, illustrate this:

> Has strong interest and desire to learn and acts with intention of solving problems... During science classes, responds well to questions raised by the teacher. Can express his own ideas. Has a wealth of knowledge. When predicting something, can contemplate the topic and can express his thoughts. Speaks clearly and confidently when commenting. (Grade 3)

> Extremely interested in scientific phenomena. Has a wealth of knowledge on topics other than those learned at school... In the unit on weather observations, began researching forecasting methods at the school library and continued researching for a week to ten days. (Grade 4)

Raises questions during lessons in any subject. Tries to investigate the point exhaustively there and then... Thoroughly researches anything he finds interesting or amusing and relentlessly explains everything to the teacher. General academic performance is not brilliant. (Grade 5)

Excels in thinking, experimentation and observation, expression and knowledge and understanding... Often asks teachers questions; asks about the lesson and about scientific topics of interest, even during class. Being unable to explain properly, often brings items in question and says, 'Look, look!' (Grade 5)

Some 2E children exhibit a high level of expertise in areas of special interest and enjoyment and such children may experience frustration with learning the basics all the time. Challenging problems can raise a child's self-esteem and sense of self-fulfilment.

'Creative'

2E children display high creativity and it is therefore desirable that opportunities for varied learning options and settings be encouraged and facilitated – for example, as noted in the interview excerpts below, involvement in science clubs or other outside science activities.

Submitted samples of plant collections for his project over the summer holiday. The stems were cut open and taped for display as if the child had been taught by a professional collector. (Grade 3)

Belongs to the science club. Very enthusiastic and has been a member of the same club for two years in a row. The child stays on alone even after club activity hours to continue to work out how to make his paper plane fly better. He is always the last to leave after everyone else has gone home. Though we hand out materials equally among all club members, this child always wants more. (Grade 4)

A hallmark of natural science is respect for 'something new'. Children's ideas that lie outside teacher's expectations and may even seem 'inappropriate' at first can be a springboard to new insights in science activities.

'Extensive knowledge'

2E science students characteristically show high-level knowledge. Provision of a wealth of resources of a multitude of types is indicated for maintaining interest and promoting further curiosity.

Generally reads a lot of books. Has a wealth of knowledge acquired through day-to-day activities. Well-versed in Kanji (Chinese characters) and can sometimes read characters he has not learned yet. Has a broad vocabulary and sometimes uses phrases that are uncommon for fourth graders. (Grade 3)

Reads a lot. If you show him a book and if it catches his interest, he will collect the entire collection or buy sequels to read. Reads volumes after volumes of thick books in no time. (Grade 4)

Has a wealth of scientific knowledge. Has intellectual curiosity in most subjects. Does well in science as well as in other subjects. Exceptional at studies. Scores 100 per cent in most tests. Does well at Kanji (Chinese characters) and calculations. (Grade 6)

'Social relationships'

In the interviews, teachers' comments pointed to differences in 2E science children's ways of interacting with peers.

Most often, problems occur not during lessons, but during break times in his interaction with friends. The child cannot take jokes and troubles arise when friends make jokes. (Grade 3)

During social studies and general studies, instead of learning about a prescribed theme with other members of the group, the child isolates himself and starts researching a particular aspect that he finds interesting... If the child does not feel like joining in, he plays alone (in the library etc.). Does not particularly seek to make friends and it is best that way. (His parents say so too.)... Does not heed caution from others, but is often bothered by other people's actions and cautions them... Consequently, inattentive. Not very good at playing with others. (Grade 4)

Sometimes unsure of how to interact with others. Does not care if he is different to other people or if he acts strangely. (Grade 5)

Cannot discreetly get others to understand his good qualities and ends up making others angry. Often sarcastic... Actively participates in experiments, but sometimes gets into trouble with other members during group experiments... Often does not participate in group activities. (Grade 6)

The implications for the classroom based on these observations are that, for activities involving observation/experiments, children should be grouped not according to child number or fixed seating position (as is typical in Japanese schools), but according to, for example, shared hypotheses or preferred methods of investigation. The inclusion of individual independent activities as well as such semi-structured group activities would also be appropriate. Science classes typically involve group activities such as observation and experiments, so it is important to consider the group make-up. When there are children who have difficulty relating to others or who need social-emotional support, as some 2E children may, seating arrangements and small group arrangements are often important considerations.

Practices of science teaching for 2E children

Project HIGH HOPES

Project HIGH HOPES (Baum *et al.*, 1995; Cooper *et al.*, 1996, 2005) was a pioneer exercise in teaching science to 2E children in grades 5–8. This project primarily served 130 students from six public schools, a private school for the learning disabled and two schools for the deaf in Connecticut and Rhode Island. Of the students identified, 55 per cent attended a special school, 15 per cent received resource room services in their school and 30 per cent were mainstreamed. These students were selected from the special education population and had been identified as having one or more of the following: learning disabilities, attention deficits, emotional or behavioural disorders, pervasive developmental disorders and hearing impairments (Cooper *et al.*, 2005).

Project HIGH HOPES provides a short activity for identifying gifted students with one or more difficulties through observation. In the domain of science, zoology, botany and physics, activities in the physical and life sciences are proposed. For example, in the physical science area, students calculate the mass of various liquids and the observer uses a 'talent discovery checklist' during the activity. The behavioural characteristics pertaining to science for screening candidates include the following: 1) displays curiosity by asking relevant questions, 2) shows considerable knowledge related to topic of session, 3) actively manipulates materials, 4) communicates clearly the results of the project, 5) systematically tests hypotheses, 6) tries to predict outcomes, 7) represents ideas in the form of a model and 8) finds means of overcoming obstacles in problem-solving.

Regarding educational content for this project, 90-minute lessons were taught by zoologists, botanists, a biological illustrator and physicists biweekly. Sample lesson topics in science included 'Liquid surfaces', 'Working with the qualities of air', and 'Experiments with hard water and soft water' (Cooper *et al.*, 1996). Observable changes demonstrating the impact of the project on students were proposed as follows: 1) improvement in self-regulation such as focusing and sustaining attention, 2) perseverance in overcoming obstacles, 3) active participation in learning, 4) willingness to extend learning both in and out of school, 5) cooperation and teamwork, 6) increased self-confidence as a learner, 7) greater ability to create products of comparable quality to those produced by gifted non-disabled peers and 8) recognition as gifted students.

Teaching science to 2E children in the regular classroom

Sumida (2010) developed a gifted behaviour checklist in science for primary school children and used it to identify 2E children in a city area in Japan. The city board of education has a three-stage systematized framework for profiling children with developmental disorders. In the first screening, all children in the city are observed using a general checklist to identify children who show characteristics of developmental disorders. The second screening is conducted using a checklist designed to specifically identify the type of developmental disorder. The third screening includes the Wechsler Intelligence Scale for Children – Third Edition (WISC-III); the Japanese Kaufman Assessment Battery for Children (K = ABC); the Illinois Test of Psycholinguistic Abilities (ITPA) and other similar developmental surveys; scholastic records; and information about home environments and early developmental history.

The checklist consists of 60 items and is focused on attitudes, thinking, skills and knowledge/understanding in science. Three 'gifted styles' were extracted: 1) spontaneous style, 2) expert style and 3) solid style. He found that LD/ADHD/HA children displayed the spontaneous style, while non-LD/ADHD/HA children were characterized under the solid style. The number of children exhibiting the expert style was the lowest, with no significant difference in their numbers between the two groups. Based on the profile of the 2E children in science, Sumida (2012) suggested the following eight points to be considered in science lessons for enriching the individual strengths and capabilities of 2E children:

1. When splitting students into groups for observations and experiments, base group configurations on the demands of the experimental and observation methods that they will be using. Including individual activities is also effective.
2. Include situations where children come up with their own methods and strategies and choose their own tools during observations and experiments.
3. Introduce situations where children use diagrams to represent their own ideas and the results.
4. Increase the amount of time allowed for working and thinking.
5. Include challenging problems.
6. Include a modelling activity in units when this is possible.
7. Provide a variety of different resources.
8. Encourage and recognize diverse opinions.

Science lessons on the topics 'How things heat up' and 'Pendulum' were designed, and conducted in a class of the 2E children identified in public primary schools. The pilot science lesson about 'How things heat up' for grade 4 includes a variety of materials to heat up and a worksheet to design the experiments and record their observations; it involves drawing, designing and making products for 11 hours in a regular classroom under the national standard curriculum. In the lessons, the 2E child considered changes and how much time elapsed while drawing complicated diagrams using colour coding and arrows, and was able to neatly represent his detailed predictions. The child carefully summarized the observed changes, such as temperature differences between the top and bottom of a rod, how much the temperature changed and so on, in detail. The child was the first student to start affixing thermal tape to a hot-air balloon as part of an activity to verify air temperature and often thought of new problems while enthusiastically participating in activities.

Discussion

This chapter considered unique children who are both gifted and display developmental challenges. It is possible that some scientists – like Einstein – demonstrate outstanding skills that will see their contributions enshrined in history books, but at the same time tend to exhibit mild developmental disorders known today as LD or ADHD (West, 1991). The pervasive LD, ADHD, HA and Asperger's syndrome are referred to as mild developmental disorders in Japan. Specialized support could be provided for each of these disabilities (e.g. Holden and Cooke, 2005; Alderman, 2008; Lupart and Toy, 2009). It has been shown, however, that the disabilities often overlap (e.g. Kalbfleisch, 2014; Muta, 2005).

Because interpretations of giftedness are diverse, and social contexts are influential, the definition of a gifted child will change over time as ideas around the topic change. Even when children are identified as gifted, it is inaccurate to view them as perfect children who will demonstrate excellence in every field. In reality, they may exhibit imbalances in their socioemotional development, experience difficulties in their interpersonal relationships, or be underachievers in fields not of interest to them (Davis *et al.*, 2011). In order to support these gifted children, educational programmes exist to foster these differences.

Barnard-Brak *et al.* (2015) show that 9.1 per cent of children who have disabilities might be identified as gifted or academically advanced, but only 11.1 per cent of these students were participating in programmes for gifted students. According to Silverman (2003), some preliminary investigations suggest that the risk of learning disorders increases as a function of IQ in the USA. Hannah and Shore (1995) compared 48 school-identified 2E students, gifted students, students with learning disabilities and average-performing boys. They found that metacognitive performance of the 2E students exceeded and resembled that of the gifted students more than that of the students with learning disabilities. Barber and Mueller (2011) compared the social and self-perceptions of 2E students with gifted students and students with learning disabilities. They showed that 2E students had less positive perceptions of maternal relationships and self-concept than the gifted students or students with learning disabilities. As described in this chapter, science classrooms have a high potential for providing a practical context for identifying and developing the strengths of 2E students. New perspectives are needed to identify the giftedness of 2E children and to enhance it so that there is both compensation for and sensitivity to their learning difficulties or disabilities.

Karnes *et al.* (2004) suggested that developing 2E students use interest and learning style inventories to become familiar with the strengths of their own strength. McGinnis and Stefanich (2007) reported that teachers who believe classrooms should be inclusive of all abilities have identified science classrooms as especially suited for students with disabilities. A strength of 2E children was that they tended to demonstrate high creative competence in science when compared with regular children (Sumida, 2010). Thus, it should be possible to design inclusive science lessons that would enable both 2E students and regular students to study together for their mutual benefit. The studies of 2E children gifted in science are an early-stage effort to spark new educational research targeting the diverse needs of all children.

Reference

Alderman, T. (2008). *Meeting the Needs of Your Most Able Pupils: Science*. New York: Routledge.

Andreasen, N.C. (2005). *The Creating Brain*. New York: Dana Press.

Barber, C., and Mueller, C.T. (2011). Social and self-perceptions of adolescents identified as gifted, learning disabled, and twice-exceptional. *Roeper Review*, 33(2), 109–20.

Barnard-Brak, L., Johnsen, S.K., Hannig, A.P., and Wei, T. (2015). The incidence of potentially gifted students within a special education population. *Roeper Review*, 37(2), 74–83.

Baum, S. (1990). The gifted learning disabled: a paradox for teachers. *Preventing School Failure*, 34, 11–14.

Baum, S.M., Cooper, C.R., Neu, T.W., and Owen, S.V. (1995). *Project HIGH HOPES: Talent discovery assessment process user's guide*. Conneticut: Area Cooperative Educatioal Services.

Baum, S.M., and Owen, S.V. (2004). *To be Gifted and Learning Disabled: Strategies for helping bright students with learning and attention difficulties*. Mansfield, CT: Creative Learning Press.

Buttriss, J., and Callander, A. (2005). *Gifted and Talented from A–Z*. London: David Fulton.

Cooper, C.R., Baum, S.M., and Neu, T.W. (2005). Developing scientific talent in students with special needs. In K. Johnsen and J. Kendrick (Eds), *Science Education for Gifted Students*. Waco, TX: Prufrock Press, pp. 63–78.

Cooper, C.R., Neu, T.W., and Baum, S.M. (1996). *Project HIGH HOPES: Talent development curriculum*. Conneticut: Area Cooperative Educatioal Services.

Davis, G.A., Rimm, S.B., and Siegle, D. (2011). *Education of the Gifted and Talented* (6th edn). New Jersey: Pearson.

DeVries, R. (2002). Physical-knowledge activities. In R. DeVries, B. Zan, C. Hildebrandt, R. Edmiaston and C. Sales (Eds), *Developing Constructivist Early Childhood Curriculum: Practical principles and activities*. New York: Teachers College Press, pp. 69–75.

Hannah, C.L., and Shore, B.M. (1995). Metacognition an high intellectual ability: insights from the study of learning-disabled gifted students. *Gifted Child Quarterly*, 39(2), 95–109.

Holden, C., and Cooke, A. (2005). *Meeting SEN in the Curriculum: Science*. London: David Fulton.

Illingworth, R.S., and Illingworth, C.M. (1966). *Lessons from Childhood*. London: Churchill Livngstone.

Japan Association of the Special Educational Needs Specialist (Ed.) (2007). *Theory and Practice in Special Needs Education II: Teaching*. Tokyo: Kongo Suppan (in Japanese).

Kalbfleisch, M.L. (2014). Twice-exceptional learners. In J.A. Plucker and C.M. Callahan (Eds), *Critical Issues and Practices in Gifted Education* (2nd edn). Waco, TX: Prufrock Press, pp. 671–89.

Karnes, F.A., Shaunessy, E., and Bisland, A. (2004). Gifted students with disabilities. *Gifted Child Today*, 27(4), 16–21.

Kumagai, T. (2015). *The Lonely Boyhood of Genius*. Tokyo: Shin-yo-sha (in Japanese).

Lupart, J.L., and Toy, R.E. (2009). Twice exceptional: multiple pathways to success. In L.V. Shavinina (Ed.), *International Handbook on Giftedness*. New York: Springer, pp. 507–25.

Masukawa, T. (2009). *Why I Won the Nobel Prize*. Osaka: Forum A (in Japanese).

McGinnis, J.R., and Stefanich, G.P. (2007). Special needs and talents in science learning. In S.K. Abell and N.G. Lederman (Eds), *Handbook of Research on Science Education*. New Jersey: Lawrence Erlbaum, pp. 287–317.

Ministry of Education, Culture, Sports, Science and Teachnology (MEXT) (2012). *Results of Research on Students with Special Educational Needs in Regular Classrooms* (in Japanese). Retrieved from http://www.mext.go.jp/a_menu/shotou/tokubetu/material/__icsFiles/afieldfile/2012/12/10/1328729_01.pdf

Muta, E. (2005). *Understanding and Support for Students with LD or ADHD: A guide for the school counsellor*. Tokyo: Yuhikaku (in Japanese).

Patton, J.R. (1995). Teaching science to students with special needs. *Teaching Exceptional Children*, 27(4), 4–6.

Silverman, L.J. (2003). Gifted children with learning disabilities. In N. Colangelo and G.A. Davis (2003), *Handbook of Gifted Education* (3rd edn). Boston: Pearson Education, pp. 533–43.

Sumida, M. (2010). Identifying twice-exceptional children and three gifted styles in the Japanese primary science classroom. *International Journal of Science Education*, 32(15), 2097–111.

Sumida, M. (2012). Meeting the needs of twice-exceptional children in the science classroom. In W. Sittiprapaporn (Ed.), *Learning Disabilities*. Rijeka, Croatia: InTech, pp. 149–74.

Sumida, M., Fukada, S., Nakamura, H., Masukagami, M., and Sakata, C. (2007). Developing young children's scientific, technological, and social competency through 'Pendulum' play activities at Japanese kindergarten. *Asia-Pacific Journal of Research in Early Childhood Education*, 1(1), 83–100.

Weinfeld, R., Barnes-Robinson, L., Jeweler, S., and Shevitz, B.R. (2006). *Smart Kids with Learning Difficulties: Overcoming obstacles and realizing potential*. Waco, TX: Prufrock Press.

West, T.G. (1991). *In the Mind's Eye: Visual thinkers, gifted people with learning difficulties, computer images, and the ironies of creativity*. New York: Prometheus Books.

Index

Taylor & Francis eBooks

Helping you to choose the right eBooks for your Library

Add Routledge titles to your library's digital collection today. Taylor and Francis ebooks contains over 50,000 titles in the Humanities, Social Sciences, Behavioural Sciences, Built Environment and Law.

Choose from a range of subject packages or create your own!

Benefits for you

» Free MARC records
» COUNTER-compliant usage statistics
» Flexible purchase and pricing options
» All titles DRM-free.

REQUEST YOUR **FREE** INSTITUTIONAL TRIAL TODAY

Free Trials Available
We offer free trials to qualifying academic, corporate and government customers.

Benefits for your user

» Off-site, anytime access via Athens or referring URL
» Print or copy pages or chapters
» Full content search
» Bookmark, highlight and annotate text
» Access to thousands of pages of quality research at the click of a button.

eCollections – Choose from over 30 subject eCollections, including:

Archaeology	Language Learning
Architecture	Law
Asian Studies	Literature
Business & Management	Media & Communication
Classical Studies	Middle East Studies
Construction	Music
Creative & Media Arts	Philosophy
Criminology & Criminal Justice	Planning
Economics	Politics
Education	Psychology & Mental Health
Energy	Religion
Engineering	Security
English Language & Linguistics	Social Work
Environment & Sustainability	Sociology
Geography	Sport
Health Studies	Theatre & Performance
History	Tourism, Hospitality & Events

For more information, pricing enquiries or to order a free trial, please contact your local sales team:
www.tandfebooks.com/page/sales